CELESTIAL FOOTY

THE STORY OF CHINESE HERITAGE AUSSIE RULES

PATRICK SKENE

Hardie Grant

MEDIA

Produced by Hardie Grant Media for the National Foundation
for Australia-China Relations.

A catalogue record for this
book is available from the
National Library of Australia

NATIONAL
LIBRARY
OF AUSTRALIA

Celestial Footy
ISBN 978 0 64687 901 7

Written by Patrick Skene
Edited by Charlie Happell
Cover design by Darcy Vescio
Typesetting by Cannon Typesetting

Printed in Australia by Griffin Press, an Accredited ISO
AS/NZS 14001 Environmental Management System printer.

FSC
www.fsc.org
MIX
Paper | Supporting
responsible forestry
FSC® C018684

The paper this book is printed on is certified against the
Forest Stewardship Council® Standards. Griffin Press holds
chain of custody certification SCS-COC-001185. FSC®
promotes environmentally responsible, socially beneficial
and economically viable management of the world's forests.

CONTENTS

CONTENTS

PREFACE

Australian Rules football holds a special place in our national life and imagination. Grand final day at the MCG is one of the most sacred dates in our national social calendar. Lance Franklin and Patrick Dangerfield are household names.

Yet few Australians associate the national game with our fellow Chinese-Australian countrymen. Though Chinese-Australians have made indelible marks on our country's development since the 1850s, they are better known as doctors, engineers and other professionals than footy players.

This book will forever change our stereotypical perception of our Chinese-Australian communities. Not only do Chinese-Australians share our national passion, but they have been kicking, handballing and taking marks since the goldrush.

Peter Cai
CEO, National Foundation for Australia-China Relations
May 2023

FOREWORD

By Darcy Vescio

Footy is a game that should be for everyone – for every community, for every person, from any background. For all of us.

The stories that we tell about footy and the people who play our great game often become folklore.

But throughout our game's history, it has been the same sorts of people whose stories are told and the same sorts of people whose deeds are celebrated and highlighted.

That is why I feel strongly about the significance of this book and the stories it contains, which salute some of football's forgotten people.

Celestial Footy shines a light on the long and special history that people of Chinese descent have with Australian Rules football and the important contribution they've made, which has gone largely unheralded over the years.

I love that this book contains so many stories from different angles and touchpoints, from out in the community to the elite level – they resonate deeply with me.

I feel so fortunate to be part of the first ever AFLW playing cohort, and the joy that has given so many footballers and supporters.

We all had unique stories coming into the game, and it's special for me to also be able to reflect on my journey through the additional lens of being an Asian Australian.

Historically, there have been challenges for Chinese-Australians looking to get into Aussie Rules, which other minority groups have also encountered to varying degrees.

As Patrick has written in this book, my grandfather on Mum's side, Cheong Lip Louey or just 'Goong' to us kids, migrated from China, via Hong Kong, after World War II.

To say that he did it tough would be a huge understatement.

He was never afforded the luxury of playing sport so, at least early on, he probably saw me playing footy as a bit of an indulgence that could ultimately end up being a waste of time and energy.

I think that's a very common migrant attitude toward work and sport in this country.

Even on Dad's side, my Italian grandparents saw my career choices as something that needed to be sustainable financially and that would set me up for the future.

Goong, while always supportive of me, loved soccer and I think he saw that as a legitimate sporting choice, whereas footy was more of a hobby, which it was for a long time for me before the advent of the AFLW.

I grew up in Markwood, a small town outside Wangaratta, which has a population of 258.

We were one of the few multicultural families in Markwood but I didn't really view us in that light because there were so few people, and we were all individuals in our own way.

We just saw everyone for the person they were.

But I know my parents tried hard to fit in whenever possible – and that came at a cost.

Once my mum started school, she and her siblings refused to speak Chinese anymore, so now she can't speak it at all.

There was a desperation to assimilate, to fit in, to be accepted – and that meant not drawing any attention to differences.

Dad speaks about the racism that he used to cop at school.

I feel like some of that energy perhaps rubbed off on me growing up, but my background wasn't really something I thought about much during my school years.

My childhood experience was different from Mum and Dad's.

We had emerged into a space where multiculturalism was starting to be celebrated and highlighted and viewed as something that makes modern Australia wonderful.

My perspective on my heritage has changed as I've grown older and become more curious.

I've gone from not even thinking of myself as from a multicultural background at all to being a proud Multicultural Ambassador for the AFL.

I came from a headspace of 'I'm just like everyone else really … I'm not *that* Chinese, I'm not *that* Italian'. So, it's been really rewarding to learn more about my family and to be able to express how proud and grateful I am.

I hope my journey resonates with people who don't necessarily see themselves reflected in the game that often.

I love my Chinese-Italian heritage. I always have, even if it's been something that I didn't really reflect on until later in life.

I've lost my Goong and my nonno, I've only got my nonna now, so I'm passionate about making sure that I appreciate and carry on the cultures that are part of me.

I'm really proud and happy that I do have a 'different' background and it's something that I get to share as an AFLW footballer.

I hope people read this book and can appreciate the time, effort and passion that the players featured have put into footy.

I think it's important for people to hear stories that are different from their own and to be able to reflect on what it would've been like for others.

I think it's important to think about the different relationships people have with footy, their journeys to the game and what it means in their lives.

For a lot of people, playing footy is just a natural part of growing up in Australia that they didn't have to consider all that much.

Others have needed to clear a few more hurdles to play a game that might be the one thing that connects them with the community ... the one thing that makes them feel like they belong.

The stories contained in this book, and the lives of the people in them, are amazing.

I hope people enjoy reading these stories and marvel at what Chinese-Australians have done for the game over the course of its history.

I know I do.

READER'S NOTES

Chinese-Australians: For the purposes of this book, the Chinese-Australian heritage community is defined by the ABS Census as those with Chinese ancestry. According to the 2021 ABS Census there were approximately 1.4 million Australians or 5.5% of the Australian population who have Chinese ancestry. The main countries of origin of Chinese-Australians are mainland China/Hong Kong/Macau and the Chinese diaspora migrant communities from Asian countries including Malaysia, Vietnam, Philippines, Indonesia and Singapore.

Use of the word football: For the purposes of the target audience, football refers to Australian Rules football and not association football/soccer.

Variation in Chinese place names: At times there are various English version spellings of Chinese names used for the same place, i.e., Toi Shan and Taishan. Different groups call them by different names based on nuances such as migration recency, old historical spellings etc. We have where possible used the 'name of the day', which explains the variation in use.

While the author has made every effort to verify the historical accuracy of this publication, which draws on first person-interviews and research oftentimes anecdotal in nature, he invites any party with further information to contact the publisher directly.

INTRODUCTION

If Tom Wills, the founding father of Australian Rules football, was able to see into the future – specifically to the Hillside Reserve in north-west Melbourne in late 2022 – he would have been amazed at how his co-creation had evolved.

On what only Victorians would call 'a perfect day for footy', the Hillside Sharks were locked in a muddy dogfight with West Coburg who would go on to play in the Essendon District Football League Grand Final later that season.

The players' body sizes, tactics, skills, athleticism and physicality would have no doubt impressed Tom, including the never-say-die attitude from Hillside who, after a mixed season, were out of contention for the finals and playing only for pride in front of their home faithful.

What would have jolted him into wide-eyed wonder was both the number of players with tattoos and the rich cultural diversity on the field featuring players with ancestries from all over the world.

Alongside the Anglo-Celtic players in both teams were Australians of African, Italian, Greek, Balkan, Pacific, Arabic and Chinese heritage.

One player that would have caught his eye was Hillside's compact midfielder, Zak Wunhym. With bleached blonde hair he stood out with his work rate and skill – linking, smothering, jinking, hustling, tackling, winning possession and delivering crisp passes via laser kicks.

Zak was continuing a proud Chinese-heritage family football tradition, which includes his great-grandfather, Footscray VFL pioneer Jack Wunhym, and dates back to his great-great uncle, Willie Wun Hym, who played in Ballarat for the Golden Point Rice Eaters in the early 1900s.

In 2016 Zak made it into the prestigious Victorian Football League (VFL), playing 16 games for Coburg. Now with a young family, he is happy to play semi-professionally for Hillside, and be a valuable contributor to his team.

Zak's sister, Brittany Wunhym, has also continued the family tradition, playing in the VFLW for the Western Bulldogs.

A crisp, bracing breeze whistles across the ground and the power of sport is in full bloom – two footy communities brought together, volunteers buzzing everywhere, parents and friends huddled in groups around the ground and the Hillside old boys sharing tales and roaring with laughter in the clubhouse, beers in hand and heartily downing the lamb and chicken kebabs fresh off the rotisserie.

Third item down on the canteen food list is dim sims, or 'dimmies' in these parts – another Chinese-Australian import to the game, first invented in the 1940s and sold outside many of Melbourne's football grounds. The Chinese footy connection runs deep.

The final siren wails and the Hillside Sharks fans and players whoop for joy – they have pulled off an underdog win, a real highlight in a lukewarm season and their players troop off muddy and satisfied.

After the match, Hillside's passionate Italian-Australian coach Charlie Denaro is thrilled with Zak's performance: 'Just look at Zak, what an inspiration.'

'He's wearing more tape than a mummy and he batters and brutalises himself for the team. His effort today epitomises why he is held in the esteem he is at our footy club.'

Denaro was raised in multicultural Coburg and is envious of the Wunhym football history: 'At my age I'm all about tradition and Zak is so fortunate to have a family name to carry on in footy.'

'I never had that luxury and he is such a proud young guy about his heritage.'

For Zak Wunhym, who topped the disposal count for Hillside with 28, it was another day at the office and after the game he sounded like any footballer: 'I've honed my whole year on consistency and putting my body on the line. Anything I can do for the team, that's what I'm about.'

What differentiates Zak is his unique football ancestry of which he is proud: 'I'm proud to have Chinese heritage and I never shy away from letting people know where I come from. I'm all about it and I'd love to learn more.'

And is the tradition in good hands with his impending fatherhood?

Zak pauses before answering: 'Like all Victorians I'll throw a soft footy in the cot and we'll see what happens.'

In the 19th century, disaffected Fujianese, Cantonese and Hakka migrants left a fractured and unstable China and sailed into the Pacific. Some struck gold in America; some made their way to Australia as goldminers, shepherds, market gardeners, cooks, merchants and as a general cheap labour force to help build a new country.

The majority group was the Cantonese, from modern-day Guangzhou, and the enabler for their mass migration was the defeat of China in the Second Opium War by Great Britain and France and the subsequent ceding of Hong Kong and the lush Pearl River Delta to Great Britain.

In return, as newly minted subjects of Empire, and empowered by the Treaty of Peking in 1860, which gave them guaranteed freedom of travel within the British Empire's vast boundaries, many packed their bags in search of adventure, family glory ... and gold.

According to Dr Siqin Wang from the University of Queensland, around 100,000 people entered Australia from China between the 1840s and Federation in 1901.

When the goldrush in Australia ended due to the accessible gold and tin reserves being exhausted, many Chinese returned but some stayed, bound in spirit to their new land.

In 1901, the passing of the White Australia policy took away many rights for Chinese-Australians, including travel restrictions and entitlements to citizenship.

Chinese-Australians became 'the other' – invisible Australians labouring under cruel stereotypes with reduced rights as citizens.

Many couldn't take the restrictions and, powerless, returned to their ancestral village, their dreams in tatters.

According to author Paul Jones, by the start of World War II there were no more than 15,000 Chinese-Australian residents left on the continent.

Those that soldiered on, planted roots in country towns or moved into the cities, working hard to build the nation, resiliently carving out their own Australian lives.

Locked out of key union jobs, the Chinese-Australians who stayed became part of the community largely as market gardeners, herbalists, cabinet makers and laundry managers.

Market gardening, which was backbreaking work, supplied the cities and regional towns with fruit and vegetables, mirroring the crucial role the Afghan cameleers performed in supplying outstations in remote Australia.

Once settled, the Chinese-Australian community adapted to Western ways and local customs. Their culinary culture was an underappreciated gift to regional towns, valued later with the fullness of time. Chinese-Australians were marginalised, reduced and vilified, but they ploughed on, a tough, resilient and adaptable community. And their sport of choice was Australian Rules football.

While other Australian global sports, such as cricket (Hunter Poon in 1916), rugby league (Billy Hong in 1932) and soccer (Johnny Wong in 1959), featured lone Chinese-Australian pioneers during the 72-year term of the White Australia policy, Australian Rules football was played by hundreds of Chinese-Australians at all levels, from the first pioneer in 1882 until the end of the White Australia policy in 1973.

The journey of the telling of the Chinese-Australian football story starts in 2006 in Melbourne in a beautiful old-school pub, the North Fitzroy Arms, first opened in 1874.

John Harms, esteemed historian, writer and publisher, was holding court after a boozy long lunch with a mixed gathering of footy fans.

As the afternoon lengthened, Sam Pang, one of the attendees who would later go on to commercial television fame as a comedian and co-host of the award-winning *Front Bar* footy-comedy show, prepared an announcement.

John Harms recalls the moment clearly: 'I have an image in my mind of Sam Pang with his hands in the air, massive grin on his face, saying "I'm the greatest Chinese footballer of all time" and a chorus

INTRODUCTION

of revellers around him saying "piss off Pang" and (then producing) a catalogue of names to challenge his grandiose claim.'

'Peter Bell and Dannie Seow were the first to be mentioned. To protect his reputation, Pang claimed Dannie Seow was Vietnamese and he claimed correctly that Bell was not Chinese.'

Harms and Pang were special guests on a 3RRR footy show in which a whole segment was devoted to the subject. After a few listener call-ins and historian testimony, by the end of the show Sam had slipped to third place behind Les Fong and Wally Koochew.

By the time Harms penned a double-page story in *The Age* in June 2008 headlined 'You're a champ China', Sam had slipped out of the top 10 – a position to which he would never return.

By the time I had finished my research for this book, Sam wasn't even the greatest Pang.

ı | | ı

In 2015 I wrote a story for the *Guardian Australia* headlined 'The forgotten story of … the Chinese Goldfields Aussie Rules leagues'.

Part of my research involved a wonderful afternoon at Victoria University with Dr Robert Hess, the inheritor of the Chinese football tradition from Sam and John and a co-author of a number of academic papers on Chinese participation in Australian sport.

All of his research was printed and stored in boxes and I spent the afternoon reading fascinating pioneer stories, none more so than one about a series of 'Celestial matches', all-Chinese charity football matches held across the Victorian Goldfields in the 1890s.

After the *Guardian Australia* story was published, various people began to contact me with further examples of Chinese-heritage players and a once-hidden story began to emerge.

The Chinese-Australian community had virtually no involvement in other national sports in the 20th century, but my records swelled to hundreds of participants in Australian Rules football.

Seven years later, in 2022, I was again seated in Dr Hess's office, combing through the latest research to begin a new journey – to write a book consolidating the stories of old and new Chinese-heritage footy players in this amazing 140-year story.

Dr Hess told me that he was 'passing the baton' on the project and wished me luck on an endeavour that would soon take me across the country.

In that moment I felt a great responsibility to ensure this group of notable Australians received their deserved moment in the sunlight.

This history can't be told contextually without the stories of the ancestral journeys that are the roots of the Chinese-Australian experience.

Journeys of industriousness and tenacity. Of isolation and suffering.

Stories of men and women who felt such a strong sense of civic pride that they risked ridicule to suit up to play footy for their village, town or suburb.

A robust group that worked hard, helped build their adopted country and deserve to have their story told as Australians.

My research uncovered a divergent view of Chinese-Australians – one of playing footy, having a go, forming mateships, tolerating racism, embracing Christianity, Freemasonry and philanthropy, serving nobly in war and trying to fit in and become Australian.

For me, Australia will not be a whole nation until all of its community's stories are celebrated, including those of the Chinese-Australians.

From Chinese-Australian ANZAC sniper Billy Sing to the proud footballers in this book, Australia will be a fairer place when these stories are acknowledged, credited and celebrated – properly.

Since the COVID-19 pandemic, Chinese-Australians have reported a reduced sense of belonging.

Some feel they have been pushed from being Chinese-Australian back to being Chinese.

This book is my attempt to rebuild the hyphen.

CHAPTER 1

Playing for Points: Port Adelaide and the China Strategy

On Thursday 23 March 2017, the Premier of China, Li Keqiang, arrived in Canberra for a whistle-stop tour of Australia. Premier Li, then the second-most powerful man in China, was on a mission to promote friendship and free trade.

During a tight schedule of arrangements, which included meetings with business and political leaders, Premier Li was also introduced to the country's premier football code, Australian Rules football.

Accompanying Li to the opening round match of the 2017 Australian Football League (AFL) season between the Sydney Swans and Port Adelaide was Australian Prime Minister Malcolm Turnbull, who just days earlier had welcomed the Premier to Parliament House.

'It would not be possible,' Turnbull said in his welcome speech, 'to imagine modern Australia without the contribution of the Chinese-Australian community.'

Turnbull, an erudite lawyer and former investment banker, was not a sports fan. However, as a Sydneysider and the Swans' local member of parliament, he wore a red-and-white Swans scarf to show support for his hometown team. He also knew the power of the AFL, Australia's most popular sporting competition and one of the best-attended leagues anywhere in the world.

The AFL is, for most Australians, shorthand for Australian Rules football, an unusual game first codified in Melbourne in the mid-19th century. 'Aussie Rules', as it is also known, has for more than a century intrigued foreign visitors to Australia. To the untrained eye, the game looks like rolling chaos with large numbers of players chasing and kicking, no offside rules, a wide, seemingly endless oval-shaped playing surface and an unpredictable, oval-shaped ball that bounced in all directions.

The game's contested origins involve three major Australian communities. For the Aboriginal and Torres Strait Islander peoples, it is an extension of *Marn Grook*, a western Victorian Indigenous game of kicking and leaping to catch a possum-skin ball. For the Irish, the open running, kicking and catching game and tiered scoring options must surely have been lifted from their own Gaelic football. And, for the English colonisers, it was an adapted version of rugby.

While the origin debate remains unresolved, most agree that Australian Rules football is one of the first genuinely Australian institutions to deviate from transplanted English traditions. From its Melbourne heartland, the game spread across the country and, over time, developed its own unique slang, rules and rituals.

From the suburbs of the big southern cities, to red-dirt derbies in Central Australia and in hundreds of small regional towns, Australian Rules football is an obsession.

Premier Li could have attended a soccer match in Sydney that weekend, to watch a game with which he would have been much more familiar. But for visiting dignitaries, the AFL represented a quintessential Australian experience.

Premier Li wore a black, white and teal Port Adelaide scarf given to him by the club's media-savvy chairman, David Koch. According to Koch, the primary reason for securing Premier Li's attendance at the match was to recognise Port Adelaide's persistence in engaging the Chinese market and to help build awareness of Port's upcoming match in Shanghai.

Of all the professional sporting clubs in Australia, Port Adelaide seemed an unlikely contender to lead Chinese diplomatic engagement. They were, in many ways, the club with the fewest natural advantages in the game to run a successful China strategy.

Founded in 1870 as a working-class club for wharfies and factory workers, Port Adelaide doggedly clawed its way to become the bluebloods of South Australian football, with a record 36 South Australian state premierships and one AFL title.

Their home ground, Alberton Oval, provided a refuge from poverty and the helplessness of social immobility. What started as a tribe became family, and grew into a religion with the men who represented them in their black-and-white prison-bar guernseys becoming their football gods.

Despite the limited horizon of working-class life, the management at Port Adelaide was always open to the world and the club had a surprisingly deep history of Chinese diplomatic engagement.

One hundred and thirty years before Premier Li's visit, in the twilight years of the Manchu Dynasty, Port had hosted touring Chinese diplomats General Wong Yung Ho and Consul U. Tsing at a match in Adelaide in 1884.

And, in 1956, Port Adelaide's legendary captain Fos Williams had hosted touring Chinese diplomats at a match at Alberton Oval, explaining the nuances of the game through a translator.

Koch unknowingly picked up where Williams left off.

He knew the 'Aussie' authenticity of Australian Rules football was a competitive advantage for international engagement projects.

'I would say that Aussie Rules is to Australia what the Bolshoi Ballet is to Russia,' he said.

'Our Indigenous game was undervalued as a bridge builder to build goodwill and an understanding of Australian culture – it's a reflection of who we are.'

As Premier Li stepped onto the corporate balcony at the SCG to watch the game, a cunning Swans fan threw him a red-and-white scarf. Premier Li obliged, despite already wearing a Port Adelaide scarf, perhaps sensing the need to avoid taking sides in front of 33,000 fans and a broadcast audience of millions in Australia.

In the humid weather, his neutrality came at a cost to his personal comfort. 'I insisted I get another scarf rooting for the Sydney Swans,' Li later explained through an interpreter. 'On this occasion, wearing two scarves is making me really hot.'

Prime Minister Turnbull also noted the jostling for club affection. 'There was a bit of scarf competition,' he told journalists after the match.

'But we're all friends here … friends of Australia, and Australian football.'

Premier Li and his delegation left the SCG at half time, missing a glorious 28-point upset win by Port Adelaide.

The English language match report on the Chinese Embassy's website noted: 'As the atmosphere of the stadium went intense, the friendly atmosphere between China and Australia went warmer and sweeter.'

Despite Premier Li's early departure, Koch claimed him as Port's 'lucky charm' and a positive omen for Port Adelaide's pending Chinese adventure.

'Yes, the Swans won the scarf war,' Koch said.

'But Port won China!'

ı | | ı

The story of how Port Adelaide won China began on Saturday 29 September 2012, AFL grand final day at the Melbourne Cricket Ground.

To many, the AFL had never looked healthier. Its first interstate club, the Sydney Swans, had that day defeated Hawthorn, a 110-year-old Melbourne club, in front of 100,000 people.

Amid the excitement of national growth, Port Adelaide was the AFL's problem child, having fallen on hard times since the heady days of its 2004 premiership. One Melbourne commentator labelled Port Adelaide 'a carcass'.

At this time, David Koch was host of a popular breakfast TV news program and Port Adelaide's number one ticket holder. He was a national media heavyweight, revelling in his role as 'Kochie'. Beyond the daggy dad persona, though, was a serious financial pundit, highly respected in corporate Australia for his insights and connections.

On the morning of the 2012 grand final, Koch took a call from AFL CEO, Andrew Demetriou. The outlook for the club was grim, Demetriou said. It had lost $7 million for the year and the AFL had been forced to sack the entire Port Adelaide board.

'Port Adelaide had an old-fashioned board and some hyper local sponsors who went broke,' Koch said. 'They were a working-class club, distrustful of outsiders and didn't think outside the postcode at the scale needed for a national brand.'

Demetriou wanted Koch, who had attended Port Adelaide games since he was a toddler, to steer his boyhood club back to stability and solvency. Koch's father, Dean, who once played for Port Adelaide reserves, had passed away five years earlier.

'I knew he would have wanted me to do it,' Koch said.

Within two years, Chairman Koch had stemmed the financial bleeding and developed a stable and sustainable business model.

But he could see that Port Adelaide, as a medium-sized club in a highly congested national sponsorship marketplace, needed to seek out new revenue streams.

At the time, China was Australia's biggest trading partner and, in 2018, the fruits of the China–Australia Free Trade Agreement (ChAFTA) signed in 2015 were clearly evident.

Two-way trade reached a record AUD 215 billion with China becoming Australia's number-one customer in exports of iron ore, coal, agricultural, forestry and fisheries products. Tourism and education were growing export industries and Australia was increasing its imports of China's telecommunication equipment, IT products, furniture and homewares.

The Chinese, according to Koch, 'wanted to sell to Australians, but Australians were distrustful of Chinese brands. So why not use footy to bridge the gap?'

Koch had learned about trust in business from his father. During the 1970s, Dean Koch had built lifelong contacts with Chinese businesspeople. 'Dad was the first westerner to trade coal into China and to trade Chinese coal outside of it,' Koch said.

'I remember as a kid, he would always say: "If you get the trust and respect of the Chinese, they will be loyal to you forever".'

First, the club sponsored the South China Australian Football League (SCAFL) and 'Team China', the Chinese national team who compete every three years in the Australian Football International Cup. Locally, they began engaging with the local Adelaide Chinese community, consulting with leaders and supporting Chinese New Year activities.

The club partnered with the University of South Australia to produce a Chinese-language 'footy dictionary' in which football concepts, words and phrases were explained to the community. Games were called in Mandarin and, during Multicultural Round,

Port Adelaide players wore guernseys with their names displayed in Chinese characters.

Next, the club engaged Andrew Hunter as General Manager (China Engagement). Hunter had graduated with a Master of Philosophy in Asian Studies from the University of Adelaide and had worked on a number of Chinese projects. According to Koch, Hunter brought 'a deep understanding of the protocols and nuances' to the club's China strategy.

Hunter added a Chinese speaker, Promise (Nuo Xu), to the team. Promise was a fluent Mandarin and Cantonese–speaking Chinese Australian who would prove crucial in diplomatic and commercial negotiations, helping to manage cultural misunderstandings.

Finally, Port Adelaide began investigating the possibility of playing a game in China, considered by many to be an outlandish and laughable proposal both within the AFL and from other competing codes.

The mocking of the disbelievers was stifled early when Port Adelaide announced they had added Shanghai Cred as a sponsor and partner for the princely sum of $3 million a year.

Over the years, several Australian, American and European sporting clubs had attempted to penetrate the Chinese market and withdrawn. China, it seemed, was too big and too complicated.

There had been a number of exhibition games featuring NBA, Major League Baseball and English Premier League clubs – and Australian A-League soccer teams competed every year in the regional Asian Champions League

But no major foreign club had ever taken the market seriously enough to host an official regular season fixture in China, with the intensity of high stakes and competition points on the line.

Port Adelaide, under Koch, Hunter and CEO Keith Thomas, decided that it would try to play for points.

Once that decision was made, the logistical challenges were itemised and the team went to work. The first step was to find a suitable ground in Shanghai that would meet AFL's specific field-of-play integrity requirements and a number of soccer grounds with athletic tracks were inspected but fell just short of the required length.

When the options of existing stadiums were exhausted they decided to make an assessment on Jiangwan Stadium, which had once hosted an AFL exhibition match in 2010 between the Melbourne Demons and Brisbane Lions as part of the Shanghai World Expo.

Jiangwan Stadium, nestled on the banks of the Qiujiang River, had once been the jewel of Chinese athletics and was built in Chinese Art Deco style by Dong Dayou, the architect behind many Shanghai landmarks constructed in the 1930s.

The stadium was built in 1934 and had been used as a Kuomintang military parade ground before hosting various National Games of China until 1983, when it fell out of favour and became a multiple-use venue.

When the Port Adelaide team arrived to inspect the facility, they found a neglected golf driving range, which had been built to cater for the growing passion for golf in China's major cities.

According to Hunter, the surface was 'horrendous'.

Underneath the neglect, the team saw an Art Deco beauty that could be brought to life if an AFL-quality surface could be laid, so they set their sights on Jiangwan Stadium.

Port Adelaide flew in grass and surface experts who agreed the task was daunting but achievable.

Once protracted negotiations about the stadium's loss of income were completed, according to David Koch, the Port team then spent more than $1.5 million on an 18-month project involving full-time gardeners who were tasked with creating a smooth, green, AFL-compliant oasis for match day.

The AFL then selected the Gold Coast Suns as their opponent, a reluctant sparring partner brought to the table by a $500,000 sweetener for Port Adelaide to purchase the rights to a Suns home game.

The final stumbling block was the Suns' choice of guernsey for the match and they insisted on wearing their primary red-and-yellow guernsey, the colours of the Chinese flag, and not their alternate guernsey, which was predominately blue and white.

The colours saga was a public-relations blow for Port Adelaide who felt they would lose any natural support from locals who were undecided about which team to follow.

After what an ABC report declared was a 'surprisingly bitter jumper spat', Port Adelaide relented and it was agreed that the Suns could wear their red-and-yellow guernsey featuring the Chinese national colours.

The game was on.

Andrew Hunter recalls that the doubters gained momentum in the media in the week before the game. Pundits questioned the wisdom of the Gold Coast Suns agreeing to the game when coach Rodney Eade's tenure was shaky.

Other media focused on the air quality and potential impacts on asthmatics. A major radio station in Adelaide ran skits with mock caricatures of Chinese accents.

Despite it all, more than 6000 Port Adelaide supporters made the trip to Shanghai, seduced by history and the potential for the ultimate away game.

Between 2015 and the first match in 2017, Hunter made 14 trips to China and even moved there for six weeks. With everything in place, he could finally relax at the gala dinner the night before the game.

'There were premiers, ministers, billionaires and one player of the century, Leigh Matthews,' Hunter wrote in his book, *Port Adelaide to Shanghai*. 'Not a bad gathering for an event, which had been for so long the subject of ridicule and ignorance.'

ı | | ı

On Sunday 14 May 2017, the Port Adelaide and Gold Coast Suns players linked arms on the field for the national anthems and an official match of Round 8 of the AFL season was about to get underway in Shanghai.

Koch, who had been mingling with both the Australian and Chinese delegation at the corporate function, had a specific role on the day to make sure Mr Gui, the main sponsor of the event, enjoyed himself.

He recalls Mr Gui and his Chinese colleagues standing and proudly singing the Chinese anthem, 'March of the Volunteers', in full voice.

Immediately after that, the Australian party stiffened in anticipation of 'Advance Australia Fair'. '(But) the Port Adelaide anthem came on instead by accident,' recalled Koch.

The AFL CEO Gillon McLachlan stared daggers at Koch but the mix-up was, in hindsight, an appropriate tribute to Port's pioneering role in the venture.

Now the national flags of Australia and China flew proudly above the newly constructed stadium, and a decent crowd watched as both teams burst through an enormous black-and-white banner that read: OPEN TO THE WORLD, HISTORY IN THE MAKING.

The first Shanghai game looked and felt like any other AFL game, with commentators, sirens, match officials, ground announcers, dugouts and umpires in yellow uniforms. The crowd yelled 'ball' if a player was caught in possession. Aussie Rules had been successfully grafted onto Chinese soil.

'It felt strange and surprisingly real – a merger of both my worlds,' Jamie Pi, the Chinese-Australian ground announcer, later recalled.

Pi was a stunning example of the new generation of Chinese-Australian AFL fans. Born in China in 1980, he had moved to

Australia at the age of 12 and fell hard for the game, both as a budding player and a Collingwood fan.

At the historic first game in Shanghai, Pi had been flown in to perform a number of roles, including ground announcer, interpreter and reporter on the ground for Channel 7's live broadcast.

Pi was paired off with a Chinese-speaking Anglo-Australian expat who was a 'minor celebrity' in Shanghai.

'They flew me, a fluent Chinese speaker, halfway around the world to announce in English while the white Aussie expat was speaking in Mandarin,' Pi remembered.

'We were quite the odd couple, and to this day I am still flabbergasted at what went on.'

Amid the fans who, according to Pi, were 'bamboozled' by the kick-and-catch football code, was an equal number of Chinese fans who were thrilled with the physicality of the contest.

'It sounds strange but I heard it and saw it. There were a lot of people who were taken by the game, particularly kids who had learned Auskick through international schools,' he said.

One stand, Pi noticed happily, was filled with fans in red-and-yellow caps, the colours of the Gold Coast Suns. Earlier that day, he'd received a frantic call from Suns' CEO, Mark Evans, who was concerned that the combined colours of the 6000-plus travelling Port Adelaide fans would visually overwhelm the Suns at the ground.

The simplest way to create a Suns presence, Evans concluded, was to order some red-and-yellow caps and give them away to fans.

Pi happily acted as his fixer and, with one phone call to a local manufacturer, 500 gold and red caps arrived at Jiangwan Stadium before kick-off.

'The Gold Coast management were amazed and relieved,' Jamie recalled.

'China is the only place in the world where that can happen.'

ı | | ı

On the field, one player that stood out was Brendon Ah Chee, a fifth-generation Aboriginal-Chinese player.

Ah Chee's great-great-grandfather, Owen Ah Chee, was a Cantonese jack of all trades who, in 1885, had helped establish the small Western Australian town of Derby.

Owen married Nellie, a Nyikina Aboriginal woman and together they had 11 children, creating a branch of the Ah Chee clan that has spread across Australia. In Derby his legacy as a founder of the town is marked through the naming of 'Owen Ah Chee Street'.

The Ah Chees are proud of their Chinese ancestry but they were a rarity in the game. In 2017 Brendon was one of just four men in the AFL to have Chinese heritage – alongside his brother Callum, Port Adelaide's Jake Neade and the Western Bulldogs' Lin Jong.

Somehow, Brendon had slipped under the radar of media scrutiny, with many of the travelling journalists focusing instead on the novelty of the match rather than the deep Chinese-Australian story that Ah Chee embodied.

'People saw my last name and may have expected a full-blown Chinese player,' Ah Chee remembered. 'My teammates joked that I was "the face of Chinese footy".'

For Ah Chee, there was a spiritual element to his ancestral return. 'Chinese blood mixing with Aboriginal blood and returning – it was poetic and felt like a full circle,' he said.

'Working in the hot streets of Derby, it would have been impossible for Owen Ah Chee, the original baker of Derby, to imagine that his great-great-grandsons would be playing an Australian sport that took us back to China. It's a beautiful thing,' Brendon said. 'I'd love to tell him that we're grateful for what he did for Derby and that we have kept his surname alive and we're carrying it proudly and the

Ah Chee brothers, our children and their children will carry a piece of him forever and wherever we go.'

Brendon Ah Chee put in a performance that would have made his great-great-grandfather proud. He was close to best player afield, lighting up Jiangwan Stadium with three goals, including the goal of the game from a tight angle on the boundary line.

'I wasn't even supposed to be playing, just over for the experience and I end up scoring three goals,' Brendon later said.

The annual Shanghai match was halted in 2020 due to COVID-19, and Brendon Ah Chee remains an unlikely but appropriate record holder.

'I don't have many records in footy, but I am the equal record holder for most goals kicked at Jiangwan Stadium in Shanghai,' Brendon said.

As Port cruised to a 72-point victory over the Suns, the jubilant South Australian fans sung the club's theme song, the INXS track 'Never Tear Us Apart'.

And, in that moment, despite all the logistical and cultural challenges – and the cynicism of those wanting the experiment to fail – it felt as if Port Adelaide's China strategy might be a winner.

Twelve months later, when Port Adelaide and Gold Coast returned to Shanghai for Round 9 of the 2018 AFL season, both clubs were more organised and able to savour the moment. The travelling media had moved beyond the novelty of the event and were on the lookout for deeper narratives.

With Brendon Ah Chee having left Port Adelaide for the West Coast Eagles in the off-season, all roads now led to his younger brother, Callum Ah Chee.

Callum, like Brendon, was an agile midfielder with roots in Broome and who'd grown up in Perth before making it as a professional footballer. Gold Coast Suns was his first club and he would later move to the Brisbane Lions.

While some of Callum's teammates preferred to avoid the soaring temperatures and stay in the familiar surrounds of the air-conditioned hotel, Callum embraced Shanghai's heat and history, visiting the 16th-century Yu Garden and City God Temple built by the Ming Dynasty master builders.

'I'm Aboriginal and really proud of that side of my heritage, but I am also proud of my Chinese side,' Callum recalled.

'It was impressive and it was quiet and peaceful in the Garden. That was when it really struck me that it's pretty amazing that I have bloodlines in this country as well.'

Nat Edwards, who was working as a reporter for the AFL website and Australian television broadcaster Channel 7, interviewed Callum. She had her own Chinese heritage footy story to tell.

Born in Melbourne to an Anglo-Australian father, Colin, and a Singaporean-Chinese mother, Jessie Poh Huay, Edwards divided her weekends between Chinese school and the local footy ground. She would sit at the table and munch on her grandmother's spring rolls while reading the football pages of the newspaper with her father.

Her mother, like many migrant parents, wanted Nat to study law or medicine or finance. Instead, Edwards pursued sports journalism, and after serving her apprenticeship in Melbourne's suburban footy leagues, she worked her way into reporting on the football for Channel 7.

Nat's broadcast career blossomed and a year after the second Shanghai game she would become the first woman to host the AFL grand final pre-game coverage on free-to-air television, all while 39 weeks pregnant.

Further success lay ahead with her appointment as the on-field MC for the 2022 AFL Finals series where she performed the formalities prior to matches sometimes in front of 90,000 fans.

Covering the Port Adelaide games in Shanghai was a surreal experience for Nat and a career highlight to that point. 'I felt this affinity and connection to the Chinese people, and here I was mixing my passion for footy with my heritage,' she said.

'It caught me off guard as far as a sense of pride and emotion because I had never put the two together and I am proud of them both.'

The 2018 Port Adelaide–Gold Coast game was better organised but less of a spectacle. It poured with rain the night before and on the morning of the match, with a number of local ticket holders deciding not to attend.

There was a smaller Port Adelaide travelling contingent than the previous year and the Gold Coast fans, one of the smallest fan bases in the AFL, did not travel in any meaningful number.

Those local fans who braved the weather were delivered a welcoming bi-cultural experience with both Chinese and Australian flags flying and both national anthems sung. Like most newcomers to the game, they would have found the goal umpires' flagwork unintelligible without explanation. But they could listen to announcements in Mandarin to help them decipher the rules and nuances of the great Australian game – and buy a pie and an Australian beer.

Port Adelaide's Shanghai experiment was, by any metric, a resounding success.

Commercially, it would lead to the club signing a lucrative, long-term sponsor in Chinese-owned car company MG. Politically, it brought Port Adelaide and the AFL into partnership with the Department of Foreign Affairs and Trade (DFAT) and Austrade – unheard of for a medium-sized club playing in an entirely provincial sport.

What could not be measured, though, was the unanticipated rewards for Chinese-Australian footy tragics such as Jamie Pi, Nat Edwards and the Ah Chee brothers.

For the average fan watching at home, Edwards' interview with Callum Ah Chee probably appeared to be no different from the thousands of other footballer interviews they'd heard.

But for Chinese-Australians watching the broadcast – and for Edwards and the Ah Chees themselves – it symbolised a merger of the ancient and modern.

Here was Ah Chee, a descendant of a Cantonese gold rush immigrant from the 1880s, chatting about his heritage to Nat Edwards, a product of post-1970s Chinese migration to Australia.

Unwittingly, Port Adelaide's China strategy had illuminated a hidden history of Chinese-Australian footy.

It is a story that stretches back almost to the origins of the game itself and reaches out from the Victorian goldfields to the pearl beds of Broome to the red heart desert of Alice Springs.

This book tells some of those stories.

CHAPTER 2

Celestial Footy: Miners and Market Gardeners

Australia was the first Western country to receive Approved Destination Status from the Chinese government in the late 1990s. Since then, Chinese tourists have flocked to Ballarat in regional Victoria to visit the mythical goldfields of *Hsin Chin Chan*, or 'New Gold Mountain'.

Generally, the tourists keep to a strict schedule. After travelling the 115-kilometre stretch of road from Melbourne's Tullamarine Airport to Ballarat, they proceed on a bus tour of the regional city which, for several frenetic years during the 1850s, was the heartland of Chinese life in the Victorian goldfields.

The jewel in the itinerary is Sovereign Hill, a recreated goldfields village and museum that employs many Mandarin-speaking guides. If time permits, the Chinese tourists might also visit an old gold mine, the Chinese section of the Old Cemetery and the Ballarat Wildlife Park.

The buses never stop, though, at the Red Lion Hotel or the Eastern Oval, despite the fact that this 19th-century pub and picturesque footy ground played host to one of the most unusual moments in Australian sporting history.

In 1892, 40 years after the first Chinese gold rush migrants arrived in Australia, more than 40 Chinese men formed two teams to play a charity match of Australian Rules football.

The clash was perhaps the first example of a non-white migrant community participating in Australia's home-grown game and provides a fascinating picture of early Chinese life in the Victorian colony.

By mid-afternoon on Friday 26 August 1892, the public bar of the Red Lion Hotel was swollen with raucous locals and eager visitors from the small towns dotted around Ballarat. Many of the men had taken the day off work to witness this unlikely sporting affair.

In the Victorian goldfields era, the Chinese were often referred to as 'celestials' or 'children of the sun' by Australian writers, and the press had duly dubbed this 'the celestial football match'.

The two Chinese teams, the Miners and the Market Gardeners, assembled in front of the Red Lion in team uniforms.

The Miners wore black stockings and red sashes, and most had their hair tied up in long Manchu pigtails. The Market Gardeners, a mix of Chinese and mixed-race players, donned grey stockings and red sashes, some team members with short-back-and-sides, European-style haircuts.

The players in the two teams represented dying professions, the death rattle of an old way of life for the original Ballarat Chinese community.

By 1892, Chinese gold mining in Australia had all but ended. However, since 1851 thousands of migrants – mostly from the modern day Guangdong province – had moved across the Victorian goldfields, operating under Confucian principles of co-operation to extract gold where others had failed.

Once settled, they faced another disruption, an annual Chinese resident tax of four pounds, which began in 1859, infringing their rights as fellow members of the British Empire.

By the late 1860s, most of the surface gold nuggets of the world's richest alluvial goldfield had been picked and panned, and so ended the rags-to-riches, strike-it-lucky stories that had originally lured the Chinese migrants to Ballarat.

With the remaining gold trapped deep in quartz reefs, big mining companies took over the industry, machines replacing pick and shovel, and some Chinese miners went underground, pushing their bodies to the limit in the dark, wet subterranean world beneath the city.

With the gold rush ended, each member of the Ballarat Chinese mining community faced a dark night of the soul: whether to stay and put down roots or return home to their families.

The Chinese market gardeners, meanwhile, had been a hidden force behind the settlement, survival and growth of small towns in regional Victoria.

Fighting off goats, rats, snakes, mosquitoes and thieves, they reliably produced fruit and vegetables, which helped townspeople ward off malnutrition, diabetes and other ailments.

But they too were under siege, by the twin threats of development and assimilation. The Chinese market gardens on the fringes of many towns were being bought up by property developers, while their children were often unwilling to put in the back-breaking work to keep the enterprise going.

Ballarat in the 1890s was split by a cultural fault line – English and Cantonese, the flutter of cards and the clacking of Mahjong tiles, whisky and rice wine, tobacco and opium, cutlery and chopsticks.

Just weeks before the celestial football match, the Ballarat Police Department had raided local Chinese gambling houses and filled the lockup with Chinese men with the *Ballarat Evening Post* noting the aim of the raid was to 'catch the Asiatics red handed at the lottery and fan-tan'.

The idea for the all-Chinese charity footy match had come from Ballarat policeman Constable T. Barrett, who estimated that 1000 people would attend, raising valuable charity funds and providing positive public relations.

Constable Barrett had worked closely with William Chow Mong, the Red Lion's publican, and the organising committee from the Ballarat Joss House on Main Street in Golden Point – and the swelling crowds were the fruits of their co-operation.

The *Ballarat Star* reported that both teams had prepared for weeks and were 'quite enthusiastic about the matter'.

On match day the players were transported from the Red Lion to Eastern Oval in a six-car procession led by a four-piece Chinese orchestra which, according to one reporter, 'moved through Ballarat on a great scale of magnificence'.

The procession was accompanied by a sonic potpourri with Cantonese opera arias punctured with firecrackers thrown to ward off the evil spirits, all to the soundtrack of the townspeople cheering them down the dusty streets.

The people of Ballarat had never witnessed such a spectacle.

Golden Point, Ballarat's Chinatown, was shut down for the day as residents left their homes, kitchens, laundries, shops, market gardens and gambling dens to watch the strange Victorian game.

To understand how a group of Chinese men ended up playing each other on Eastern Oval in 1892 requires an appreciation of what football meant to the people of the colony of Victoria.

Founded and codified in Melbourne in 1858, football quickly seized the imagination of Victorians, spreading from the city to the country throughout the 19th century. Ballarat Football Club was established in 1860, the third foundation club after Melbourne FC and Geelong FC.

The sport was propelled, in part, by the introduction of the eight-hour working day, which opened up serious leisure opportunities that had been previously filled by work.

By 1875, the annual periodical *The Footballer* recorded 96 clubs in Melbourne and 42 in country regions. With no offside rule, football was a game of running and open spaces, an optimistic free-spirited sport for all Victorians to share.

English journalist John Stanley James wrote in 1876 that the new Australian football was unique in its social cohesion, unlike sports in England, which were divided on class lines.

James compiled an impressive list of Melbourne football tribes that were bound together by the game: 'larrikins, mechanics, clerks, young aristocrats, tradesmen, free selectors and squatters, shopmen, members of Parliament, ex Cabinet ministers, bagmen, betting men, publicans, barmaids, working girls – a truly democratic crowd.'

Football clubs soon became an extension of the local community as businesses, churches and schools all got behind the endeavour to make sure their best men were fully prepared to defend the town's honour.

During the Victorian economic boom of the 1880s, Melbourne was one of the world's most prosperous cities, doubling in size to more than a million people.

The population boom provided both spectators and a deeper funnel of participants for the nine Victorian Football Association teams that began competition in 1877.

Within 15 years, it was not unusual for crowds of more than 30,000 to congregate at the Melbourne Cricket Ground, while in country areas football was used as a tool of social cohesion.

The 1892 'celestial match' in Ballarat was one such example.

The men that ran onto the Eastern Oval for the 'celestial match' had come from interstate, satellite towns, remote market gardens, mining camps and the Chinatown communities of Ballarat and Bendigo.

The game was officiated by Mr James Henry Lepp, likely the first Chinese man to umpire a footy match in Australia. His journey, which had landed him at the centre of Eastern Oval, was a familiar one to many of his Chinese-Australian compatriots on the field and in the crowd.

The son of a Cantonese father who came to Ballarat in 1853, and an Irish mother who had escaped the potato famine, Lepp and his brothers discovered football at school.

In 1886, while working as a miner, Lepp decided to become an umpire. At the time, the central umpire was a crucial part of the game, who bounced and threw the ball to restart play, managed the flow of the action and had the final, indisputable word on any incident.

Before he officiated the celestial match, Lepp had been the central umpire in two interstate matches in which South Ballarat took part: against Port Adelaide and New South Wales. The *Ballarat Star* published match reports and letters that testified to his fairness, including one that noted: 'In my opinion, Mr James Lepp is one of the most impartial umpires we have in Ballarat.'

The fact that there was a Chinese-Australian available to officiate the celestial match is a testament to the growing popularity and spread of football.

The presence of 42-year-old Sydney merchant Mei Quong Tart as captain of the Miners further illustrates the importance of the occasion.

The son of a shopkeeper and grandson of a farmer, Quong Tart migrated to Australia in 1859 from Taishan, escaping a Manchu-ruled China that had descended into chaos since its defeat by the Western powers in the two Opium Wars in the 1840s.

In 1854 a civil war had broken out in Taishan as the 'Red Turban' peasant movement rose up, causing chaos and mass destruction.

Taking advantage of the British Empire's freedom of movement opportunities for those governed under British treaty ports in China, Quong Tart left his ancestral home, at the age of nine, with an uncle, to set sail for Australia, migrating to the Braidwood goldfields in the New South Wales Southern Tablelands.

He was apprenticed to a local Scottish family who educated him in the ways of the Western world. As a young boy he accompanied his adopted father and mine owner, Percy Simpson, on a small pony and acted as an interpreter for the mostly Chinese miners.

Quong Tart's English was delivered in a full Scottish brogue, and by the age of 21 he was naturalised as an Australian.

Quong Tart played a number of sports in Braidwood and was a central part of town life, but already a wealthy man from mining, he outgrew the town and set off for Sydney to open a tea business.

His flagship 'Elite Hall' in Sydney's Queen Victoria Market could hold 500 patrons and it was the social centre and a neutral place for important meetings between members of Sydney's high society, with many major transactions concluded over a cup of Loong Shan tea. His tea rooms were also the site of the first meetings of Sydney's suffragettes women's rights movement.

The businessman would embrace all comers, treating politicians and workmen equally. His wife, Margaret Tart, recalled the culture he impressed on his staff in her biography, *The Life of Quong Tart*:

'His employees were ordered to treat all alike, whether they wore silk dresses or cheap prints, for Quong Tart had long learned that the silk dress did not make the lady, nor the fine black coat the gentleman.'

He took up unfashionable causes like advocating for lepers, and showed compassion for the sick and disabled with a particular interest in helping the inmates of mental asylums.

Quong Tart married a Ballarat Englishwoman, Margaret Scarlett, and was so enamoured with the city and its historic Chinese connection that he chose to spend his honeymoon there in 1886.

Tart was the quintessential multicultural man, comfortable in a kilt or Chinese robes. He was a bagpipe-playing, poetry-reciting honorary Mandarin; an athlete, philanthropist, merchant, humanist, freemason, diplomat and the first Chinese-Australian celebrity.

'Quong Tart is as well-known as the Governor himself and is quite as popular among all classes,' the *Daily Telegraph* once reported.

Although he moved now in the elegance of his opulent Sydney tea rooms, Quong Tart's early years working in the Braidwood goldfields made him eligible to captain the Miners team and he travelled down to Ballarat specifically for the historic first celestial match.

The game began at 2.00 pm and was soundtracked by the Chinese orchestra and the boom of firecrackers that kept evil spirits at bay. Schoolchildren shouted their support for the players in Cantonese and watched Chow Mong, the resident publican of the Red Lion Hotel, deliver the half-time entertainment.

'The large attendance of the public were much amused by the wild movements of the Mongolians, many of who appeared to think that seizing the ball and making off with it was the main point,' reported *The Age*.

The most startling moment, though, was when a white spectator ran onto the field and took a swing at one of the Chinese players. The player, later described as 'John, a muscular son of the sun' by the *Ballarat Evening Post*, 'seized the offender and soused him in some adjacent mud amid applause and laughter of a large group of onlookers'.

The crowd was on 'John's' side according to the *Post* report: 'The young fellow, who looked a pitiable object, besmeared with mud, was escorted off the ground by an officer in blue, and the general verdict was 'serve him right'.'

The 25–17 victory by the Market Gardeners was reported nationally as an 'unusual spectacle' and a 'splendidly contested' match.

In front of an estimated 5000 fans – five times the number expected by match organiser Constable T. Barrett – the healthy attendance allowed 'the Mongolians' to distribute '93 Pounds of the takings' to various local charities, sports clubs and a local widow.

A report in the *Ballarat Evening Post* on 29 August 1892 noted an unusual impact of the match on the Market Gardeners: 'One outcome of the recent Celestial football match is that numerous housewives in Ballarat have wondered at the late and in some instances non-appearance of the vegetable man.'

Four years later, in June 1896, the Ballarat Police decided to run another Chinese celestial match to replicate the success of the original. When the match was announced in Ballarat newspapers, the call went around Golden Point and the surrounding towns for able-bodied Chinese-Australian men to sign up.

Again, the match would be played to raise money for charity, and this time the recipient of the gate takings was the Ballarat Hospital and the Benevolent and Orphan Asylum, which had come under serious strain due to the financial depression during the 1890s.

This depression was particularly severe in Victoria, with more than 114,000 people departing the colony between 1892 and 1900. According to the *Ballarat Star*, there was 'evident appreciation by the public of the efforts of the Chinese residents of the City to assist the local charities'.

After weeks of feverish planning in the Golden Point Joss-House temple, on the morning of Friday 12 June 1896, organisers woke to bleak weather, which threatened to impact attendance numbers.

Despite the gloom, the Miners and the Market Gardeners once again assembled at the Red Lion Hotel and began their procession towards the Eastern Oval with a mounted police escort.

'From early morn yesterday the Chinese were highly excited,' the *Ballarat Courier* reported. 'The streets were lined with spectators and as the footballers, with their large and gorgeous banners, marched through the streets, considerable difficulty was experienced in keeping the crowd back.'

The *Courier* also noted the demographic differences in the teams with the Gardeners being 'principally full-blooded Chinese', and the Miners, captained by umpire James Lepp's brother George, fielding mixed race players: 'Altogether there were thirty full-blooded Chinese and ten half castes on the field.'

Despite the unfavourable weather, a sell-out crowd of more than 5000 roared as the two teams alighted from their carriages. This time, the Market Gardeners wore white jumpers, blue sashes, blue bloomers, blue-and-white caps and red stockings, while the Miners were attired in blue jumpers, white bloomers, red sashes, red caps and red stockings.

The other differentiator was their haircuts, with the Miners sporting short-back-and-sides and the 'full-blood' Market Gardeners maintaining their long Manchu pigtails.

Both the European and the Chinese bands began to play as James Henry Lepp, the same umpire from the 1892 match, strode onto the field in his Chinese silk slippers and ornate outfit.

The *Ballarat Star* report described in detail an unorthodox match that finished in a 12–10 victory to the Miners:

> The game commenced punctually, and its start was the signal for a burst of merriment on the part of the spectators, which continued without interruption until the final bell had rung.
>
> The play was a revelation to those accustomed to ordinary displays of football, and the frantic attempts made by the Chinese to perform feats of which a first-class footballer of the orthodox type might have well been proud, were provocative of uncontrolled laughter.
>
> All rules were disregarded, and the object uppermost in the minds of all was to kick the ball in whatever direction or by whatever means first presented themselves.
>
> It almost invariably happened that the player attempting the mark caused the ball to rebound upon his face or fly away at a tangent in a different direction from that in which he desired it to go.
>
> A few such experiences taught the players wisdom of a kind, and thereafter, when desiring to favour another with a mark, the ball was struck upon the knee or politely handed to the comrade.
>
> Under these circumstances it will be plain that the ball did not remain long in the vicinity of either goals, and in addition it did not appear to occur to the minds of many of the players that the object of the game was to secure a majority of the goals.
>
> At times the Gardeners' forwards joined their forces with the Miners' backs, and manfully assisted in beating back the attacks of their own comrades, and when a player found himself unable

to reach the ball by reason of friends or adversaries interposing he did not hesitate as to his course of action.

With the ball in the ruck he flung himself upon the backs of others and dragged men to the ground or seized them by the heels and threw them bodily upon the struggling mass of humanity in front. Legs, arms, and bodies became intermingled, and confusion reigned at times.

Players heedless of the possibility of their opponents obtaining goals, ceased their struggles for a few moments to toll up the pigtails which in the melee had been torn from their fastenings, or stopped to remonstrate with, sometimes to retaliate upon countrymen who had been the often innocent cause of their 'coming to grass.'

And during all the exciting passages of the game the Gardeners' captain (James Chung), gorgeously apparelled, maintained the same position in the centre of the field, smoked his cigarettes and surveyed his team and his opponents with a lordly air of disdain and a delightful unconcern as to the result of the struggle.

The central umpire performed his duties with the strictest impartiality. Protests from aggressive players were thrown away upon him, and when not engaged distributing a free kick or awarding marks, he was not above taking a hand in the game and rendering assistance to either side according as the ball reached him, and the direction in which he was running at that particular moment.

But though the game continued for a long time in the utmost good humour it was not allowed to finish without recourse to fisticuffs – a proceeding that is also known in the Europeans' game.

The trouble arose in consequence of a Gardener failing to kick for goal from the point at which the mark had been awarded him. It was an angle shot, and the would-be goal sneak desired to pass round so as to stand directly in front of the goal, but of course this could not be permitted.

Words were bandied, and at length an indignant Miner enforced his protest with his fist, and thereupon a general melee ensued. Hands and feet were used freely, but with very little effect.

The spectators were convulsed with laughter. That which had gone before had been of the tamest as compared with the spectacle of nearly 40 excited Chinese chattering volubly in their own language and striking blindly at one another.

The disturbance, however, was quickly quelled, and the game proceeded, fresh objects of mirth being revealed every instant.

The *Ballarat Courier*, meanwhile, noted a violent incident that was caused by the Manchu pigtails worn by the Market Gardeners.

This hairstyle featured a high shaved forehead and a long-braided, snaking ponytail and was considered an act of obedience and fealty to the Manchu dynasty since 1644. For Chinese men – even those in Australia – to cut it off was considered an act of treason and defiance.

'The pigtails worn by the Celestials became loose and entangled amongst the players and a foul occurred through Yet Way's pigtail being pulled by one of the half-castes,' reported the *Courier*.

This incredible scene illustrates the tensions between Chinese migrants in Australia, some who remained emotionally tied to China, while others had withdrawn their loyalty to the Manchu.

In the dying days of the Manchu Qing dynasty, the pigtail pull could be seen as a statement by the 'half-caste' Miners to their ancestral countrymen to show some gratitude and sever ties with the old country. Whatever the case, the *Sydney Bulletin* noted that the pigtail pull 'was wrong, because the half-castes should have remembered that their fathers were Chinese'.

Other Chinese charity football matches would be played in the 1890s in Victorian goldfields towns, such as Bendigo, Bright and

Beechworth, while the very first Australian Rules international match was played between a Chinese team and an Indian team in Melbourne in 1899 to raise money for St Vincent's Hospital.

For Victoria University professor Rob Hess, these early matches featuring Chinese teams deserve greater recognition: 'These are amazing Australian stories. Chinese players lining up to play the quintessential Australian game in the shadow of the White Australia policy.

'Football was able to bring the European and Chinese communities together and created an era of tolerance and harmony across Victoria.

'There's a rich history that historians have ignored, hidden or marginalised.'

These matches prove that by the turn of the 20th century, Chinese-Australians had taken up Australian Rules and were prepared to use the game as a means of expressing their own communities.

At times, footy showed the divided loyalties of a community balancing their relationship with their country of birth and their country of residence.

Above all, the celestial matches show the Chinese community's deep philanthropic streak, willingness to participate in Australian life – and 'have a go'.

CHAPTER 3

Wally and George – the Pioneers

The Carlton fans who streamed into Princes Park on the afternoon of Monday, June 8 1908 had grown to expect success from their team.

They were drawn from the full spectrum of Melbourne's social classes and arrived at the ground by tram, train and on foot, their eagerly anticipated King's Birthday public holiday capped off by a game of football.

These supporters had every reason to be buoyant and their ascendancy to excellence was a reflection of the wider success for the Victorian Football League (VFL).

Eleven years earlier, in 1897, the stronger clubs of the old Victorian Football Association (VFA) had started a breakaway league, tired of carrying the financial burden of the smaller teams.

In a show of strength, the VFL hosted the 1908 Jubilee celebrations – which featured the first interstate competition – to mark 50 years since the first official game of Australian Rules football. Victoria was the powerhouse state, and Carlton was its leading club.

One opponent, Richmond's Barney Herbert, would later tell the *Sportsman* newspaper that the Carlton side of 1907–1911 was without peer. 'I do not think that that side will ever be excelled in the League for strength, balance and brilliance,' he said.

'No team playing today can show the football genius of the Blues in those years.'

Carlton's all-conquering team had won the previous two premierships, in 1906 and 1907, and were unbeaten in the first six games of the 1908 season. Led by captain Fred Elliott and coached by former elite footballer and Test cricketer Jack Worrall, Carlton's players and fans were overwhelmingly white, reflecting Australia's dominant Anglo-Celtic population.

But Wally Koochew, a rover playing just his third game for Carlton, was one of two Chinese-Australians listed on the match program for the Round 7 match at Princes Park. The other, also a rover, was Geelong's George Tansing.

In a convincing 77-point victory to Carlton, Koochew kicked one goal and, according to *The Argus*, was 'prominent' in the play, while the *Geelong Advertiser* noted that Tansing 'roved with good judgement'.

If these two Chinese-Australian pioneers acknowledged one another, it was not publicly recorded. But both men had remarkably similar stories. Both were born to mixed marriages between a Cantonese man and a European-born woman. Both grew up in regional towns 75 kilometres outside of Melbourne, and both came from families in the greengrocery business. Both had merged surnames – 'Koochew' came from the original 'Kou Chow'; Tansing from 'Tan Sing' – and both would play a few games of the 1908 VFL season before returning to country football.

One key difference was their pathway to the big time.

While George Tansing was able to live and play VFL in his hometown of Geelong, Wally had to leave his familiar environment in Central Victoria and move to Melbourne to play the game at the highest level.

This is the story of how two Chinese-Australians came to cross paths in Victoria's premier football league.

Wally Koochew's father, James, left his village in Whampoa in Canton in 1865 after word of the fortunes that could be made on the Victorian goldfields activated his wanderlust.

Upon his arrival in Melbourne, immigration officials changed the surname on his papers from Kou Chou to Koo Chew.

After failing as a gold miner, James entered the fruit and vegetable game as a market gardener in Geelong, and Bairnsdale, a town 300 kilometres east of Melbourne.

By 1880, James had become a citizen of the British Empire and married Mary Dalker, an Irishwoman who had once been imprisoned for public drunkenness. Somewhere on his journey, James changed his name from Koo Chew to 'Koochew', making it easier for Australians to say while retaining its distinctive Chinese sound.

'It's quite remarkable that Wally chose to keep his name and didn't anglicise it,' football historian Dr Robert Hess says. 'It's quite clear he was proud of his heritage.'

James and Mary Koochew put down roots in Macedon, a town in the Macedon Ranges, located between Melbourne and Bendigo in Central Victoria. They started a greengrocer shop in the heart of the thriving town and settled down to have a family.

Their first son, Walter 'Wally' John Henry Koochew, was born in 1887 and, in the mountain air, he would develop as an all-round athlete. Wally loved to sprint, and speed would become his calling card for the nearby Woodend Football Club.

From the early days of the game, VFL and VFA clubs and representative teams would tour regional Victoria to play against the cream of local footy associations, often identifying talented prospects to bring back to the city. And when VFA club Brunswick came to play Woodend in May 1907, they discovered 19-year-old rover Wally Koochew.

His general play and accurate kicking earned him an invitation to come to Melbourne and he made his debut for Brunswick immediately, the *Coburg Leader* reporting that he played 'a very good game'.

Wally's form for Brunswick began to attract attention further afield and, in 1908, he joined the Carlton Blues, enlisted in their mission to win a third straight premiership. Of the clubs in the VFL and VFA, Carlton had been the most successful in their recruiting and development of talent, having assembled the greatest team in the history of the VFL or VFA to date.

For the Carlton coach and committee to have prioritised the slightly built Chinese-Australian speedster from the Macedon Ranges speaks volumes for Wally's potential.

On Thursday 13 May 1908, the Carlton selection committee met in the club rooms at Princes Park. Missing a few players to injury ahead of the Round 3 match against Essendon, the committee decided to select Wally to make his debut.

Both key decision-makers had previous exposure to Chinese communities in regional Victoria. Captain Fred Elliott, a tailor by trade, had learned his craft in Bendigo, the Chinese capital of regional Australia, while coach Jack Worrall was from Maryborough, an hour from Ballarat, where he would have undoubtedly come across the local Chinese community

However, after the team announcement, one Carlton member immediately resigned his membership in a bitter complaint at the selection of Koochew, whom he viewed as a racial gatecrasher.

As documented by *The Blueseum* history website, the Carlton committee recorded a minute on the affair that read:

From C.W. Richardson, 640 Drummond St., Carlton, presenting his membership ticket to the club and requesting that his name be struck off the membership list; for the reason that the Society of Druids, to which he belonged, believed that the Carlton Club, by including a Chinaman in the team, was dealing a death blow to the White Australia policy.

On the motion of Mr. Oxlade, sec. by Mr. Gurr, it was carried that the request contained in the letter that the writer's name be struck off the membership list be complied with; Mr. Richardson to be notified to that effect.

The Ancient Order of Druids was introduced to Australia in the 1850s by English migrants and, by the early 1900s, there were branches spread across regional Victoria.

To their credit, Carlton stuck by their selection of Wally and accepted the member's resignation.

With the support of his club, coach and captain, Wally ran onto Princes Park wearing Carlton's navy blue lace-up and chamois yoke, the first footballer of Chinese heritage to play for a VFL club. The date was Saturday 16 May 1908.

His role in the Blues' 11-point win against Essendon was lauded in the press, with *The Age* noting that he 'performed creditably' and *The Weekly Times* listing him as one of eight 'heroes of a day of heroism'.

An item in *The Herald*, published on 22 May, illustrates the curiosity that Wally generated in the VFL. 'Somebody wishes to know how to pronounce the name of little Koochew,' the columnist wrote. '"Kashoo" is the nearest phonetic spelling I can give.'

In Wally's second game against Collingwood, at Victoria Park, he scored his first VFL goal from the half forward flank. 'Koochew, though on the light side, is clever, and makes the best of his opportunities,' *The Argus* noted.

Fifteen days later, George Tansing made his VFL debut for Geelong against St Kilda at Corio Oval. There was no reported outrage or letters of membership resignation upon his selection.

Born Kimjue Sing on 25 March 1884, George Tansing was the son of Cantonese migrant Sang Sing and his English wife, Ada Mary Stephens. Sang Sing, from Canton, had met Ada in London, where he'd worked for 10 years as a mixed business trader.

They migrated to Melbourne, got married, contracted the family name to Tansing and moved to Geelong to establish a grocery store. George, their first child, learned to play Australian Rules football at school.

As a young adult in 1907, the 23-year-old George Tansing married an Anglo-Australian woman, Wilhelmina Ellis, and played for local club East Geelong in one of the three leagues in town. His best-on-ground performance for East Geelong, in late May, was a key factor in him being promoted to VFL side Geelong, the only regional club in the league.

Geelong, 75 kilometres south-west of Melbourne, was a shipping and rail hub known as 'the Pivot'. The football team, then nicknamed 'the Pivotonians', raised the hopes of the town's working-class population, who travelled by foot, tram or horse-drawn buggy to Corio Oval, deemed by many to be the 'prettiest' ground in the VFL.

On Saturday 6 June 1908, Corio Oval hosted Geelong's Round 6 clash against St Kilda. Geelong's team contained an Asian surname for the first time in its history: Tansing.

Despite Geelong recording a three-point loss, George scored his first VFL goal, described by *The Argus* as a clever snap kick.

According to *The Geelong Advertiser*, George 'put in a lot of clever work, made a distinctly good impression and should prove an acquisition to the team'.

But after Geelong lost its next four games, George was dropped from the team, never to return. His 21-day stint yielded five appearances and two goals – one in both his first and last games for the club.

As Geelong went on to finish bottom of the VFL ladder, George returned to East Geelong and captained the team to a premiership. When he took on the captaincy, George became the first reported Chinese-Australian captain of a mainstream football club.

In that suburban league grand final, George kicked a crucial goal in the final quarter to set up the 19-point win. It was the first of his two premierships with East Geelong.

Meanwhile, Wally Koochew was on a similar trajectory, playing just one more game for Carlton, making four in total, before heading back to his hometown, Macedon. His VFL career had lasted a little longer than George's, but he left Melbourne with one less game to his name.

Reports from the time suggest his departure may have been caused by the depth of talent in Carlton's squad. 'Carlton's difficulty is to give a game occasionally to the several smart players they have in reserve who would be better employed as regular members of weaker teams,' *The Argus* reported in June 1908.

The most likely reason was the illness and premature death of Wally's mother, Mary, who passed away, aged 49, in 1909. A report in *The Herald* on 2 July 1909 noted that Wally had been granted permission to transfer to Brunswick, his former VFA club, but did not take up the offer.

By the end of 1909, Wally had resettled in Macedon. He worked in his father's greengrocer store and became a first-time father after his wife, Axelina, gave birth to a son, Frederick, who would be joined by four brothers and a sister.

Wally signed up for the local footy team and immersed himself in the community, becoming secretary of the club and spearheading its fundraising endeavours.

In 1909 and 1910 he played for the Kyneton Football Association's representative team, which would travel by train to challenge city teams such as his old club Brunswick and the Victoria Police.

However, Wally's post-VFL career in Macedon was marred by an ugly racial incident during a match. As the *Woodend Star* reported in October 1909, a spectator named PJ Mahony was charged by a Constable Tucker with using insulting language to provoke a breach of the peace.

'When Wally asked him to stop, he was called a "dirty little Chow" to which Wally responded by "hitting at him",' reported the *Star*.

A witness named McKenzie corroborated the evidence and the defendant at first denied the charge and then said he apologised, which was not sufficient for Constable Tucker to 'repair the wrong'.

Had the aggressive language been allowed to continue, according to Tucker, if he wasn't there to intervene, the defendant would have been 'roughly handled by the crowd'.

After witness corroboration, Wally received a caution for 'striking at the defendant', while PJ Mahony was found guilty, fined 20 shillings and ordered to pay costs. Goldsmith's judgment included a warning that is still relevant today: 'There was a danger in people outside of the players interfering in football games.'

The manner in which the crowd, police and community rallied behind Wally demonstrates the fair-mindedness of the townspeople and the power of country football as a tool of belonging. Despite his

Chinese heritage, Wally was a member of the Macedon football tribe, and abuse of him would not be tolerated.

Within a year, the local press returned to reporting on Wally's good football form, noting that he 'excelled in meteoric dashes and showed his great pace off to perfection' in Macedon's top-of-the-table clash against Kyneton.

In 1912, Wally opened his own greengrocer's shop on Woodend's High Street. He worked hard to make the business a success, travelling by horse and cart to bring produce back from Melbourne, a significant 140-kilometre round trip.

According to the Woodend and District Heritage Society, Wally was a deeply involved community member, singing at the St Mary's Anglican Church, fighting fires with the Woodend Fire Brigade and pitching in to help working bees around town.

In 1914, he helped Woodend Football Club win the premiership. One local dignitary, Ernest David Gardiner, later wrote that Wally 'was a star for Woodend and many of us will remember this clever footballer'.

World War I closed down the Kyneton League from 1916–1918 and Wally never played seriously again.

In 1925, Wally's father, James, passed away, breaking Wally's connection with China. Until his passing, James had been running an unofficial Chinese consulate in Kyneton, helping the local Chinese community out with naturalisation, legal and other matters.

Wally's heart was no longer in Woodend and, when he left town, in 1926, a report was published in the *Woodend Star* with the headline, 'Businessman Departs'.

Before his death in 1932, Wally was known to sell hot dogs to football fans outside North Melbourne's Arden Street Oval.

Few, if any, of the people who stopped to buy a hot dog would have appreciated the significance of the figure standing before them: Wally Koochew, the first Chinese-heritage VFL player.

ı | | ı

However, the Australian Rules football family line did not die with George Tansing's retirement. His son Bill Tansing played in the Geelong reserves team in 1936 and 1937. Bill was the leading goal kicker in both years and played a starring role with four goals to help the Geelong reserves win the 1937 premiership, while George's great-grandson Damien Tansing played for a number of years in Geelong's amateur league.

Today, the names Koochew and Tansing still ring out in country football. In the Geelong and District Football League (GDFL), the annual medal for the best and fairest in the GDFL is named after George's nephew Ivan Tansing, who was a prominent player for Herne Hill in Geelong in the 1950s.

Football stayed strong in the Koochew clan, too, with Wally's son, Walter Jr, playing seconds for the Melbourne Football Club and achieving some fame as a top-level country sprinter.

Wally's grandson Leslie was awarded life membership of the VFL Umpires Association, and his great-grandson James served as the official statistician for the Blues' 1995 premiership-winning coach, David Parkin.

'It says something about Australian Rules football that 87 years after Wally Koochew made his debut at Carlton, there was still a Koochew involved with the club,' James says.

Wally's great-great-grandson, Jack, plays for Melton South in the Riddell District league. Jack's grandfather Ross – a country footy legend in his own right for Robinvale, near Mildura – never misses a home game.

'The Koochews,' he says, 'are still here and they're still playing football.'

CHAPTER 4

Les Kew Ming – the Longest Kicker in the Land

The moment Tom Wills and the founding fathers of Australian football agreed that there would be no offside rule, the game philosophically seceded from its English rugby origins.

Players in the new expansive Victorian game would not have to go through their opposition with brute force – they could tactically kick over their opponents and exploit the wide-open spaces and possibilities on either side of them.

Kicking became the most fundamental and essential skill of the sport – the only way to score a goal and the fastest and most efficient way to move the ball around the ground. Crowds loved the spectacle of a long kick and appreciated the subtlety of an accurate kick delivered to a teammate's chest over distance.

'To be able to kick a ball well would appear at first glance to be a cardinal qualification of every league footballer,' once proclaimed *The Sporting Globe*.

Founded in 1922, *The Sporting Globe* was an influential newspaper with a reputation for in-depth tactical analysis, player profiles and news items. In 1928, it convened the first national kicking contest in Melbourne.

The event organiser, *Sporting Globe* journalist and former Geelong player, Wallace 'Jumbo' Sharland, might have anticipated the winner to come from one of the glamorous VFL clubs in Melbourne.

Instead, the winner came from Echuca, a bush footy stronghold on the Murray River, 220 kilometres north of Melbourne.

ı | | ı

On 20 September 1928, a mixed group gathered at Echuca oval to witness an Echuca player, Les Kew Ming, step up and measure his punt and drop kicks.

Assembled to bear witness to the event were club officials, curious onlookers, *Sporting Globe* representatives and, most importantly, a licensed surveyor engaged by the *Sporting Globe* to measure and certify the exact distance of the kicks.

They were there to watch Les Kew Ming kick and he looked the part in his Echuca football outfit and boots.

Due to work commitments, Les had been unable to make the kicking contest finals to be held at the MCG the following day featuring the long-kicking heavyweights from the VFL, VFA, Victorian country football clubs and even an entrant from the Newtown club in Sydney.

Because of Les's long-kicking reputation, the *Sporting Globe* had convened a special advance event to allow Echuca's superboot to compete.

After the line was marked out, Les unleashed a 67-metre punt kick, followed by a 66-metre drop kick.

The next day at the MCG, the best kickers in the country could not get even get close to Les's pair of monster kicks. In the punt kick, the closest was 59 metres from Geelong's George 'Jocka' Todd, who played 232 games for Geelong and was famous for his long punts.

Les won the drop kick by seven metres, with A. Bliss from Williamstown a distant second after a 59-metre kick.

The following day the *Sporting Globe* ran a story proclaiming 'a triumph for L. Kew Ming of Echuca who won both the punt and drop kick competitions'.

Les received a £25 prize for each kick. The longest kicker in the land, according to the *Sporting Globe* rankings, was a Chinese-Australian from a small Victorian country town.

The *Riverine Herald* reported: 'His kicking ability is so well known to Echuca and district residents, it needs no eulogy in these columns. His success goes to prove that all champions are not found in the metropolis.'

Leslie 'Les' Henry Kew Ming was born in 1897 in St Arnaud, a town in Victoria's Wimmera region, three hours' drive north-west of Melbourne. His father, Kew Ming Lok, came from Kwangtung (now known as Guangdong) province. His mother, Louisa Cum Moon, was born in Minyip from a Chinese father and an Irish mother.

Kew Ming Lok settled in the Chinese camp in north St Arnaud, running a market garden and store. He was reportedly a popular figure in the town and would travel to houses and stations in a horse and buggy to deliver the fruits of his market garden – fresh tomatoes, cauliflowers, cabbages, carrots and other root vegetables, all providing important nutrition for residents across the district.

St Arnaud was an important town for the Chinese community in the Wimmera due to its thriving Chinatown north of the town centre. The town still contained many Chinese miners from the gold rush who had flocked to 'New Bendigo', as St Arnaud was originally named.

Chinese New Year was widely celebrated, as was 'Ching Ming', the annual tending of the graves of ancestors.

In 1883, St Arnaud's Senior Constable Moncton was quoted as saying: 'The Chinese of St Arnaud were the most law abiding citizens he had ever in his official capacity met with and also the most charitable.'

Compared to other some areas in Victoria, there were largely harmonious relations between the St Arnaud European and Chinese communities, a success built on the Chinese propensity for hard work and providing of invaluable services to the residents. One of those services was the All Nations Hotel and general store, run by the Kew Ming family.

But on 22 December 1900, the St Arnaud Chinatown burned to the ground including the All Nations Hotel with three-year-old Les Kew Ming and his family escaping. Later in life, Les would hear stories and theories about the source of the fire, but for now his parents were in crisis.

A decision was taken not to rebuild the Chinatown; the town's Chinese footprint was erased and its residents scattered throughout the region, becoming market gardeners or finding work on surrounding farms.

For Les, this meant a major disruption and a move 70 kilometres deeper into the Wimmera to Minyip, where he lived with his Chinese grandfather, Cum Moon, went to school and was later apprenticed as a bootmaker.

In its heyday, the streets of Minyip were alive with bustling commercial activity, the town servicing the region as a grain hub.

At various times it had bursts of prosperity, which underwrote the building of a beautiful town in the 1880s.

Cum Moon's bootmaker shop was located on Napier Street, the main street of St Arnaud, and he was a permanent fixture of a mostly transient Chinese community that worked as traders, gardeners and labourers.

One local historian, Shirley Smith, wrote that Les's grandfather Cum Moon was 'a tiny man' who would generously hand out threepence coins for the town's children to buy lollies.

In Cum Moon's shop, Les learnt the bootmaking trade, a skill that would serve him well later in life.

Les played at the Minyip Football Club, which was his passport to acceptance in the town. In the Minyip museum's collection, there is a photo of 15-year-old Les in 1912, arms folded with his junior teammates – he seems comfortable as one of the Minyip footy lads.

Les was 17 when the call came to the colonies of the British Empire to supply troops for World War I. According to the Minyip Historical Society, 168 volunteers enlisted from a population of just 500. Les tried to enlist in 1914 but could not get past the Defence Act of 1909, which excluded him because of his Asian background.

However, two years later the Australian Imperial Force (AIF) relaxed the restrictions and Les – who had returned to St Arnaud and joined both the local army cadets and the rifle club – enlisted immediately. In October 1916, he boarded the HMAT *Borda* with his new mates in the 5th Reinforcements, ANZAC Cyclist Battalion.

Les was a no-nonsense character and three weeks after his ship left Melbourne, he was charged with insubordination for slapping a higher officer in response to an alleged racial slur and was given 24 hours to cool down in the ship's brig – a prison room for soldiers who had breached military rules.

Still, Les was a popular member of his battalion. According to the official newsletter of the AIF's 23rd Battalion, he helped his battalion to victory in a football match and a sprinting relay.

His experience, calm demeanour and ability to lead men saw him promoted through the ranks to Lance Corporal and later to junior Section Commander. In 1917, he was wounded leading his men through gunfire in the battle for Broodseinde Ridge as part of the Ypres offensive.

'Corporal Kew Ming was a man among men when it comes to leading his soldiers to rescue their mates under shellfire and protecting the communication trench, helping save the lives of dozens of soldiers and helping our men get back from a desperate situation,' says Brad Manera, a senior historian and curator of the Anzac Memorial.

When assessing Kew Ming's legacy, Manera has studied the actions of many brave soldiers, especially at the bloody battle for Broodseinde Ridge.

'Terms like hero are very difficult to apply when more than 38,000 Australians were killed or injured in four months trying to take that ridge line,' he says.

'Certainly, Corporal Leslie Kew Ming was among those heroes. I reckon you can call him a hero.'

Les returned to Australia and received the prestigious Military Medal engraved with an official account of his actions in which he set: 'a fine example to his men, encouraging them to complete the work though under heavy shell fire, remaining on duty though wounded and helping the Australians to take the ridge and hold it despite the German artillery bombardments.'

In an interesting footnote to World War I, Alastair Kennedy, the author of *Chinese Anzacs: Australians of Chinese Descent in the Defence Forces 1885–1889*, notes that despite most of the approximately 260 Chinese-Australian Anzac soldiers being kept out of front-line roles, they served Australia nobly and were over-represented in gallantry awards.

Les finished his military career as a sergeant and came back to Australia for demobilisation with the respect of the military and the wider community.

In 1919, Les returned to Minyip to live and work with his grand-father Cum Moon in his bootmaking shop. He rejoined the Minyip Football Club and immersed himself in the Minyip Fire Brigade, where he excelled in hydrant events at inter-brigade competitions.

He decided it was time to make a move on his own and he found a gap in the market at Wedderburn, a growing town 120 kilometres east of Minyip. He packed up his belongings and set off to establish his own bootmaking business.

In September 1920, a 'Public Notice' for the business appeared in the *Wedderburn Express*: 'LH Kew Ming (Late 23rd Bat AIF), Bootmaker, formerly of St Arnaud – All Classes of Repairs Done at Moderate Prices. Sewn work a specialty.'

Les soon became a star of the Wedderburn Football Club, helping the team to win the 1920 Korong Football League premiership. He was 22, in great physical shape, and his match-winning performance in the grand final capped off an impressive year that attracted the attention of North Melbourne Football Club, who approached him with an offer.

Les accepted and moved to Melbourne to play for the 'Shinboners' against the best in the Victorian Football Association (VFA).

It was every young footballer's dream to have his photograph on a 'cigarette card', the ancestor of the modern day 'footy card' that young fans still collect. Les was granted his own cigarette card at the start of the 1922 season, but in his photo he is frowning, perhaps a signal that the country boy was not enjoying city life.

That season, a report in *Smith's Journal* headlined 'Kew Ming, Melbourne's brilliant half-back' noted Les's performance in a spirited match against Hawthorn.

After the game, an 'enthusiastic' North Melbourne supporter approached Les with a ten-shilling note to reward him. Les refused the money and directed the supporter to give the ten shillings to 'Johnny', an unemployed teammate who was in financial hardship.

North Melbourne made the finals series and although they lost to Port Melbourne, Les was reported among the best players on the ground. However, in the 1923 season he broke his finger and then his collarbone. *The Argus* described the succession of injuries as 'Kewming's unfortunate year.'

In the off season, Les made a decision to return to the country, choosing Echuca for his next hometown.

He married his partner, Vera, joined the Echuca Football Club and volunteer Fire Brigade and opened a bootmaking business in town.

Les had always been a quick runner and he began training in preparation to compete on the circuit of 'Gift' handicap sprint races, the main feature of regional athletics carnivals that were a central part of the Victorian country sporting tradition.

In 1925, Les won the sprint at the Shepparton Gift. At the Echuca Football Club he made the fullback position his own, his booming kicks becoming famous throughout the region, sometimes reaching the centre with one mighty kick.

Any doubt that he could still match it on the football field with the game's elite was dispelled in 1927 when he was reportedly among the best players on the ground for a Bendigo representative team in its one-point loss to a VFL representative team.

The following year, legendary Port Melbourne player and ex-soldier George Ogilvie joined him at Echuca and the club won the 1928 Bendigo League premiership.

Different match reports in the *Riverine Herald* were peppered with praise for Les's play: 'he cleared brilliantly' with his booming kicks, and dazzled fans with his exciting 'dashes from goal'. He was also instrumental in 'saving the day' and 'repulsing attacks' and his skills were noteworthy: 'The way he picked the ball off the ground was one of the most outstanding features.'

Echuca's winning run to the Bendigo League premiership meant increased focus on Les, who had to endure both racial abuse from spectators and physical abuse on the field.

Newspaper reports from the season noted that at various times he was deliberately punched, kicked and kneed in the back. His wife, Vera, chose not to attend either his country or city football matches because of the abuse he received.

'He found that if you showed emotion as to why the comments were said, that it played into their hands,' Les's daughter Berenice later explained. 'So he used to ignore them as though they weren't there.'

After he won the *Sporting Globe*'s kicking contest in September 1928, the president of the Bendigo Football League 'extended to him the league's congratulations,' according to the *Riverine Herald*. 'The players also congratulated him, while the crowd cheered.'

When World War II broke out, Les was keen to enlist but was deemed too old for active service.

At 42, he was appointed by the Army to the dual role of machine gun and physical fitness instructor.

Heeding the call to arms, Les closed his bootmaking shop in Echuca and moved to Brunswick in northern Melbourne to prepare young recruits for war.

His own fitness was maintained by playing football for Watsonia in the inter-services competition against fellow soldiers who were often 20 years younger than him. He also coached his daughter Berenice's netball team, joined the Brunswick snooker club and settled into suburban Melbourne life.

In February 1960, at the age of 63, Les died from a massive stroke while driving back to Melbourne after visiting friends in Echuca.

Although Berenice describes her father as 'Aussie through and through', she remembers him staying in contact with the Chinese community in Melbourne. 'One thing I can say for sure is that Dad was not ashamed of being Chinese.'

Although she was too young to see her father play top-level football, she came to understand his reputation through his interactions with fans at North Melbourne's Arden Street Oval 'We couldn't walk 10 metres without someone stopping for a chat,' she says.

And he will never be forgotten for that special day in Echuca in 1928 when he kicked long and true and would go on to be crowned the longest kicker in the land.

CHAPTER 5

From Country to City:
Melbourne's Young Chinese League Team

For most of the Cantonese and Hakka Chinese fortune seekers who arrived in Victoria in the 1800s, Melbourne was literally a stopover on their way to regional areas rich with gold.

Accordingly, the first Chinese-Australians to play Australian Rules football in Victoria were almost all from regional towns.

The first recorded Chinese player, Henry George Chin Kit, ran on for Eaglehawk in the Bendigo League in 1882, followed by Ah Tie for the Golden Square Imperials and Ni Gan and Ah Poo for Valentine Hill in 1883. In Ballarat, the Lepp brothers George and James were followed by Willie Wun Hym and the Sing brothers.

Outside the major regional centres, Thomas Chin Chee won a premiership for Inglewood in 1895 and William Ying won a flag for Dunolly in 1903.

That year, Echuca's James Hing became the first recorded Chinese-Australian to be suspended and face the disciplinary tribunal after soundly thrashing an opposition player, from Moama, in response to being racially vilified.

In the big leagues of the VFA and the VFL, almost all of the pioneer Chinese heritage players came from the bush. Carlton's Wally Koochew from Macedon, George Tansing from Geelong, Les Kew Ming from St Arnaud, Jack Wunhym from Ballarat and South Melbourne's Ian Chinn from Bendigo. The exception was Ernie Foo, who played four games for St Kilda in 1914, and was raised in Melbourne's inner-city suburb of Fitzroy.

The Chinese-Australian football story in Melbourne mirrors the urbanisation of the Chinese community in the early 1900s, following the Federation of Australia and the introduction of the White Australia policy in 1901.

The Australian-born children of the early regional Chinese migrants were less restricted in their occupational options and came to the big cities to participate in urban life and join white collar professions.

In Melbourne, the Chinese community clung tightly around the inner-city suburbs, with Chinatown, centred on Little Bourke Street, serving as the spiritual, commercial, social, cultural and culinary hub.

This inner-city area also housed six founding VFL/VFA clubs – Melbourne, Carlton, Collingwood, Richmond, North Melbourne and Fitzroy – and the Chinese community lived cheek by jowl with the most hardcore football supporters.

In 1922, the Chinese Progress Association team to take the field was the first reported all-Chinese footy side, followed by a second from the Chinese Athletics Association in 1923.

These teams provided cultural strength, safety in numbers and, more importantly, a gathering of the community around the Australian game. Within a decade, they would merge to form the Young Chinese League (YCL).

The story of the YCL was one of advancement and integration.

As author and footy academic Rob Hess notes: 'On the eve of World War II, the Young Chinese League was a well-established, if not significant part of the broader Australian football milieu in Melbourne.'

ı | | ı

The two Chinese teams that played in Melbourne in the 1920s were an urban version of the all-Chinese teams that had played in the Victorian goldfields in the 1890s. A key difference was the occupations of the players.

Where the goldfields teams were made up of miners, furniture makers and market gardeners, Melbourne's Chinese teams were made up of both working-class and middle-class Chinese community players.

The Melbourne Chinese teams were not considered a novelty like their goldfields counterparts, perhaps due to the fact that most of the players had grown up with a sound understanding of the game.

The first high-quality player who played for both the Chinese Progress Association and Chinese Athletics Association in the 1920s was Leslie Lew Shing, a third-generation Chinese-Australian who ran a produce stall in Melbourne's Queen Victoria Market and played 10 matches for Carlton's VFL reserve side.

The Lew Shing family, wrote author John Fitzgerald in his book *Big White Lie*, were 'battlers who made good'.

Leslie's grandfather William Lew Shing (anglicised from Leu Sen) was a See Yup native from Toishan in Canton who emigrated to Ballarat where he met and married an Irish woman named Bridgit Gavan.

The couple left Ballarat and chased their fortune in the tin mines of Garibaldi in north-east Tasmania in the 1870s and had three boys, including Arthur Lew Shing.

They moved to Melbourne, and Arthur and his brothers cut off their Manchu pigtails in commitment to their new home. William Lew Shing's pigtail was kept in a box, and it was buried with him when he passed away.

Arthur's son Leslie was born into football and he had skills comparable to his Anglo-Australian teammates at the Carlton Rovers.

The family went all in on the game and while Leslie and his brothers played for the Carlton Rovers senior team, their father, Arthur, ran an illegal bookmaking business through a back gate beer bar.

In 1924, a journalist from the *Sporting Globe* attended a Chinese Athletics Association match in Melbourne and wrote positively of the experience. 'China is fast disassociating itself with the pigtails and flowing robes that have made her ancestors unique figures in the pages of world history,' the reporter noted.

'She has entered fields previously unexplored by her countrymen and into all branches of sport, China is slowly forcing her way. The Chinese of Victoria have not been lagging behind those of their motherland and have formed an athletic club worthy of the best traditions of sport.'

Meanwhile, in 1925, the Chinese Progress Association played against VFL side Richmond and VFA powerhouse Brunswick, who would win the VFA premiership later that year.

The Chinese Progress Association team competed hard before losing to Richmond and, although they lost heavily to Brunswick, *The Argus* reported that the Chinese players 'performed creditably in view of the fact that they were of much slighter build and much younger than their opponents'.

The match report also noted their 'good sportsmanship' in taking 'many hard knocks from their powerful adversaries'.

The 'determined spirit' of the Chinese Progress Association 'brought a cheer of acknowledgement from the spectators'.

Seven years later, the Young Chinese League football team was formed as a merger of the Chinese Progress Association and the Chinese Athletics Association. One of its founders was Frank Chinn, who served as president for 34 years.

Chinn, a tin miner turned fruit and vegetable salesman, saw the Young Chinese League as a moral alternative to the gambling and drinking houses in and around Chinatown's Little Bourke Street.

In an interview with *The Age* in 1971, Chinn said the League provided not only a football team but organised picnics, dances, the annual ball, tennis tournaments and other 'positive social activities that would further the Chinese community's advancement'.

By 1938, weekly Young Chinese League matches in Albert Park were a much-anticipated fixture on the calendar of the Melbourne Chinese community; a meeting point to build friendships and keep community strong.

They would play regularly against a range of teams, including bookmakers, jockeys, boxers and bankers.

The acceptance of the Young Chinese League in Melbourne's sporting life was a reflection of the Chinese community's integration into the city.

By the mid-1940s, Melbourne's Chinatown had gone from being known as a hotbed of vice and depravity to a lively hub of fine furniture and food.

During World War II, as Melbourne was flooded with American and Australian soldiers, hundreds of Chinese restaurants and cafes opened across the city.

For the duration of World War II, Chinatown underwent a renaissance and the smell of hundreds of different dishes wafted through the lanes, arcades and alleys from packed restaurants and cafes.

Chinese food was so highly sought after for its bold flavours of the orient that even prior to the war immigration restrictions were relaxed to allow the importation of Chinese cooks and cafe workers, a move that helped reverse the declining Chinese population in Victoria.

Among these migrants was William Chen Wing Young, who arrived in Melbourne in the 1930s and opened his Wing Lee restaurant in Chinatown. Today, he is known as the inventor of the 'dim sim', the pork and cabbage dumpling that has become so popular in Victoria and elsewhere.

According to Chen's daughter, celebrity chef Elizabeth Chong, the dim sim comes from the popular 'siu mai' dumpling served with tea in the Wing Lee restaurant. Chen took the little parcels of pork out of the restaurant and into the streets, employing the old Chinese men who hung around Chinatown as salesmen and delivery drivers.

'They were like the leftovers from the goldfields days,' Chong told US network CNN in a website interview in 2021, 'They didn't make it back home to China and were too old for heavy work.'

One day, Chen's son Tom gave a dim sim to a Greek friend, Joe, who ran a fish-and-chip shop in Melbourne's southern suburbs. Joe threw the dumpling in the fryer, and an Australian institution was born. 'Before the next day was over, Joe rang Tom at Wing Lee and said every one of his mates were asking where he got these dim sims,' says Chong.

Chen soon opened the Wing Lee Dim Sim company, the first Chinese factory to commercialise a fast food for the Australian mass market.

Dim sims, or 'dimmys' were soon found at football grounds, such as Footscray's Western Oval, and fish-and-chip shops across the nation. Later, the chop suey rolls produced by Chen's factory would be adapted by a Bendigo businessman and football stadium caterer into the iconic 'Chiko Roll'.

Taken together, the dim sim, the Chiko Roll and the Young Chinese League football team played a crucial bridging role between the Chinese community centred around inner-city Melbourne and their Anglo-Celtic Australian neighbours.

ı | | ı

After World War II ended, the Chinese Youth League resumed its football activities and was a beacon for Chinese-Australians who moved in and out of the city from regional Victoria.

One such player was Phillip Esmore, a Chinese-Australian who, in 1947, played for Dunolly in the country leagues, Oakleigh in the VFA in Melbourne, and the Young Chinese League on Sundays.

In June, the *Dunolly Advertiser* commented that Esmore was 'unbeatable' on the wing, and 'what he lacks in size he more than makes up for in tenaciousness'.

A month later, the official Oakleigh Football Club reserve grade match report read: 'Esmore's pace and uncanny position play and long driving drop kicks made him outstanding in the Oakleigh side.'

ı | | ı

In a typical season from the 1950s to the 1980s, the Young Chinese League team would play between 10 and 18 matches against local teams and business houses including the Bank of NSW, Department of Trade, Commonwealth Bank, and the Board of Works.

After certain matches, both teams would go back to the See Yup Temple in Albert Park to feast together.

While the players honed their skills and represented their community in the regular season, the highlight was the end-of-season road trip to play against country teams. In 1949, one of those end-of-season trips was down the Great Ocean Road to play the Lorne Dolphins.

The joint team photo shows both teams blended together, a perfect illustration of the Young Chinese League's role in bringing disparate communities together through football.

One player who built his social life around playing football for the Young Chinese League was veteran player Harold Chin Quan, a third-generation Chinese-Australian who played more than 250 games between 1964 and 1986.

Harold grew up immersed in Melbourne's Chinatown and speaks fluent Cantonese.

He had no choice with the first 12 years of his life mingling with guests and staff out the back of his father's restaurant, Weng Sheng, which was located at 182 Russell Street before being demolished for an eight-storey car park.

Harold's grandfather Wah Quan Chin arrived in Darwin in 1897, fleeing the famine that had devastated his village in Toishan county in Sze Yup in Canton.

Wah Quan Chin came over to Australia as a general merchant but found opportunity beyond being a successful shopkeeper, starting a farm including a major market garden and a piggery to serve the pork needs of the top-end Chinese community.

When he started a family he appended his middle name to the end of his surname creating a family name unique to his descendants which, according to Harold, now extends to almost 300 people from Wah Quan Chin's original seven children.

After the Japanese bombed Darwin in February 1942, Wah Quan Chin's family was soon evacuated to Melbourne and they began a new life.

When his family did not return to Darwin after the war, his old farm was subdivided into the golf course and Gardens Park, the old Palmerston Park famed for its public mango trees planted by Wah Quan Chin in the 1920s.

The road dividing the two is today named Chin Quan Road and flanks Gardens Oval, home of the Waratah Football Club.

ı | | ı

In 1971, Harold Chin Quan and The Young Chinese League team were the subject of a feature story in *The Age* newspaper. 'Although Oriental in appearance they are a mix of old, new and temporary Australians from all walks of life including doctors and students,' journalist Ken Knox wrote.

'Some are born in Hong Kong; some are born here. Others are fifth and sixth generation Australian-Chinese.'

The result, Knox concluded, 'has been that the Chinese community in Victoria makes up one of our happiest and best-understood migrant groups.'

Indeed, when Knox asked Chin Quan if the team had an advantageous 'secret weapon' by being able to 'use a foreign tongue to confuse their opponents', Chin Quan shot down that line of inquiry. 'I'm afraid quite a few of our players don't speak Chinese too well,' he said.

In 1986 the Young Chinese League Football Club ceased operating and the club had 'done its job of bringing Chinese and Australians together', according to Harold, not just in football but across the board with all of its social activities.

As per Harold's statistics, the Young Chinese League played 123 games in the 1960s, 157 in the 1970s, but only 40 games in the 1980–86 period.

They had one last hurrah in 1981 when they were unbeaten in their 11-game season, a feat that Harold feels was the YCL Football Club's peak moment.

Harold attributes the demise of the club to a number of factors, both societal and demographic.

Beyond the traditional challenges of computer games and competing with a plethora of options in attracting the younger generations, the YCL faced a decline in relevance for the new Chinese migrants.

'We were the club made up of old Melbourne Chinese families and the new Chinese migrants had no interest in assimilating through football, they had other priorities,' he said.

'And the players all sort of disappeared.'

ı | | ı

Today, Harold Chin Quan serves on the Young Chinese League committee with three former teammates.

Although the football side is long gone, the committee still organises a social tennis club, made up mostly of ex-footballers.

'We all made so many friends from different teams,' he remembers of the Young Chinese League's glory days. 'We played bankers, government workers, pilots, jail warders, jockeys, boxers. Through footy, we fitted right in as another group of Aussies – with a twist.'

Reflecting on the Young Chinese League's legacy, Harold says one of the most satisfying feelings was the shock Chinese community spectators would receive when they attended matches: 'They would see Chinese players running around and kicking drop kicks, torpedoes, stab kicks, hard tackling – and they couldn't believe we played footy and could win.

'We won about half our games overall I reckon which was good for the fans.'

Although several Young Chinese League players crossed over to mainstream leagues – including William 'Billy' Kiefer, who played 26 games for Coburg; Dr Robert Yee, who captained the Fitzroy Under-19s; and Stephen Brown, who played for Carlton's reserves in 1974 and 1975 – none was ever able to crack the big time in the VFL.

Perhaps the best-known product of the Young Chinese League is Trevor O'Hoy, who played three seasons for St Kilda's reserve grade side from 1972–74, highlighted by the 1973 season when he came second to Carlton's Vin Catoggio in the prestigious Gardiner Medal for the best and fairest player in the VFL reserves competition.

'I think looking Chinese made me stand out in a strange way because I seemed to collect a lot of umpires' votes,' O'Hoy says.

Later, O'Hoy would move into business, serving as the CEO for Fosters Group and serving on the boards of the North Melbourne Football Club and Cricket Australia.

'My father was conceived in Bendigo and born in Hong Kong, so his side of the family is Hong Kong-Chinese,' O'Hoy says. 'My mother Marie is half Japanese, a quarter Chinese and a quarter Australian.'

They met, of course, at Albert Park, on the sidelines of a Young Chinese League match. 'I'm a throwback,' O'Hoy says.

CHAPTER 6

Big Man Jack from Ballarat

Every year since 1966, Ballarat's best junior athlete receives the Wunhym Trophy, named in honour of one of the city's finest all-round athletes, Jack Wunhym.

According to the organisation that runs the awards, the Ballarat Sportsmen's Club, Wunhym 'spent many years of his life in the watching and encouragement of junior sports people in more than one sport'.

John (Jack) Stevenson Wunhym passed away in 1965, aged 57. Like many of his contemporaries, he played Australian Rules football in the winter and cricket in the summer. During the 1920s and 30s, he moved between Melbourne's premier cricket competition, the midweek industrial football leagues and the big-time clubs of the VFL and the VFA, before returning to his hometown in Ballarat as a player-coach.

The most famous image of Wunhym is from a 1930s-era cigarette card, with arms folded across the red, blue and white guernsey of the Yarraville Football Club, a short-back-and-sides haircut and a happy grin.

The bio on the back of the card reads: 'A big follower and one of Yarraville's most consistent performers, Wunhym has a fair amount of pace, uses his weight rigorously, and is a fair mark and kick.'

At the time in the late 1920s, he was the only known Chinese heritage footballer in either the VFL or the VFA.

Like his predecessors Wally Koochew, George Tansing and Les Kew Ming, Wunhym was the descendent of a Chinese man and a European woman. The name Wunhym, like Koochew and Tansing, was a contraction of the family's original Chinese surname.

Jack's grandfather, David Wun Hym, was born in 1839 in Canton and migrated to Australia in the 1870s. David married an Englishwoman and they settled in Ballarat to raise nine children. They lived in Golden Point, the heartland of Ballarat's Chinese community, not far from the mines where many of the Chinese community worked.

Before Jack began to show promise as a junior athlete in the 1920s, his uncle Willie Wun Hym played for the Golden Point football team and captained the Ballarat Chinese side that would play invitational matches against visiting teams.

From an early age, Jack Wunhym's size and raw talent set him apart from his teammates and also from the previous Chinese football pioneers, who were of smaller frames and played as rovers or wingers and not in a 'big man' position like ruckman.

After dominating junior sport in Ballarat, in 1924 Wunhym moved to Melbourne's western suburbs, where he played for Sunshine Cricket Club and Sunshine Football Club at Barclay Reserve in Sunshine.

Under the guidance of Sunshine's experienced coach – Geelong future Hall of Famer Alec Eason – Wunhym played well enough to earn a trial with Footscray, which was going through a rebuild after winning back-to-back VFA titles and joining the rival VFL in 1925.

At the beginning of Wunhym's debut season in 1927, the *Sunshine Advocate* noted that the 19-year-old ruckman 'turns the scale at 14 stone' and was 'a big man of possibilities'.

That year, Wunhym played seven matches and kicked one goal in what was a dismal year for Footscray, which finished third last with a win-loss record of 3–12.

The following season, he played mostly in reserve grade, with Footscray coach Paddy Scanlan lamenting to reporters Wunhym's 'silly mistakes', 'stage fright' and 'inexperience'.

Hopes had been high for Wunhym, who performed strongly in the final 1928 pre-season trial, and an article on the front page of the *Footscray Advertiser* on 14 April spoke glowingly of his character: 'Jack Wunhym in a football match is the antithesis of Jack Wunhym off the field. On the field he is a grim battler, dealing out force to all and sundry. Off the field he is one of the quietest and most genial youths one could wish to meet ... a lad of such splendid physique and heart is surely worthy of special tuition from the coach.'

Wunhym's development seemed to stall under his coach, Scanlan.

In an article headlined 'Wunhym's Reappearance', on 1 July 1928, the *Footscray Advertiser* argued that for his lone appearance in the senior team for the season, Jack had 'justified his inclusion' by noting that he was 'the embodiment of pluck and has rare strength and stamina. He is enthusiastic and anxious to learn and when play became fiery, he played his part well.'

Much of the media commentary on Wunhym focused on his physique. Standing six feet tall (183 cm) and weighing 96 kilograms, he was the tallest and heaviest in the Footscray side.

After helping Footscray beat Fitzroy in the opening round of the 1929 season, the *Footscray Advertiser* noted that: 'Wunhym played with the heart of a lion and threw his weight about in the packs with good effect.'

But after Footscray lost its Round 2 match against Essendon, Wunhym was dropped to the reserves – and then released to VFA side, Yarraville.

Formerly known as 'The Villains', Yarraville had recently been promoted to the VFA and was a club with big dreams. Wunhym's size, experience and personality soon made him an anchor for the club's success.

For five seasons between 1929 and 1934, he played 88 games, kicked 17 goals and was appointed captain. *The Herald* described him in 1931 as the team's 'mainstay'.

Wunhym's peak season came in 1932 when his form earned him selection for the VFA All Stars team to play the VFL All Stars in a showdown of Melbourne's rival professional leagues.

The match – held at Carlton's Princes Park in front of 31,000 fans – went right down to the last quarter, with the VFL All Stars winning by eight points.

A year later, the *Sporting Globe* noted that Wunhym was 'one of the outstanding followers in the Association'; a hard but fair player whose 'stamina enables him to carry on in the most rugged company'. He was a crucial part of Yarraville's run to the finals in 1933, taking over the captaincy after Ted Bourke resigned.

Wunhym was the first known Chinese heritage player to lead a VFL or VFA club, even though his one match in charge – the first semi-final against Port Melbourne – ended in a narrow loss by three points in front of 4000 fans at Olympic Park.

'The added responsibility as captain did not appear to affect Jack Wunhym's play,' reported *The Herald*.

'He was an untiring worker for Yarraville and, keeping well up with the play throughout the game, was always a force in the ruck. He gained the knock-out more than his opponents, and never once let up in a rough game that was a searching test of stamina.'

That year, Wunhym also played football for his employer, Railways, in the midweek competition against other Employers teams – a paid afternoon off work and a chance to impress his bosses.

The midweek Employer league matches were often played with ferocious spirit and represented the only opportunity for amateur footballers to match up against the elite VFL and VFA players in a competitive environment and make a name for themselves. On at least one occasion, Jack was suspended for his part in a fight when willing exchanges boiled over.

Playing for the Railways team was a worthy investment in an employer that would support him after his football career finished, providing him stability and security through the Great Depression of the 1930s.

One report in *The Age* noted his leadership role as captain of the Railways team: 'He is a tower of strength to the side and great encouragement to young players.'

Wunhym played in an era where it was common for former VFL and VFA players to head to the regional areas in the final years of their career, where they were often paid handsomely to play for and coach a country team.

A much-loved figure in the Ballarat district, Wunhym was renowned for mentoring young talent.

This tribute, published in the *Horsham Times* in 1935, speaks volumes of his reputation in regional Victoria following his stint as coach of the Ballarat Imperials in the Wimmera-Ballarat Football League: 'Mr. Wunhym's coaching methods, his knowledge of the game, and his ability as a player stamp him as an ideal leader. His popularity with every official, player and supporter is undoubted.'

During a decade where he played and coached several clubs in and around Ballarat, the highlight was captain-coaching Ballarat North (named North City Football at the time) – as a 39-year-old – to its first premiership in 1946.

Playing under and alongside Jack Wunhym in that Ballarat North premiership team was fullback Harold Foo, a Chinese-Australian who had just returned from serving in Papua New Guinea in World War II and was then working as a boilermaker.

Harold's great-grandfather, Chin Ah Foo, arrived in Ballarat in 1865, operating a general store in Creswick close to Ballarat and enjoying a well-documented friendship with Dr Robert Lindsay, patriarch of the famous Lindsay family of painters.

Ballarat North club historian Stanley 'Digger' Roberts remembers Harold being a valuable addition to the club: 'He was a good fella, a quiet, lead-by-example type who was a great fullback and a beautiful kick of the ball – one for the purists.'

Foo played for six years at Ballarat North, rising to be vice-captain of the club and winning the Best and Fairest award in 1950.

From its humble working-class origins, Ballarat North would go on to become the powerhouse of Ballarat football, winning 22 senior premierships, all built on the foundations of the 1946 champions and the contributions of Harold Foo and captain-coach Jack Wunhym.

To this day, Stanley 'Digger' Roberts remembers Wunhym as 'a striking man' who was 'highly respected as a coach and the architect of our first premiership'.

CHAPTER 7

Old Buffaloes Never Die: The Survival and Success of the Darwin Football Club

On Christmas morning 1974, Darwin football legend Bennie Lew Fatt woke to 'an unforgettable noise' as Cyclone Tracy tore through his city.

The Category 4 storm hit Darwin's coast at around 3.30 am and left a devastating trail of destruction in its wake.

Hardy stone landmarks, such as the Palmerston Town Hall, the Old Police Station, the Court House and Cell Block were all destroyed, as was the sturdy Chung Wah temple in Darwin's Chinatown, which had survived several earlier cyclones.

'Buildings had disappeared, wreckage was everywhere, trees were stripped bare of their leaves,' recalls Lew Fatt. 'It was like a bomb had been dropped.'

Eighty per cent of the city's houses were demolished, creating an instant humanitarian crisis with tens of thousands of residents left homeless. The Lew Fatts were one of the fortunate families after Bennie recalled a vital piece of advice from his father, Walter.

'My father told me to open all sides of the house and just let it come through,' says Lew Fatt. 'It was a hard decision that went against my instincts, but it's what saved us.'

Cyclone Tracy was one of Australia's worst natural disasters, taking 71 lives and leaving 645 people wounded. The city's electrical grid and telephone system were rendered useless, with residents unable to communicate with each other or their families interstate, amplifying the horror and uncertainty.

More than 30,000 Territorians were evacuated on 'flights to anywhere' in the biggest air evacuation in Australian history.

Some never returned, broken from the harrowing experience. It was a landmark event, so apocalyptic that locals would, from that moment onwards, mark time as 'pre-Tracy' and 'post-Tracy'.

In the immediate aftermath, the 1974–75 Darwin footy season was cancelled as its players scattered across Australia.

When Darwin's residents filtered back, its football teams scrambled to secure players and rebuild their clubs. It was felt the season had to proceed for the morale of the town and as a signal that the residents would not be beaten by Cyclone Tracy.

Each club committee was faced with the decision to pause, or continue on for the 1975–76 season. Even foundation clubs such as the Darwin Buffaloes were imperilled, with the *NT News* reporting that the 'club may fold' in June 1975.

The Buffaloes, bound together by a web of intergenerational families, had survived three cyclones and a bombing. With many of the senior members of the club still involved, they decided that their club must be saved at any cost.

As members and supporters rallied, two leaders emerged, both of whom had the club deeply embedded in their psyche: president Riley Wing, a Chinese-Australian sprinter-turned-accountant, and captain-coach William 'Nungah' AhMat, a powerful midfielder who had recently won the 1974 Northern Territory

Sportsman of the Year award and belonged to the famous AhMat footy family.

According to Nungah's nephew, Robbie AhMat, Nungah and Riley were very close and could be described as 'besties'.

Although Riley Wing grew up with football and played for the Darwin Buffaloes, he made his name as a sprinter, famously winning South Australia's richest foot race, The Bay Sheffield, as a 21-year-old in 1947.

His victory earned him a unique status in Darwin and, combined with his accounting skills and iron will, he was the perfect foil for 'Nungah' AhMat who was deeply engaged and respected in the football community.

Together, Riley and Nungah represented a long history of cooperation between Chinese and Indigenous people at the Darwin Buffaloes.

ı | | | ı

The deep connection between Chinese and Aboriginal communities in the Top End of Australia dates back to at least the 1850s. Although often hidden, this history of cooperation and social interaction was crystallised in the Darwin Buffaloes.

The club began in 1917 and was known for many years as Vesteys, after the British multinational meat works, which opened in Darwin a few years earlier. It was one of three teams in the Northern Territory Football League (NTFL), a competition that was cleanly divided along Darwin's class structure lines.

At the top was the Waratah club, recruited from public servants, bank employees and cable company workers. The next rung down was the Wanderers, whose players were drawn from the Post Office and the Overland Telegraph. At the bottom was Vesteys, a multiracial, working-class club.

The teams all played at Darwin's Esplanade Oval, a rocky patch of grass perched on the ocean behind Darwin's CBD.

According to Matthew Stephen, the author of *Colour Bar: Remembering and Forgetting Northern Territory Football*, the Esplanade Oval 'became a theatre of dreams where social, political and ideological battles were played out weekly. These battles emphasised sport's paradoxical nature in both connecting and disconnecting socio-cultural groups within Darwin.'

Stephen sees a direct link between the respect forged in those on-field battles and the creation of a single mixed identity – 'Territorians'.

He wrote: 'Football played a crucial critical role in developing cross cultural allegiances that forged a multi racial identity that is central to the Northern Territory identity today.'

When ABC veteran broadcaster Charlie King reflects on modern Darwin's success story, he agrees with Stephen's assessment of the importance of the Buffaloes' battles with the 'mainstream clubs': 'Darwin wasn't always the harmonious and diverse society it prides itself on being today and the story of those battles on the Esplanade is a story about the fight for rights.'

By 1926, Vesteys was a majority Aboriginal-Chinese club, fielding players with names such as Lee, Ah Fook, Ming Ket and Chan.

The club had won back-to-back premierships and was home to Reuben Cooper, Darwin's first Indigenous footballer and arguably the best player in the Northern Territory at the time.

In 1924 Reuben wrote a letter to the *Northern Standard* that described the racist abuse he and his teammates received on the football field.

Sir, – As one of the players of Vesteys Football Team I wish to protest against the insults which I, and other coloured players have to put up with from so-called sports barracking for their respective clubs. On Saturday last we were called black____'s, chocolate soldiers and other vile names which only foul debased minds could think of. These gentlemen (?) take advantage of the football ground to indulge in what can only be classed as filth. Not one of these dirty barrackers would be game to utter the same expressions off the ground for fear their worthless hides would suffer.

In late 1926, a match was organised between an NTFL team and a Katherine invitational team including some Vesteys players who were working on the construction of the Katherine Railway Bridge. After some allegedly poor umpiring, the Katherine team walked off the field in protest.

The protest escalated into an unprecedented moment of racial apartheid as the white players, led by the Waratah club, decided to form a new 'whites only' league called the North Australian Football League.

To compound the injustice, the management of the Vesteys club decided to pledge their allegiance to the new league and remove the Aboriginal and Chinese players from their club.

The expulsion of the original, multiracial Vesteys was 'the only way they could think of to stop Vesteys from winning the premiership,' wrote Harry Edwards, a white blacksmith and Vesteys' club representative in a letter published in the *Northern Standard*.

'In the face of the facts it is difficult to understand what objection anyone can have to playing with the coloured lads, except perhaps, their superiority of play.'

During those years of sporting apartheid between 1927 and 1929, Tommy (Gee) Ming Ket, the president of Darwin's Chinese Recreation Club, invited the excluded Indigenous players to play soccer with his community in the four-team Darwin Chinese Soccer Association.

Tommy got to know the new Aboriginal players and felt compelled to help them work around the cruel colour bar that now existed in Darwin's Australian Rules football community.

Darwin had been a majority Chinese city until World War I, an anomaly on Australian soil, and its Chinese residents were influential at the centre of town life and not confined to isolated clusters like the major capitals 'down south'.

Some, like Tommy Ming Ket, were so attached to Darwin and its people that they felt it was their civic duty to assist with the Aboriginal community where they could.

The Darwin Buffaloes' unique racial unity was captured in a *NT Times* match report on 18 December 1923 regarding a match at the Esplanade Oval: 'Chinese joining Aboriginal kids kicking the ball at the breaks, "footballers in embryo" rushing the oval in the intervals and putting up a grandstand performance worth watching.

'None of them are more than hip high, but they know every phase of the game and amuse themselves, and onlookers to their hearts content.'

Under Tommy Ming Ket's leadership, the Darwin Chinese Recreation Club agreed to fund the newly minted Darwin Football League (DFL), which featured the best Aboriginal, Chinese and other Asian heritage footballers. To keep things even, they created two teams, and 25 players from the Darwin Chinese Soccer League came across to play footy.

Darwin became the stage for a surreal moment in Australian Rules football history, the city's football teams divided on racial lines.

On Saturdays, the whites-only Northern Australia Football League (NAFL) played at the Esplanade Oval, while on Sundays the multiracial Darwin Football League would take over the ground and entertain crowds with their exciting play.

Over time, the superiority of play in the Darwin Football League won over more fans, and by 1929 the all-white NAFL was running at a loss.

The Waratah club delegates reluctantly agreed to allow some coloured players in the NAFL league, and in season 1929–1930 the colour bar was lifted. The Darwin Football League, with its coalition of Aboriginal and Asian players, had won, forcing the freshly reconstituted NTFL to represent all of the communities in its broad multicultural spectrum.

'There is the football match on Saturday afternoon, with barrackers in 25 languages and the "yachahoi" of the tribes, with swarthy half castes in bright blazers, the big majority of the teams, leaping eight feet into the air to catch the shining rain-wet ball, and running with the swift grace of a deerhound,' reported Darwin's *Northern Standard* in 1933.

'In Darwin it is more an Oriental ballet than a football match.'

From 1930 to 1939, the Buffaloes competed in every NTFL grand final, winning four premierships.

One of the star players was veteran Indigenous goal-kicker William 'Put' AhMat, who had been with the club since 1919 when they were known as Vesteys. 'Put' AhMat's career spanned 20 years and he won seven premierships.

'Put' played alongside Walter Lew Fatt, the first Aboriginal-Chinese superstar of Top End football.

Born in 1911 to a Cantonese father and a Larrakia-Aboriginal mother, Walter came to prominence as a skilful midfielder for the Darwin Buffaloes in 1930 and spent his entire career at the club, helping them to three consecutive premierships in 1933, 1934 and 1935.

His son, Bennie Lew Fatt OAM, remembers a generous man who mixed freely with all of Darwin's communities.

'My father Walter was an excellent hunter and fisherman and would go out for a couple of days shooting geese and bring back 50 or 60 – some for us, some to sell and he would give to those that couldn't afford it,' he says.

'He'd do the same with prawns he netted and fish he caught – always sharing with the neighbours, who were a mix of Chinese, Indian, Timorese, Aboriginal and Anglo Aussie.'

After Walter retired from football, another Chinese heritage star Joe Sarib picked up where he left off. In 1949, aged 19, Joe won the first Nicholls Medal for Best and Fairest in the NTFL, and between 1947 and 1955 he helped the Buffaloes to four premierships.

According to the family story, Joe's father, Thomas, was a Javanese Muslim who in 1880 fled Indonesia on a pearling lugger to escape an abusive father. To avoid detection in Australia, Thomas changed his surname to Sarib.

He then married a Malaysian-Chinese woman, Marion Wu, who came from a prominent Darwin family and for many years ran The Oriental Cafe on Cavenagh Street in Darwin's old Chinatown precinct.

Joe Sarib's son, Rob, is proud of his father's legacy. 'People would share stories about Dad being the best centreman they had seen, or that he had a great left foot stab,' Rob says.

Northern Territory music legend Ted Egan remains in awe of Joe's all-round ability in football, athletics, tennis, golf and basketball. 'I've seen most of them and Joe Sarib is the best all-round athlete the Territory has produced,' he says.

'I remember watching him play football one day and he sprang, took a high mark and landed like a cat. He moved so beautifully.'

Egan recalls Joe playing for the Buffaloes alongside another Chinese-Australian star of the 1950s, Chin Chui Hoonga – aka Ron 'the Flying Chinaman' Chin.

'What a man: tall, handsome, a great athlete, a great singer, very funny and generous and without any malice. "Hoonga" is one of the great Territorians,' says Egan.

Ron Chin was born in 1926 in Katherine, 260 kilometres south of Darwin. His father, Chin Loong Tang, was the son of a Chinese migrant from Toishan in Canton.

Ronald's mother, Lizzie Chin, was the daughter of Granny Lum Loy, a much-loved market gardener who would walk through Darwin every day carrying a yoke balancing her fruit and vegetables, which she would sell or give away.

Ron won four premierships with the Buffaloes, thrilling crowds with his speed and intensity.

'He was a safe mark, great drop kick and great contester for the ball,' Egan says.

Bennie Lew Fatt also has fond memories of Ron: 'It was one of the great sights to see the flying Chinaman scooting down the wing. He was very quick.'

Off the field, Ron was a larger-than-life character with Egan remembering many nights when he would get up on the table and sing his signature song, 'Donkey Serenade', or the Chinese national anthem. Bennie Lew Fatt recalls Ron performing 'the Buffalo shuffle' at functions and dances.

The next significant post-war Chinese-Australian Darwin Buffaloes player after Joe Sarib and Ron 'The Flying Chinaman' Chin was John 'Bubba' Tye.

When the Northern Territory Football League announced its Team of the Century in 2016, it contained three players of Chinese descent.

Walter Lew Fatt was named on the interchange, Clifford Lew Fatt as a fullback and John Bubba Tye on the wing alongside AFL legends Andrew McLeod and Michael Long.

The first Melbourne vs. Chinese-Australian Rules football team who participated in a St Vincent's Hospital charity game in 1899.
(Newspapers Collection, State Library of Victoria)

Ballarat's James Henry Lepp was the first recorded Chinese-Australian umpire in the 1880s in addition to being an early pioneer player.
(Mark Lepp private collection)

Portrait of Quong Tart (Artist Unknown). Tart was a philanthropist, merchant, freemason and sportsman who captained the Chinese Miners team in the first ever 'Celestial match' in Ballarat in 1892.
(State Library of NSW)

Team photo of the 1908 Carlton Football Club VFL side. Wally Koochew, the first Chinese-Australian player in the VFL is seated in the middle row, second from the left.
(Carlton Football Club Archive)

The 1903 Dunolly premiership team. William Ying is seated bottom row, third from the right.
(Dunolly Museum)

George Tansing played five matches for Geelong in 1908 and was the second player of Chinese heritage to play in the VFL.
(AFL Photos)

Les Kew Ming played for North Melbourne in 1922 and 1923. He was known as the 'Fighting Footballer' for his service in the AIF, in which he won the Military Medal for his gallantry at the Second Battle of Bullecourt in France in October 1917.

(Australian War Memorial)

A 1933 W.D. & H.O. Wills cigarette card of Yarraville's Jack Wunhym. Wunhym was raised in Ballarat and played 10 games for Footscray in the VFL in the late 1920s before moving to Yarraville in the VFA.

(Supplied by the Wunhym Family)

Team photo of the 1947 Young Chinese League team who played across Melbourne and regional Victoria.

(Chinese Museum Collection, DQ017, P00788, D. Peebles Private Collection)

The Darwin Buffaloes 1950–51 premiership winning team. Joe Sarib, who won the Nichols Medal for the best and fairest player in the NTFL in 1949, is seated in the middle row, fourth from the left. Ron Chin is standing in the top row, third from the left.
(Darwin Buffaloes Football Club)

Darwin Buffaloes players Ron Chin (left) and Joe Sarib (right) walking in Darwin in the early 1950s.
(Robert Sarib Family collection)

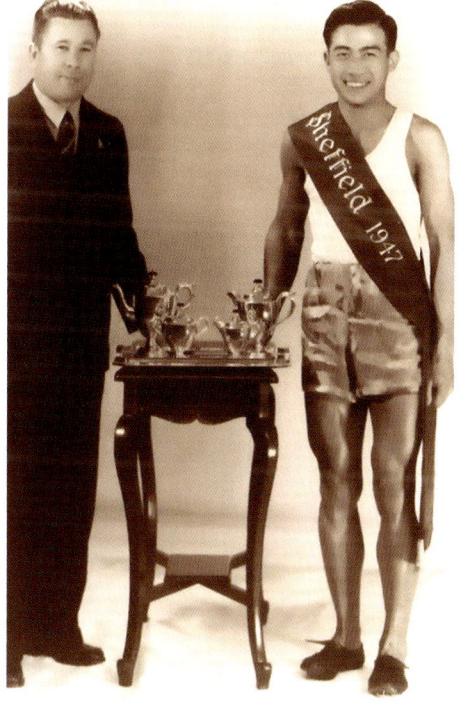

Darwin Buffaloes player and president Riley Wing was also a sprinter, pictured here after winning the Bay Sheffield Sprint in South Australia in 1947.
(Supplied by South Australian Athletic League)

Paul Ah Chee preparing to kick for goal for the North Adelaide Roosters in 1979.
(North Adelaide Football Club)

Brothers Les Fong (left)
and Neale Fong (right)
training together for the
West Perth Cardinals (now
Falcons) at Leederville
Oval in 1985.
(The Fong Family collection)

Team photo of the 1907 Mooroopna premiership winning team. Billy Wong, the son of market gardener Ah Wong, first played for Mooroopna in the 1896 premiership winning team and is standing in the back row, second from the right.
(The Mooroopna Museum)

Billy Wong played 312 senior games for the Mooroopna Cats including two senior premierships in 1985 and 1986. In 2019 Billy was inducted into the Goulburn Valley Football Hall of Fame, only the fourth Mooroopna Cat to achieve this honour.
(Mooroopna Cats)

Dannie Seow (right).
(AFL Photos)

Russell Goldfield Jack (far left in white uniform) trialling for South Bendigo in 1951. He eventually agreed to play with Eaglehawk in the Bendigo Football League.
(Russell Goldfield Jack personal collection)

Team photo of the 1922 Golden Point Rice Eaters team from Ballarat. Clarence Lepp was the first Chinese-Australian captain of the club and is seated in the middle of the bottom row with the ball on his lap. Chinese-Australian trainer Freddy Foon is standing on the far right of the middle row.
(Mark Lepp private collection)

Tye is largely unknown outside the Northern Territory as he only had a brief time playing in the SANFL, but he played such exquisite 'wet season' football that he was voted: 'The greatest footballer since Cyclone Tracy' by the NTFL.

John Henry Bubba Tye was born in Darwin in 1951, the son of George Tye and his mother, Mavis, who was a famous midwife in the town.

He was a hard-living, hard-drinking bushman who was described as 'The Real Crocodile Dundee' by his brother Arthur at his funeral in 2014.

Bubba played the first part of his career for the Darwin Buffaloes, winning three premierships before switching to Nightcliff and delivering them a premiership as well.

He also played six games for the Norwood Redlegs in the South Australian National Football League before returning home to Darwin.

Fellow SANFL Chinese heritage player, Paul Ah Chee, recalls Bubba being a brilliant footballer wherever he played: 'He played a bit like Cyril Rioli – a mix of pace, style and skill. I know that he missed the Territory when he was away from it – the bush was in his blood like few others I met.'

Paul remembers a unique man among men who was proud of his cultural identity: 'I knew him well and he was an amazing, magnificent man, who looked oriental and knew about his Chinese heritage.'

Bubba Tye was inducted into the AFL Northern Territory Hall of Fame in 2010 with the following summary:

There are not enough superlatives to describe 'Bubba' Tye's football ability and there is no doubt that had he so wished he could have plied his trade in the VFL.

Fortunately for NT football he chose to remain playing in the NTFL, entertaining legions of fans every week.

A spectacular, high energy player, his inspirational play earned him the respect of all football followers. His fierce attack on the ball sent shudders through all his opponents.

A brilliant mark and a superb kick, to watch Bubba play would often give all his supporters goose bumps.

ı | | ı

Prior to Cyclone Tracy, the Darwin Buffaloes in their various guises were the most successful club in NTFL history with 19 premierships.

After the cyclone, the Buffaloes – guided by Riley Wing and William 'Nungah' AhMat – won the 1975–76 premiership.

'More important than the victory was the fact that the club was becoming financially sustainable,' says Costa Karaoliasi, who co-ordinates the Darwin Buffaloes' club history.

'The Buffs were in massive trouble and Riley galvanised the club.'

According to Nungah's nephew, Robbie AhMat, Nungah was a 'loyal' coach who built close relationships with his players.

'He would be very honest as well, and really prioritised getting a good education and staying on a good pathway,' says Robbie who was himself a proud junior Darwin Buffalo before 'going south' to play a combined 67 AFL games with Collingwood and the Sydney Swans.

'He was an asset to the community well beyond the football field.'

Nungah finished up coaching at the end of the 1978–79 season after he and Riley delivered their final premiership for the Buffaloes in a fitting finale for their club-saving relationship.

Riley carried on to serve a record nine-year term as president, during which he was awarded an MBE for his tireless community work.

In 2023, William Nungah AhMat is alive, fit and healthy and living in Darwin. At 74, some of his Buffaloes memories have faded but not the contribution of Riley Wing.

'He was a good bloke, a very good man,' says Nungah. 'But don't get on the wrong side of him.'

For Nungah, Riley's biggest success was in bringing order to the previous chaos of the 1960s and early 1970s when the club was run by the players.

'He turned it around like a business, get everyone in line to do their bit,' he says. 'And it worked.'

Before his death in 2018 at the age of 92, Riley Wing was made a life member of the Northern Territory Football League and Northern Territory Netball.

His obituary would contain the same line used for hundreds of fallen Buffaloes before him: 'Old Buffaloes don't die, they simply fade away.'

CHAPTER 8

From Alice to Adelaide to Amunda: Fast Times and Footy with Paul Ah Chee

In 1975, as Darwin rebuilt its football clubs following the devastation of Cyclone Tracy, it was business as usual in Alice Springs, a frontier town located 1500 kilometres to the south.

In 'Alice', footballers in the Central Australian Football League (CAFL) battled it out in the red desert heat, a world away from the humid tropics of Darwin.

Football had real meaning in Alice Springs and, like every season, the lead up to the 1975 grand final was the most vibrant time of the year. Shops and cars were adorned with streamers: light blue and dark blue for Rovers; green and yellow for the Pioneer Football Club.

Since the founding of the CAFL in 1947, Pioneer had been known in Alice as the club for Indigenous players. 'The first team played barefoot, with only a couple wearing work boots,' Betty Rawson, sister of club founder Mick Costello, later told *The Australian*. 'The team became known as the Sons of Pioneers because, although the boys were Aborigines, most of their fathers were white settlers who pioneered the region.'

Between 1947 and 1974, the club won 14 premierships – including five in a row during the 1960s. The 1975 grand final was Pioneer's first in three seasons, and one of the club's star players was Paul Ah Chee, a skinny teenager with family links to China's Pearl River Delta and Australia's red centre.

At 18 years of age, Paul's speed and skill helped Pioneer to a famous victory in that 1975 grand final. His brilliant individual performance earned him the Mail Medal for best on ground, and the Minahan Medal for the best and fairest player in the league.

Over the next two years, Pioneer would win two more premierships.

Paul, though, took off after the 1975 grand final and headed north to Darwin. He was a man accustomed to being on the move.

Football in Alice Springs took inspiration from Adelaide and its mighty South Australian National Football League. For Alice Springs youngsters such as Paul Ah Chee, playing for SANFL heavyweight clubs such as Norwood or North Adelaide was as attractive as playing for a Melbourne club in the VFL.

After all, the Northern Territory had been administered by South Australia until 1911, and its Adelaide roots ran deeper than football.

In 1870, when Sir Charles Todd connected Adelaide to the world by stringing the Overland Telegraph Line across the red heart of Australia to Darwin to link up with an undersea cable from Asia, Alice Springs was its most important repeater station.

The Ah Chee story traces that line, beginning in Oodnadatta, a remote South Australian town 700 kilometres south-east of Alice Springs. The town was once a thriving outback 'tower of babel', with residents from Europe, Asia and other parts of Australia mingling with the local Aboriginal people.

Paul's great-grandfather, Cherry Ah Chee, was one of the market gardeners working a patch of land on the banks of the Neales River.

Born in Canton in 1840, Cherry arrived in Australia in the early 1870s and, according to family legend, helped lay the Overland Telegraph Line. In 1898, Cherry started a large market garden at Hookey Waterhole, south of Oodnadatta, and would cart a stunning array of fruit and vegetables around the town from his garden of plenty.

In Oodnadatta, Cherry married Minnie Bell, an Arrernte woman who was born on the Finke River and spoke three Aboriginal languages fluently. In 1912, Cherry was accused of supplying local Aboriginal people with alcohol, a charge he vehemently denied. After he was unable to clear his name, he committed suicide by poison and was found in his shed by his son, Arthur.

'It's a tragedy, because his little dog was poisoned alongside him. They went together,' says Paul, who remains grateful to his pioneering ancestor.

'Chinese have "saving face" and the Aboriginals have "shame", but it's the same thing. That humiliation in public has a deep impact.

'No matter what happened, I tell my family, "We come from that fella, Cherry Ah Chee. Without him I'm not here, you're not here and we have to respect this man's journey."'

Cherry's eldest son, Arthur, was a famed fettler who helped build and maintain the Adelaide to Oodnadatta rail line, and once singlehandedly repaired the Southern Cross aeroplane of Sir Charles Kingsford Smith when he landed in Oodnadatta.

Arthur's second son, Fred, married Paul's mother, Myra Kanakiya Taylor, a traditional Aboriginal woman who was born and raised in Oodnadatta.

When they moved to Adelaide and got married, their wedding featured on the cover of the *Australian Women's Weekly*. 'Dusky Bride

Wore White Satin – Aboriginal Wedding Had a Film Star Touch',
read the headline.

Three years later, in 1957, Myra gave birth to Paul in the Adelaide
Hills, before the family moved again to Alice Springs. There, Fred
became an initiated 'wati', committed to the responsibilities of tribal
lore and country.

'Every weekend was on Country visiting places like rock holes
where you could find water, which is a significant part of our story,'
Paul recalls.

'We would take care of sites and live off the land on bushfoods –
kangaroos, goannas, berries.'

However, after excelling as a junior for the Pioneer club, Paul
decided to return to Adelaide to chase his football dream.

At 15, he moved in with his uncle George and aunty Maude
in Adelaide's northern suburbs, and quickly earned selection for
South Australia's Under-16 representative team at the 1973 national
schoolboys competition.

South Australia won the competition for the first time in
45 years – beating powerhouse Victoria along the way. Paul was one
of five South Australians picked in the All-Australian team.

From that point on, Paul recalls having no choice but to play for
North Adelaide. 'The pathway was laid out for me,' he explains.

'We lived close to Prospect Oval, my uncle George and his family
all barracked for the North Adelaide Roosters, so he took me down to
North Adelaide Under-17s training and introduced me to the coach
and I was in the system.'

In 1975, Paul returned to Alice Springs to win a premiership with
Pioneer. He also starred in the National Aboriginal Football Carnival
in Launceston, where he was selected in the All-Australian Aboriginal

side and spotted by Syd Jackson, a two-time VFL Premiership winner with Carlton.

On Jackson's recommendation, Carlton flew Paul to Melbourne for a trial. He was immediately homesick, alone in a big city with 'strange weather'.

'I had no mentor; I was signing things I had no idea about and the thought of making new friends and networks was just too much – it was just difficult and confusing,' he says.

'I just didn't really understand the enormity of what was in front of me. I really didn't have anybody there to grab me by the ear and say, "listen, stick at it."'

After a few weeks of training, including a senior trial at Carlton's home ground Princes Park, Paul left for Adelaide, shredding his VFL prospects. It was the 'loneliest' period of his life and he took a season away from football, escaping the expectations by drinking alcohol and 'smoking ganja'.

At one stage, Aboriginal legendary civil rights activist Charles Perkins collared him.

'You're a fool, what are you doing here, you're supposed to be in bloody Melbourne, playing with Carlton,' Paul recalls Perkins furiously telling him.

Eventually, Paul pulled himself together and, free from expectation, rejoined North Adelaide in 1977. Over five seasons in the SANFL, Paul played 22 league games and scored 15 goals, with media reports often commenting on his speed and his smooth moves.

'I was one of very few Aboriginal guys playing and definitely the only one with any Asian heritage,' he says. 'After a succession of injuries I went off the rails. I didn't really put in as much as I should have.'

'Footy wasn't my destiny; I wasn't hungry for a 10-year career like my teammates and it wasn't going to be the vehicle that was going to elevate me to the levels that I wanted to get to.'

At the end of the 1981 season, Paul left footy and went to work for the South Australian Highways Department, before returning home to Alice Springs in 1983.

Two years later, he formed a band called Amunda, with Paul the vocalist and guitarist alongside Charles Perkins' daughter Rachel, who would later go on to become a famous film and television producer.

Amunda was the first Alice Springs band to go mainstream and they took the stories of Alice Springs around Australia. They produced three studio albums and for 10 years rocked nightclubs and festivals, including the Big Day Out in Sydney.

'Music replaced the adrenaline of footy – it took me to another level and opened up new worlds,' Paul explains. 'It's a form of expression, just like football is a form of expression.'

Today, Paul lives in Alice Springs and serves on the committee of his local footy club, Pioneer. He works as the Director of Engagement and Cultural for NT Major Events, chairs the Aboriginal Tourism Committee and is a director of Tourism NT.

'I'm very fortunate because I know where my Country is, I have a direct spiritual connection with it and it provides me with a greater understanding of who I am,' he says.

'We have ceremonies that keep respect in place that remind you that you're part of a bigger story.'

He is also enjoying discovering more about his Chinese ancestry dating back to his great-grandfather, Cherry Ah Chee.

'The discipline and work ethic comes down from him to his son to his son to me. You have to go out and deliver on your word and not do anything that's detrimental to your family,' Paul says.

'I tell them all that my great-grandfather was full Chinese, that's not very far away, only three generations. We wear it as a badge of pride.'

CHAPTER 9

Captain Courageous and Chairman Fong

In 1980, the Western Australian National Football League shortened its name to the Western Australian Football League (WAFL), heralding a new decade that promised an uncertain future.

Over in eastern Australia, its Victorian competitor, the VFL, would soon become the dominant national competition with expansion clubs in Brisbane and Perth, and a relocated club (South Melbourne) in Sydney.

For diehard fans of the WAFL clubs, the period between 1980 and 1985 would come to represent the final era of WAFL greatness. One player that typified the fast, tough style of the old WAFL was West Perth's Les Fong.

At the beginning of the 1980 season, 23-year-old Les was a leading rover in the competition.

He had won a premiership with West Perth and played for Western Australia in interstate competition. That year, he also achieved his childhood dream by becoming captain of the West Perth Cardinals – the youngest ever leader of the club.

With a solid frame and quiet demeanour, Les led by his actions and was respected by teammates and opponents alike. 'To captain the club at WAFL level at 23 was an absolute honour,' he said. 'I felt I was in the right place and deserved to be there.'

But while Les was elevated to the captaincy role, his younger brother, Neale, was heading in a different direction.

Neale, who played in the West Perth reserves, was a midfielder/defender with great stamina and strong handball skills, though he was not blessed with his brother's goal sense or marking ability. Two years earlier, he'd badly injured his Achilles tendon, forcing him to miss the entire 1979 season.

As he tried in vain to crack the first team, Neale's frustration at the lack of opportunity led to a confrontation with the West Perth senior coach, Graham Campbell.

The Fong brothers' paths diverged in 1980. Les began a golden period in which he captained West Perth for a record-breaking seven seasons, while Neale appeared to be headed for obscurity in the lower leagues.

Neale soon departed to continue his medical studies and play for the Nollamara club in the Western Australian Amateur Football League (WAAFL), where he would win the CJ Jamieson Medal for the competition's best and fairest player in three consecutive seasons between 1981 and 1983.

But over the next two decades, as Les earned the nickname 'Captain Courageous', Neale would rise to the very top of the game's administration and be labelled 'one of the most important figures in Western Australian football history'.

This is the story of how two brothers from a working-class, Chinese-Australian family earned themselves positions in the WAFL Hall of Fame.

When Les Fong made his debut for West Perth in 1973 it had been 57 years since a Chinese heritage player had played in the Western Australian Football League.

Frederick Nomchong was born in 1885 and raised in Braidwood in the NSW Southern Tablelands, the son of a Cantonese gold rush migrant who ran a general store servicing the Braidwood goldfields.

Frederick's father passed away and, with his mother and stepfather, he moved to Western Australia as a teenager to join the Kalgoorlie gold rush, adopting his stepfather's surname, Mitchell.

Frederick Mitchell (Nomchong) joined the Boulder Football Club, winning four premierships between 1907 and 1910, and was impressive enough to be selected for South Fremantle in the WAFL, playing 49 games between 1912 and 1916.

Curiously he wasn't the first person of Chinese heritage to play in the WAFL.

That honour belongs to Job Fong, a distant relative of Les and Neale Fong, who after learning the game at Perth's Scotch College, played one game for South Fremantle against Perth in 1906 before heading back to Hong Kong under his father's orders to continue his education.

Les and Neale had never heard the story of their football ancestor Job Fong, and instead trace their Chinese-Australian story back to their grandfather, Andrew, who migrated to Australia from Toishan in Canton in the 1890s.

Andrew's journey was, in many ways, typical of the movement of many Chinese migrants to Australia: he began on the goldfields, then moved to a regional centre before seeking the stability and diverse employment and education options available in a major city.

After a stint on the Kalgoorlie goldfields, Andrew settled in Geraldton, working in a co-operative named after his brother, Sydney Fong, which was a classic Chinese-Australian mixed business general store and included a greengrocer, fuel agency, ship chandler and an export-import agency.

Later, Andrew moved to Perth and set up Fong's Greengrocer in Northbridge, in the heart of Perth's Chinatown.

According to Neale, the circumstances of how his grandfather lost the family store remains shrouded in mystery.

'Something happened; we don't know the full story, but basically the shop got taken away from him with debt owing, or it was stolen from him,' Neale explains. 'Nobody in the family wanted to talk about it.'

When Andrew Fong passed away in 1941, those stories and the connection to Chinese culture were effectively lost.

Les and Neale's father, Alan, was just 12 years old at the time, and grew up not knowing about his heritage during the era of the White Australia policy.

'My father grew up in a fairly strong anti-Asian community in the 1940s,' Neale explains.

'He didn't get bashed or anything like that but, because of what was happening, our grandmother Minnie wanted to basically disassociate from the Chinese community.'

Part of the Fong family's integration into the wider society was Australian Rules football.

Alan played for Wembley Magpies, an amateur team based in Perth's western suburbs, before settling in Nollamara, a new state housing commission suburb located 10 kilometres north of the Perth CBD.

The Fongs found a housing commission home on Collier Street and settled in among their Anglo-Celtic and southern European neighbours.

'Dad was a truck driver and Mum used to do a bit of cleaning,' Les explains. 'We certainly knew what it was like to be relatively poor.'

Although it was not a traditional Chinese upbringing, Les was made aware of his heritage at primary school. 'Neale looks a lot less Asian than me, so he was noticed less,' Les recalls.

'I had jet black hair and almond eyes and looked Asian, and I used to cop quite a bit from the kids in the schoolyard. It got to one stage where I threw a guy quite strongly against a locker because he had called me something. I told him to never do it again and nothing happened thereafter.'

Les's best defence, though, was the language that every schoolyard understands – sporting excellence. He was an accomplished athlete from his early years, excelling in footy, cricket, basketball and athletics. 'When I'd win or do very well, eventually the respect would come,' he says.

The Fongs were a typical footy family. Les and Neale honed their craft in the front yard with their two older brothers Graham and Stephen, taking 'screamers' and occasionally bringing down powerlines with their high kicks.

Les was the boy most likely, winning the first of three consecutive Under-12 best and fairest awards at the age of nine. His mother, Daphne, later told a reporter: 'I honestly can't remember him playing a bad game.'

On weekends, little Les would take the bus to Leederville Oval on his own to watch the West Perth senior team play.

'I will never forget the intense excitement I felt when the league team ran out on the ground,' he recalls. 'It gave me a great buzz.'

In 1971, Les was appointed vice-captain of the Under-16 Western Australian State Schoolboys team. The team went undefeated in the National Secondary Schools Championship and were crowned champions after twice defeating traditional heavyweights, Victoria.

Les finished third in the J.L. Williams Medal for best and fairest and earned selection in the All-Australian Schoolboys team, instantly becoming a hot property for VFL recruiters.

Les's parents, Alan and Daphne, soon received a telegram from the Richmond Football Club, signed by Secretary Alan Schwab, one of the most respected officials in VFL history.

'They were willing to pay a sign-on fee, which would have been a reasonable amount of money,' Les recalls.

Daphne, though, wanted her boys to play for West Perth.

'We didn't make a big thing about it at the time,' she said later. 'He was too young to give it serious consideration.'

Within two years, Les became the youngest West Perth senior player when he ran onto Lathlain Park at 16 years of age. He was given the nickname 'Chopsticks' because of his Asian heritage, which was soon abbreviated to 'Chop'.

By 1975, Les, then 19, was a permanent fixture in the West Perth team. It was a special year for a young man playing in a tough competition filled with greats of the WAFL game.

'I was up against legends like Bill Walker, Barry Cable, Bryan Cousins and Maurice Rioli,' he remembers.

'I consider myself very lucky to have played at the pinnacle when the standard was unbelievable.'

In the 1975 grand final, held at Subiaco Oval in front of a record 51,000 fans, Les's West Perth side took on its old rivals, South Fremantle. 'When we ran out, I thought, "This is what 50,000-plus people sound like,"' he says.

Les rose to the occasion and was amongst the best on ground for West Perth, tackling aggressively, gathering 16 disposals and constantly finding teammates with his hand-passing.

After West Perth recorded a crushing 104-point victory, Les partied with his teammates and thousands of supporters.

'It was an incredible experience for a 19-year-old,' says Les. 'I never won or played in a grand final again.'

There were other honours, though.

In 1977, Les was selected for Western Australia in an interstate match against South Australia. The game was the centrepiece of the centenary celebrations for South Australian football, but Les and his teammates spoiled the party, defeating South Australia by seven points. In doing so, the WA side removed an interstate curse that had existed since 1938.

Over the next six years, Les would go on to represent his state six more times, but it was a good performance against Victoria in a losing Western Australian team in the 1980 State of Origin series that gave him national exposure and attracted interest from VFL clubs.

In the race for his signature, Collingwood emerged as the leader and club president John Hickey flew to Perth to meet him with former Collingwood player Peter Eakins who was the Magpies' representative in Western Australia.

'They pulled out the chequebooks and said, "we'll give you $10,000 today and another $10,000 when you land at Tullamarine to join us,"' Les recalls. 'I was bamboozled and had never heard of this sort of money.'

Once again, Les spurned the VFL offers. He had just finished building a new house in Perth and his eldest son was in primary school. He could not stand the thought of being stuck in Melbourne's traffic or what might happen if he got injured.

In the end, he decided to stay with West Perth to repay those who had invested in him: 'You can't blame players for wanting to go for financial reasons but I did not want to let people down, people that had believed in me and backed me.'

Les's decision to stay in Western Australia was welcome news for the Chinese-Australian community in Perth, for whom Les was a superhero and their only mainstream role model in football.

'On the field, I saw one player that looked remotely like me and that was Les Fong,' Graham Miller, a renowned Western Australian photographer and artist, recalls.

'He was a brilliant and courageous player who was well respected in the community for his leadership and footy prowess. I didn't know anyone who didn't like Les Fong.'

Miller arrived in Australia as a 10-year-old from Hong Kong and was put straight into boarding school. His mother was Hong Kong Chinese; his father Anglo-Australian. It was, he says, a tough personal assignment for a mixed-culture kid.

'I was a small, English-accented, half Chinese boy and there was some anti-Asian sentiment due to the first wave of Vietnamese refugees,' Miller later told Art on the Move, a Western Australian arts organisation.

Miller knew nothing about the game, except for the fact that it was the key to building an Australian identity. In boarding school in the late 1970s, footy was the dominant topic and, according to Miller, the football community's respect for Les Fong helped him find a place in the boarding school.

'I would be called names for being Chinese and I could always point to Les Fong – even though he was Chinese, they respected him and liked him,' Miller says.

'And in some small way, all that social capital that filtered down into my little world in the boarding school. I think it really helped me, so I'm grateful to Les for that.'

Another of Les's fans was Hong Kong–born Howard Collinge, a Chinese-Australian who played seven matches alongside his hero at West Perth between 1985 and 1987 before embarking on a successful post-football career as an author and creative director in New York.

Collinge, who was raised in Perth by his Hong Kong Chinese mother, once wrote that Les helped him embrace his Asian heritage. 'I was never comfortable revealing my Chinese background when I was playing,' he said.

'My thinking at the time was "Why would I reveal something that would expose myself to racist remarks like 'chink' and let them have that one on me?"'

But Les, he continued, was 'the Bruce Lee of Australian football: a cool Asian dude, tough and highly respected by all, and that gave me some strength.'

Despite the parochial nature of footy at the time, Fong's celebrity spread beyond Western Australia.

In 2019, comedian Sam Pang, who once played for Collingwood's Under-19s team, spoke about Les's impact on his life.

'This footy card,' he said, brandishing Les's player card, 'is like my passport.'

What people like Pang, Collinge, Miller and hundreds of thousands of fans in Western Australia could not fully appreciate was the cumulative amount of racism Les received from spectators and players who targeted him with abuse.

'I copped it and got called everything from a slopehead to a chink, told to go back to China,' Les recalls. 'One guy yelled, "We should have shot your dad."'

Les just smiled at his abusers and stuck to his mission: 'To prove to everyone that just because I had a Chinese surname, didn't mean I couldn't play football.'

By the time Les retired from top flight football in 1987, he'd played 284 games, kicked 331 goals and won a premiership, two club best and fairest awards and induction into the Halls of Fame of both his club and the league.

In addition to his spectacular output, he was known throughout the state as 'Captain Courageous' for his loyalty, his bravery and his warrior leadership.

Of all his achievements, it was his record seven-year term as West Perth captain that was the most satisfying of his career.

'I rate that higher than anything else I achieved,' Les told a reporter in 1988. 'It gave me more satisfaction than the prospect of playing in the VFL or winning awards.'

'He often said the right thing,' former West Perth teammate Corry Bewick recalls of Les's captaincy. 'But it was his actions – the way he put his body on the line, how hard he worked and the way he lifted everyone around him. It was an honour to play alongside him.'

In 1988, Les was granted a testimonial year by West Perth, which included the production of a small book to mark his career achievements.

The opening tribute from club president, Brian Atkinson, spoke of his legacy at the club:

On rare occasions during the history of a football club, a footballer emerges who makes such a contribution to his club that his name becomes synonymous with the club itself. Such a player is Les Fong and his name will live on as long as the club itself.

A measure of the importance of the impact Les Fong has had on the West Perth Football Club is the enormous respect he has earned from members and supporters of other clubs, as well as our own.

Such respect is difficult to earn in what is a very parochial setting.

This respect was won by the tremendous courage shown by Les, by the fanatical and inspirational example he set, and by the unwavering loyalty he has always shown to his club in a remarkable playing career.

The entrance gates at West Perth's new home ground, Joondalup Oval, would be named the Les Fong Gates in his honour, while the award for the best player in West Perth Under-16s team is called Les Fong's Futures Best and Fairest award.

ı | | ı

Les's departure from the WAFL coincided with the end of an era.

Australian Rules football was undergoing seismic change in Western Australia as a brand new club, the West Coast Eagles, entered the VFL in 1987. For the first time in history, the WAFL clubs were no longer the premier option for footballers in the state.

As a result, the old WAFL clubs went into decline, losing sponsorship dollars and supporters. In 1993, Neale Fong joined the board of West Perth as a director.

West Perth, like most of the WAFL clubs in the 1990s, were navigating a turbulent and confusing time and were no longer the primary focus of the state's top administrators.

The dissipation of focus was exacerbated in 1994 with the launch of a second Western Australian AFL team, the Fremantle Dockers, which further diminished crowds and the significance of the WAFL.

When the inevitable consolidation phase came with talk of club mergers and relocations to outer metro areas, it was West Perth that was the only club to change, moving its home ground to Joondalup in 1994.

Neale, like many Western Australians at the time, had a foot in both WAFL and AFL camps. In the same year he became a director of West Perth, he was appointed the inaugural chaplain of the West Coast Eagles, with his role counselling the players not deemed a conflict of interest.

Outside of football, Neale was CEO of Australia's largest private hospital, in Subiaco, so it was perhaps no surprise that he was elected to the Western Australia Football Commission (WAFC) in 1999.

He became chairman in 2001, a historic appointment placing Neale as the first Australian major sports chairperson of Asian heritage.

Neale assumed the role at a low point for the state at all three tiers of the game: the AFL, WAFL and grassroots. The West Coast Eagles and the Fremantle Dockers were at the bottom of the AFL ladder, and grassroots participation had stagnated.

Previously the pathway to senior football was through the WAFL clubs and as their pre-eminence faded, key indicators, such as membership, fan attendance, merchandise and participation, all trended downwards.

The WAFC addressed this with an integrated strategy to grow the game by targeting players, parents, volunteers, fans and coaches and eventually the game stabilised and blossomed.

One of Neale's great legacies was the Westar Planning Committee Report, which became known as 'The Fong Report' due to Neale's strong leadership in addressing the problems facing local football, especially the WAFL.

'My contribution, I think, was to bring the whole football fraternity together, because it was very disunified,' he said in 2022.

'Everyone, frankly, disliked and mistrusted each other … There was no money, and footy was in real trouble with $30 million in debt, and an ageing stadium at Subiaco.'

Neale's dual role was trouble shooter and builder, driving sustainability, growth and prosperity that befitted the status of the sport in Western Australia.

'I worked closely with the new CEO of the WA Commission, and we got football back on the map financially and turned it around over the next five years.'

Between 2002 and 2010, West Coast Eagles won a premiership, the WA government committed to a new stadium in Perth's inner suburbs, and the WAFL and community football stabilised.

'More people played the game; more people were involved in the game and more support came for the game,' Neale says.

In 2010, after 11 years of service, Neale stepped down from the WAFC Commission and was duly awarded Life Membership. Beyond his leadership role in football, his leadership in the WA and national health industry has been extraordinary by any measure.

He helped establish the Curtin University medical school, co-founded the Bali International Medical Centre and served as both the Director General of the WA Health Department and as National President of the Australasian College of Health Service Management.

Dr Neale Fong is acknowledged in the Perth Football League Hall of Champions as 'one of the most important figures in Western Australian football history'.

Over a period of almost 40 years, Les Fong became one of the last great WAFL legends while Neale drove great change in the administration of the game.

However, for all their on-field and off-field achievements a career highpoint for the Fong brothers was the two seasons in the mid-1980s when they were teammates.

After Neale completed his medical studies in 1982, he returned to West Perth as club doctor. During the 1985 season, he decided to do pre-season training with the team to maintain his fitness.

His hard work and good form in reserves earned him an unexpected call up to play in the senior team, a dream he thought had passed him by.

Neale's debut against Subiaco at sacred Leederville Oval in Round 9 of that 1985 season sits in a special place in Les's memories.

'Every time I think about my little brother Neale running alongside me onto Leederville Oval, I start tearing up,' Les recalls. 'It was fantastic.'

Neale ended up playing 14 matches over the next two seasons and could never forget 'the buzz of playing in front of 20,000 crowds with my brother Les.'

CHAPTER 10
Drought-breaking Dannie Seow

In 1973, the White Australia policy was dismantled by the Labor Government, paving the way for a new wave of Asian migration beginning in 1975.

Following the end of the Vietnam War, tens of thousands of Vietnamese refugees and migrants arrived in Australia. It was an early test of Australia's new commitment to multiculturalism.

The first cracks appeared in 1984, when distinguished historian Geoffrey Blainey cast doubt on Asian migration levels in an address to a group of more than 1000 Rotary Club members in Warrnambool, a regional town deep in south-west Victoria.

That year, arrivals from Asia increased to 42 per cent of the total migrant intake – the highest since Federation in 1901. Mostly, the new migrants came from Vietnam and Cambodia, but there was also an increased intake of Chinese migrants.

'The pace of Asian immigration is now well ahead of public opinion, particularly in the suburbs and work places where Asians are,' Blainey said.

Arguing that the Australian government had made 'the minority the favoured majority in its immigration policy,' Blainey said that an 'increasing population of Australians' seemed to resent the South-East Asian migrants who he claimed were living, 'through no fault of their own, at the taxpayers' expense'.

Blainey's speech highlighted the disconnect between an old, mostly white Australia and the growing progressive class committed to multiculturalism and deeper engagement with the Asian region.

It led to the ferocious 'Blainey debate': a year-long frenzy of media attention, demonstrations and event cancellations. For some, Blainey was simply raising genuine concerns, while others accused him of racism.

It was in this environment that Dannie Seow, a 17-year-old Collingwood player, made his entry into the VFL.

On Sunday 9 September 1984, 176 days after Geoffrey Blainey's incendiary speech – Dannie played for Collingwood's Under-19 side in a curtain-raiser semi-final clash against Fitzroy. With 15 minutes to go in the match, Fitzroy was ahead by five goals and cruising to victory.

Then Collingwood staged a stirring comeback, kicking three goals to pull within 11 points.

With five minutes remaining, Dannie took a 'speccy' mark and then kicked a goal to bring Collingwood within six points and the big crowd, mostly Collingwood fans who were now settled in their seats waiting for the senior semi-final to begin, roared in unison.

'It felt like I was floating on air!' Dannie recalls.

'It was like the whole MCG lifted through the roar of 70,000 people. I had tingles through my body.'

The crowd's roaring over Dannie's mark and goal intensified when Gordon Sumner kicked the winning goal from the outer boundary line to put Collingwood a point ahead.

Dannie says he will never forget the crowd chanting 'Collingwood, Collingwood.'

Over the next two seasons, Dannie would work his way into the senior Collingwood side, becoming the 'drought breaker', the first Asian-heritage player in 44 years to play in the VFL.

Dannie Seow was born in Melbourne in 1967. He got his surname from his Chinese-Singaporean father, Boon Seng Seow, but was raised by his mother, Vion, an Anglo-European woman, after the family separated from their troubled father when Dannie was six.

His maternal grandmother, Agnes, was a footy fanatic and she would ride an emotional wave with her young grandson every time they watched a Collingwood match together.

Every spare moment for Dannie was devoted to his passion. 'I had a footy with me all the time, walking to school, recess, lunch,' he says.

When asked by one of his primary school teachers what he wanted to do when he grew up, Dannie wrote 'professional footy player'.

'I just wanted to play footy, that's what I wanted to be,' Dannie explains. 'That was it and I knew I could do it.'

As a star performer for the Strathmore Football Club Under-11s, Dannie was selected to play for the 'Little League' team of VFL side Essendon.

The Little League was made up of junior representative teams in each of the VFL club 'zones' that played at half-time of VFL matches for fan entertainment.

Yet despite the cheering and fun, the AFL Record match programs from the time illustrate how seriously the Little League was taken, with scores and competition tables published alongside the VFL results.

Dannie's efforts in the Little League were his first taste of big crowds, and he was given number 18, which was the number worn by Essendon fan favourite, Paul Vander Haar.

Dannie quickly became a cult hero in the Little League for taking spectacular marks. 'The Essendon Cheer Squad affectionately named me "The Flying Chinaman,"' Dannie recalls. 'I loved it.'

Away from footy, though, Dannie was experiencing significant disruptions. Due to his family's deteriorating financial situation, he was forced to leave Essendon Grammar, the plush private school he had been attending since kindergarten, and move to Montmorency Secondary School, a 30-minute drive away in Melbourne's north-east suburbs.

For the first time, he experienced racism in the schoolyard, and although he promised his mother he wouldn't fight at school, he was pushed to limits by the resident school bullies.

'They used to get into my ear on a daily basis with racial comments,' Dannie recalls. 'The usual: "Ching Chong Chinaman", "Nip", "Chink", "Why are you here?", "Better watch yourself"!'

He recalls elbowing one of them in the face, which drew blood and earned him a warning from the school principal.

The racism experience prompted Dannie to reflect on his Chinese heritage. Without his father to guide him, he escaped into Chinese martial arts movies starring Bruce Lee, Jackie Chan and the Run Run Shaw movies, revelling in their wisdom and their core messages of respect and honour.

The only initial positive about his move to Montmorency was that he was now in the recruitment zone of Collingwood, his favourite VFL club.

After he won premierships with Montmorency Football Club and a best and fairest award in the Diamond Valley League, Collingwood recruiters approached him with an offer to sign for their Under-19 squad.

His mother and grandmother were in shock when a letter arrived with his first payment and an off-season training program for him to follow.

In his first Collingwood training session, they played a handball-only game and Dannie was smacked in the face by one of the older players.

'You've got to prove yourself so it didn't worry me,' he remembers.

In 1984, at the age of 17, he was selected in a touring VFL representative team alongside future stars Ross Lyon, Stephen Silvagni, Garry Lyon, Dean Bailey and Ron McKeon.

After playing in Ireland for the VFL side in a hybrid-rules match against the best young Gaelic footballers, Dannie returned to Australia to play in the schoolboy national championships with the same talent-packed team.

'We smashed everyone by 20-plus goals,' Dannie says. 'It was football at the next level.'

Worryingly, later in the year playing against the Hawthorn Under-19 team in a curtain-raiser at Princes Park he was knocked out cold after backing into a pack to take a mark. In those days, players were encouraged to return to play – a far cry from the advanced concussion protocols governing player health and wellbeing in today's contact sports.

Dannie's concussion was so severe that he was taken from the field and, after showing no negative signs during the week, he played the following match.

On reflection, Dannie feels that the players were in such hot competition for places that even in his case, after suffering two concussions in a season, both the club and player would push for a return as soon as possible without any regard for long-term brain health.

ı | | ı

Two years after the Blainey speech, there was an increase in hostility towards Asian communities. For Dannie, the football club was a controlled environment with cross-cultural exchanges limited to friendly banter.

Dannie was given nicknames such as 'China' and 'Sweet'n' – short for 'Sweet and Sour' – but they never caught on. 'I never worried about it and it was a laugh – other guys got it a lot worse and theirs stuck,' Dannie says.

The abuse from opposition teams was much more serious, with some players prepared to cross the line to throw Dannie off his game. On some days a monsoon of abuse would rain down from his opponents, particularly as he started his run up to kick.

According to Dannie, they would yell 'Chinks can't kick the ball,' and 'Go back to where you came from, you stupid nip.'

'Some of them thought I was Japanese, so I copped it for the war as well!' he says. 'I saw it as part funny and part childish.'

Dannie refused to be provoked: 'I was so focused on playing and lining up for a goal. I would hear it every now and again, but it just focused me more.'

On Saturday 10 May 1986, Dannie made his senior debut for Collingwood, under legendary former VFL player Leigh Matthews who, previously an assistant coach for Collingwood, had come in to replace Bob Rose as coach after a disastrous start to the season.

Dannie was the first Chinese-heritage footballer to play for a VFL club since Ian 'Snow' Chinn played for South Melbourne in 1942, and the first since the end of the White Australia policy in 1973.

The breakthrough was not correctly reported in the press, with Collingwood match committee member Ron Richards telling radio reporters that Dannie was the first Vietnamese player in the VFL. The mistake was incorporated into the news bulletin and spread far and wide.

Dannie's grandmother was not impressed. 'She called up the station in a fury to say I had Chinese heritage, not Vietnamese,' he says.

Eventually, Dannie was given the opportunity to set the record straight, telling his local newspaper that his father was from Singapore and his grandfather had come from the Xiamen region in China.

That season, Dannie played 14 games for Collingwood before he was handed a two-match suspension for striking Richmond's Michael Pickering, a decision he still questions.

'I swear that I never meant to hit him,' Dannie says.

'That wasn't my game. I went to do a two-handed punch to clear the ball and it got him flush in the side of the head as he jumped in front of me.'

Under the tough love of Leigh Matthews, Collingwood recovered from their poor start to the 1986 season, narrowly missing out on the finals after finishing the season in fifth spot on the ladder.

'Footy was becoming easy, I was never panicked, and felt comfortable,' Dannie said. 'Even training became easier and fun.'

The 1987 pre-season began with Dannie suffering a severe concussion at an intra-club match.

'I passed out for a moment until I heard someone yell, "Dannie, get up,"' he says.

But he kept playing, and after training passed a rudimentary health test, which he says was 'basically a guy with a mini torch shining it in your eyes.'

For the first time, he began to feel flat, as if he was a 'step behind' the play. At the next pre-season match, he felt sluggish, with pressure on his brain.

It all came to a head in the Round 3 match against Hawthorn. 'I was running through the centre, received a handball and collapsed on the ground,' he recalls. 'I had blurred vision, short breath and nausea – it all hit me at once.'

Yet when he explained his situation to the coaches, he was told he couldn't leave the field.

After being dropped to the Collingwood reserves, he underwent an 'EEG' to measure brain activity in response to different questions.

Dannie says the doctor told him that he had abnormal electrolysis of the brain. 'Stop all exercise for the rest of the year. Especially footy,' Dannie recalls the doctor saying.

When Dannie passed the results to his Collingwood coaches, they were sympathetic but couldn't offer him much time or energy while in the middle of the season.

So Dannie said his goodbyes and went back into the 'real world'. Then 20 years old, he decided to use the time to complete some unfinished business – graduate from high school.

Dannie decided to enrol in the Virginia Episcopal School in the United States, close to where friends of his mother's were living. 'I'd started footy at a high level so young and I felt unless I could play, I'd rather finish school somewhere interesting,' he says.

His grades were good enough to be accepted into the University of North Carolina, where NBA superstar Michael Jordan had graduated three years earlier.

However, before he played any sport, there was one hurdle to overcome.

Due to his background as a professional footballer, it took the stringently amateur National Collegiate Athletic Association (NCAA) two weeks to rule whether he was eligible for college sports.

After he was given the green light, he was selected for the university's American football squad.

'It was an eye opener training for football in college. The professionalism and open and clear communication was at the next level,' he says.

Sadly for Dannie, his college football career ended before he could get any momentum, when he learned his mother was sick with what was later diagnosed as chronic fatigue syndrome.

'She couldn't get out of bed and the family was worried,' Dannie says. 'I was sad to leave college behind but it was Mum first always.'

While acting as a carer for his mother, Dannie kept a low profile and very few in the football community knew of his return to Australia.

Then boredom kicked in and, after a session of kick-to-kick with his brother, he decided to give his former Collingwood coach Leigh Matthews a call about a return to the club.

After Matthews refused to play him in a crucial interclub game, Dannie decided he would leave. It was Melbourne that won the race for his signature and in his first game for the Demons – in Round 1 of the 1989 season – Dannie was one of the best players in Melbourne's five-point victory against Fitzroy.

He kicked two goals, including an electrifying passage of play in which he fooled a Fitzroy player with a sidestep, glided over the 50-metre mark and kicked a perfect long distance goal.

In the match report in *The Age*, journalist Martin Blake described his impressive return to top-flight football. 'Dannie Seow's stint of gridiron has done him no harm,' wrote Blake.

'He was the best of the debutants playing a solid game at centre half-back on Paul Roos. He was particularly effective in the first half and even scored two goals.'

However, within weeks Dannie pulled out of football due to health concerns. 'My brain wasn't right and it was starting to impact other parts of my body as far as hand-eye co-ordination and, occasionally, shortness of breath,' he says.

That season, he also suffered an ankle injury in an exhibition match against Geelong in Toronto, Canada, after landing awkwardly on the rock-hard astroturf.

The club doctors continued to use cortisone but, on his return to Australia, Dannie says independent doctors told him he had 'a long bone spur with shattered bone'.

He remembers being appalled when the doctor told him that the blood in his ankle was 'dark brown'.

By 1990, he had retired from footy, with head trauma ending his career.

'Our club's physiotherapist at the time was doing a study on computers and concussion and mentioned to me that with my bad concussions, computers can bring back concussive symptoms,' Dannie says.

'And he was right. It made a great deal of sense. If I'm on the computer too long my vision gets funky, I get a headache, my brain sometimes feels tense and, if I'm on too long, I get nausea.'

When Dannie Seow retired from Australian Rules football, his next goal was to reconnect with Chinese culture. He moved to Shanghai for five years, travelling often to meet his brother, Ben, who had moved to their father's ancestral city of Xiamen to train with a martial arts grandmaster.

Dannie forged a deeper cultural connection through three pillars: martial arts, food and learning Mandarin. 'I was up to about 1200 Chinese characters when I was living there, reading and writing,' he says.

His Chinese experience was funded by working as a fashion model for three years, which evolved from strutting the catwalk to organising various major fashion events.

On his return from China, Dannie reunited with his father, Boon, who Dannie says came close to dying in a factory accident in which he was crushed. In 2023, Boon is in his 80s and suffers from bad dementia, with Dannie the only family member he recognises.

When asked to summarise his legacy in football, Dannie relates an event that took place when he was playing for Melbourne and doing a footy clinic at Richmond Primary School where almost all of the kids were Vietnamese.

One of the kids stood up and said, 'Can we have Dannie Seow speak please?'

'When I got up to speak there was a silence – all the kids sat bolt upright and listened to everything,' he says.

He recalls the class bursting into applause when he told them: 'Asian or otherwise, you can play the sport or do what you love, regardless of the obstacles.'

In that moment, he realised that for a group of Asian schoolkids in Richmond, he was their pioneering hero. 'It really showed me the power of role models,' he says.

'I always think that if even one of those kids went on to have a kick, it would be a great achievement.'

CHAPTER 11

'Pangy' the Perfect Teammate

In 1989, high school boys from every state and territory met at the Darwin Showgrounds for the National Secondary Schools Australian Football Championship.

The Australian Capital Territory (ACT) team were the surprise of the tournament, beating their much larger neighbours, Victoria and New South Wales, and although they finished mid-table, they earned genuine respect having not won a game at the previous three championships.

At the start of the season, the ACT Schoolboys team had no coach and manager and they were true underdogs; second-class citizens in a fanatical rugby league state in the year that the Canberra Raiders would win their first NRL Premiership.

One of the best players for the ACT was Richard Pang, a scrawny 15-year-old half-back flanker from Canberra's Phillip College. In an ACT squad list full of Anglo-Celtic kids – Ryder, Dickinson, O'Halloran, Gregory – Richard was the only boy with an Asian name.

Richard was a recent convert to football, having picked up a Sherrin for the first time that year at the encouragement of his neighbour, Charles, and Richard's development was then accelerated through a classmate and friend, Ryan Kearney.

With Ryan's support, Richard rose quickly, and both boys were star performers at the 1989 Schoolboys Championship.

Today, Richard still has a treasured bottle of port that he and his teammates received for beating Victoria, a prize that he says was 'a bit odd' considering none of them was of legal drinking age at the time.

That tournament, he says, was the launchpad for his professional career, which took him from Canberra to Subiaco: 'That's when I said to myself, I can actually be okay at this game.'

ı | | ı

Richard was born on 11 November 1972 to a Chinese father and a New Zealand mother. Despite his diverse heritage, he led a typical Australian childhood in the nation's capital.

'My dad was from a traditional Chinese family, however my grandparents who were very traditional Chinese encouraged him to be as Australian as possible,' Richard explains.

His father's assimilation into Australian life did not extend to a love of contact sports, though, and he tried to ban Richard and his brothers from playing football.

After all, Henry Pang was a doctor, and he felt the game was too dangerous. When he finally relented, Richard arrived home from his first junior game with a broken wrist.

Richard never learned Cantonese from his father but his name and his features attracted unwanted attention in the schoolyard. 'In Canberra there wasn't a lot of Chinese guys and at school we used to cop a bit of crap,' he says.

'If it got a bit heated, I'd just call my brother over and he'd tell the guys to back off, so it never affected me.'

After Richard finished school, he was selected in the Eastlake senior team in the ACT Football League. 'We had the tightest group of mates at Eastlake footy club,' he recalls. 'Most of my lifelong mates have come from that group of people.'

Despite their tight bond, his teammates would occasionally remind him of his status as a cultural pioneer in the league.

'It was quite funny when I told all my non-footy mates from Canberra that I was playing Australian football, they laughed and said, "You're the first one,"' Richard recalled.

'They used to always call me "the first Chinese footballer," which was quite funny.'

After five years of senior footy in Canberra, Richard arrived at a crossroads. His consistent form for Eastlake earned him selection three times for the ACT representative team and his job as an electrician gave him the flexibility to train three times a week and do gym work during lunch.

His consistent improvement as a footballer in the ACT culminated in his towering performance in Eastlake's 1996 grand final victory when he won the Alex Jesaulenko Medal for best player on the ground.

He would also consistently be playing with or recovering from injuries, particularly to his knees, which brought his career longevity into question.

He felt, 'it was time to reach as high as I could.'

When he was invited to participate in the 1997 AFL Draft Combine, he jumped at the opportunity and flew to Melbourne.

As a 24-year-old man among 17-year-old prospects from around Australia, Richard was an odd presence.

And although he enjoyed the physical examination, his skills let him down. Australian Rules football at the elite level was becoming a possession-oriented game, which Richard says was not beneficial for him.

'I could run, jump and get the ball, but I came very late to the game so it was harder to compete with guys who had been kicking since they were five or six years old,' he says.

He didn't get drafted and returned to Canberra, 'a little bit down in the dumps but happy that I had a crack at the AFL.'

Despite the setback, he went back to Melbourne to do a pre-season with Essendon, a club that he'd supported since he was a kid. He moved in with a friend near the Bombers' home ground and trained hard for three months alongside Essendon legend James Hird, who also grew up in Canberra.

'I realised then what it takes to be an AFL footy player,' Richard says. 'They were big and fit with amazing skills.'

The pivotal moment came one evening after training when Richard was kicking the footy with 17-year-old Essendon player Mark Bolton, who would go on to play 124 matches for the Bombers.

Watching on was Essendon coach Kevin Sheedy, who Richard says told him: 'See "Bolts"? He's 17 and I can teach him to kick. You're 25 soon; we can't teach you to kick.'

Richard says Sheedy then told him: 'You'll need to move out of Canberra if you want to play high level footy.'

After taking a voluntary redundancy from his job as an electrician, Richard started making plans to leave Canberra. He trained with South Australian side West Adelaide before following some of his Eastlake teammates to Perth Demons in the Western Australian Football League (WAFL).

The step up in professionalism was immediately apparent.

Perth players, unlike most at Eastlake, trained at high intensity, worked out in their own club gym and utilised sports science in preparation and recovery.

At the start of the 1998 season, Richard was proud to wear Perth's black guernsey with the red sash – an identical colour scheme and design to his beloved Essendon.

He was on a contract and, for the first time in his life, was being paid real money to play. 'Perth wasn't a wealthy club, but they looked after a whole lot of things for you,' he recalls.

That year, Richard played 18 consecutive matches for Perth, consistently getting his hands on the ball and feeding it to the set-position specialists.

His good form was rewarded with selection in the Western Australian State of Origin team.

Under the traditional State of Origin selection criteria, Richard couldn't have represented his new state of residence but the rules had changed to allow teams to select players who had been imported from other states.

Although Western Australia lost to South Australia, for Richard it was 'the next best thing' to playing in the AFL. 'It was a great experience with a bunch of really good blokes and we had a big night out on the booze afterwards,' he says.

Although Perth narrowly missed the finals in 1999, Richard thrived alongside future AFL stars such as Darren Glass, Chance Bateman and Leon Davis.

'It was a fun year and great to play with these young fellas,' he says, adding that 'sometimes they'd just turn it on and run amok and we'd blow teams out of the water.'

Richard's stunning run of form was acknowledged when he finished second in the Sandover Medal for the WAFL's best and fairest player and won the Butcher Medal for Perth's best and fairest player over the season.

'Pangy was effectively the perfect teammate,' Perth player and friend Richard Kelly says. 'Off the field he was always up for a laugh at the gym or training and on the field he was a fantastic player and always lifted our team. He was a hard runner and I was a hard hitter and would protect him with shepherds. It got to the stage where we were just connecting by visuals; no comment needed.'

There was a 10-year age gap between the two Richards and Kelly will never forget the first time he saw Pang in the gym: 'Here was an Asian guy with an absolutely phenomenal body, like I'd never seen before.'

| | | |

At the end of 1999, after a failed player coup to remove Perth coach Gary Armstrong, Richard joined a mass exodus from Perth and signed with Subiaco.

To Richard, the move was an opportunity to win a premiership, increase his pay, and play at Subiaco Oval, widely acclaimed as the most beautiful ground in the WAFL. 'I'd been playing with a lot of injuries and my time was running out – I really thought we had a good chance of winning the flag,' Richard explains.

His Subiaco teammates gave him a new nickname. 'Although most of the boys at Subiaco called me "Pangy", a couple called me "China", which I don't have an issue with as they were all my mates and nicknames simply manifest themselves,' he says.

'We had an amazing bunch of players who had really good camaraderie. We'd all go out and do stuff together and train hard, party hard and had heaps of fun. We had a really good team.'

Although Subiaco failed to win the premiership, Richard played one of his best games that season, securing a titanic 48 possessions against Peel Thunder. His standout performance overshadowed that of teammate, and future Sydney Swan, Richard Ambrose, who had also played the game of his life.

'Bloody hell, Pangy: the day I take 20 marks, you go and get 48 possessions,' Richard recalls his mate saying post-game.

In 2001, Richard's knee injuries kept him out of the first team for most of the year. He drained fluid from his knees weekly to train, eventually recovering to be selected for the final game of the regular season.

Playing through the pain, he says, was 'the most stupid thing I did in my whole football life.'

In what would be his final footy match against the Perth Demons, he was called a 'traitor' by Perth fans before exiting the game early with a broken collarbone.

'It was a bit sad for me – that was the end of my footy life. Abused off the ground that had given me so many good memories,' he says.

After Richard retired from football, he started working for a Perth-based software company, which led to 10 years living and working in Singapore.

He also took up surfing, a sport that does not aggravate his knees, and he makes regular trips to the Mentawai Islands off the coast of Sumatra to indulge his passion.

'Unfortunately, I've had 13 knee operations including four major grafts where they stitch the cartilage back on the bone. I also broke both collarbones and both wrists,' he says.

'And you feel it all when you finish.'

CHAPTER 12

The Wongs: Four Generations of Chinese-Australian Footy

It's a six-minute drive from the heart of Shepparton to neighbouring Mooroopna but, despite their shared geography, the two Victorian towns are worlds apart.

Located 190 kilometres north-east of Melbourne, Shepparton is the commercial capital of the Goulburn Valley and Mooroopna is its smaller, poorer cousin across the Goulburn River.

Mooroopna, which gets its name from the Yorta Yorta word for 'deep water hole', has always been defined by its relationship with the river.

After heavy rains, the 'deep water hole' often rises up to flood the town. Residents are now accustomed to living with flooding, and the town's houses and businesses are routinely fortified with sandbags when flood warnings reach critical levels.

On the Midland Highway between Shepparton and Mooroopna is a sign that proclaims 'Fruit Salad City', a nod to Mooroopna's history of fruit production.

From 1925 to 2011, the Ardmona fruit canning plant was the engine room of town life, providing steady employment for its Anglo-Celtic, European and Chinese-Australian residents.

The Chinese settlers had a deep impact on Mooroopna. Today, every traveller from Shepparton must cross the 'Ah Wong Bridge', named after Chan Ah Wong, a Cantonese gold rush migrant and market gardener who almost drowned in the flood of 1889 while trying to deliver fruit and vegetables to the townspeople.

'A Chinese market gardener, in attempting to cross this morning with his cart nearly lost his life,' reported the *Shepparton News* in August 1889.

'He clung to his cart until he was rescued some three hours afterwards by some persons in a boat. The cart and horse were carried down the torrent, and the horse was drowned.'

The Ah Wongs were at the mercy of the seasonal floods of the Goulburn River floodplain and their market garden periodically would turn into a lake after heavy rains. During the good times, Ah Wong was famous for delivering fruit and vegetables on the back of his horse and cart, travelling as far as Undera, a 60-kilometre round trip.

He was known as a great 'barterer' and would supply produce to the needy, particularly during the Depression in the 1890s. He also contributed funds to the hospital, an institution that treated him and his family with respect.

After the floods of 1916, Ah Wong's land was taken over by the government. The fertile loam soil he had nurtured for 40 years was dug up, then carted throughout the city to enrich the flower beds of the public street gardens and median strips.

Ah Wong finally moved into the town, to a house in Morrell Street, where he grew vegetables until he passed away at the age of 90.

There is a picture of Ah Wong from the 1920s in front of his market garden. His clothes are smart but he looks tired and haggard, with a long beard and unkempt hair. He chose a difficult life but his legacy lives on through hundreds of descendants sprinkled throughout the region.

Ah Wong's descendants left their most visible mark on the football field for the Mooroopna Cats.

On match day, visiting fans could cross Ah Wong's bridge, pass by Chinaman's Reserve, stop for lunch for a John 'Tangles' Wong burger at the art deco Verong and Vittles Cafe Diner, and enjoy an afternoon beer at the John 'Tangles' Wong Bar at Mooroopna Oval.

'For a bridge to be named after a Chinese market gardener, he must have been something special,' Billy Wong says of his great-great-grandfather.

'It's a very special honour for our family and you get a nice reminder every time you come in from Shepparton.'

In June 2019, Billy Wong was inducted into the prestigious Goulburn Valley Football League Hall of Fame for his sustained excellence for the Mooroopna Cats as a ruck rover/forward.

A life member of the Goulburn Valley Football League (GVFL), Billy had a storied career playing 312 senior games, winning back-to-back senior premierships in 1985 and 1986. He was awarded the club's best and fairest trophy twice and made 10 appearances for the Goulburn Valley representative team.

Beyond fitness, skills and tactics, the most important element of his success with Mooroopna was mateship. He grew up with the same group of friends and they won a number of junior premierships together. 'That's a great platform to build off,' Billy explains.

Although the 1985 premiership was the town's first flag in 47 years, it was the back-to-back grand final victory over Shepparton United the following year that entered the region's folklore.

By half time, Mooroopna trailed Shepparton by 24 points and their fans were anxiously hoping the Cats could turn around the deficit in the second half.

And then, Billy Wong recalls, 'something amazing happened.'

In an effort to recharge his flagging players, Mooroopna coach Chris Smith reached into his bag of tricks that he had acquired from playing 10 years in the VFL for Fitzroy.

'We were just about to run onto the ground when Chris Smith stopped us,' Billy says. 'He then made us sing the team song twice.'

This ritual, exclusively reserved for the victors at the end of the game, psychologically jolted Mooroopna into action and they kicked nine goals in a row to win by 16 points.

Later, Smith glowingly summarised Billy Wong's contribution to the season: 'He was hard at the ball, a great team player and a dream to coach.'

Billy, meanwhile, was in awe of the impact the victory had on the community. 'My dad was over the moon, everyone's parents and grandparents came out,' he remembers.

'Mooroopna is a working-class club – lots of tradies, not corporate – so a win just meant so much to them.'

The Mooroopna Museum has a section devoted to the successes of the Mooroopna Cats – a celebration of their 11 premierships since the Goulburn Valley League was inaugurated in 1894.

The display includes some original guernseys, newspaper clippings, pennants and a large number of team photos from over 120 years of club football.

The Wong surname is sprinkled throughout the display of photos, and in every generation there is a Wong helping out in some way with the footy club.

The Wong family football story in Mooroopna mirrors the Chinese-Australian experience – collectively it is a story of triumph, tenacity and tragedy; of overcoming adversity and fitting in.

In 1896, Billy Wong's great-grandfather – also named Billy Wong – was part of the first Mooroopna team to win a premiership.

The pictures of Billy Wong Snr in team photos from the early 1900s show a lean, muscular man with thick black hair, sinewy forearms and a big moustache, at home with tough working-class men and farmers. His gaze carries an intensity befitting his tough day job, helping his father Ah Wong in the Mooroopna market gardens.

After Billy Wong Snr retired from the Mooroopna Cats in the early 1900s, his son Laurie continued the tradition in the 1930s, serving on the committee before becoming the head trainer after World War II and coaching the club to the 1946 premiership.

Laurie's cousin, James Wong, was killed when hit by a car while riding home after football training in 1940.

James was 23 years old and a popular figure at the club, having been part of Mooroopna's 1939 premiership side. The *Shepparton Advertiser* reported on the tragedy with the headline, 'Premiership Flag at Half Mast'.

In 1962, Les Wong played in the Mooroopna seniors team that came runners-up and in 1969 John Wong won a reserve grade premiership. The Wong tradition was continued into the 1970s by long-haired Neville Wong, who played in the Mooroopna senior team.

Billy Wong Jr says Mooroopna's two premierships in 1985 and 1986 were underpinned by excellent off-field administration led by his father, John.

John 'Tangles' Wong played briefly for the club in the 1950s, was a trainer in the 1960s and devoted the rest of his life to serving the Mooroopna football club in a variety of committee roles.

'Tangles' passed away in 2012, and to mark his passing the club officially named a bar, The John 'Tangles' Wong Bar at Mooroopna's home ground.

'He wasn't a great footballer but he loved the community spirit,' says his son, Billy Wong Jnr. 'He got a lot of enjoyment out of watching me play, which makes me really proud.'

Billy is proud to carry the Wong name but it has caused him some confusion and funny moments in his footy career and beyond.

'I was a pale skin red-headed kid but I used to cop a fair bit of abuse over the fence about being Chinese. You name it I got called it,' he says.

'And our rivals [Shepparton] United would always get stuck into me a fair bit about it. Sometimes it was funny, sometimes it wasn't.'

His Chinese heritage sometimes catches him by surprise, especially when he travels.

He has received some confused looks from hotel staff at check-in expecting to see a Chinese person attached to the surname Wong, and his honeymoon in Queensland took an unexpected turn when he and his wife were booked with Chinese tourists on a river cruise and he couldn't speak a word with them.

'We laughed pretty hard at that one,' Billy recalls.

How does he feel being a fourth-generation Chinese heritage footballer descended from Ah Wong, the famous market gardener?

To be Billy Wong, the son of John Wong, who was the son of Laurie Wong, who was the son of Billy Wong, who together proudly span a century of Mooroopna footballing history?

'I don't think about it that much but now and then people remind me that it's an amazing family history and it is,' Billy Jr says.

And although his great-great grandfather Ah Wong the market gardener didn't play footy, his memory is still cherished by the family.

'I think the Chinese weren't really looked after well in those times, so it makes our family achievements more meaningful – respect to Ah Wong for working hard and building a family in those days,' says Billy.

In summarising the Wong legacy in the town, Billy is upbeat.

'If you look at it, the Wongs haven't done too badly in Mooroopna,' he says. 'We've got a bridge, a bar and a burger shop!'

CHAPTER 13

Russell Goldfield Jack and the Big Gold Mountain Footy Tradition

Bendigo, a regional city 150 kilometres north-east of Melbourne, holds a special place in Chinese-Australian history. In the 19th century, up to 20 per cent of its population was Chinese and Bendigo even had its own name in Cantonese – 'Dai Gum San' (Big Gold Mountain).

The centre of Chinese life in Bendigo was the Ironbark Camp, built in 1855 by the city's appointed 'Chinese Protector' to segregate the Chinese from the other communities. Market gardens were established and the camp became a self-sustained village with bath houses, laundries, blacksmiths, carpenters, butchers, goldsmiths, scribes, gambling rooms, opium dens, piggeries, cookhouses, churches and temples.

There were once seven Joss House temples in Ironbark, each erected by different clans. Today, the beautiful Bendigo Joss House Temple at Emu Point is the sole survivor, maintained for a long time by elderly ex-miners and market gardeners who used to pray there for good fortune.

Although in disrepair, fenced off and closed to the public, the Joss House's handmade red bricks still attract the attention of passers-by.

Many Chinese people in early Bendigo embraced Christianity – as well as 'European' activities, such as gambling on horses and greyhounds.

But they persisted with their style of cooking and introduced 'foreign' spices and flavours to the Bendigo community in food shops that were a portal to the East.

The Toi Shan Chinese restaurant was established in 1910 and remains the longest continuously operated Chinese restaurant in Australia. Originally a 'cookshop' named 'On Loong' in the old Bridge Street Chinatown, it moved to its current Mitchell Street location in 1942.

The Bendigo Chinese community worked hard to raise money for local hospitals and were a central part of the first Bendigo Easter Festival in 1871. Led by 'Loong', who at 40 metres was the longest imperial parade dragon in the world and first imported to Bendigo in 1892, the Chinese participated every year in the Easter Parade in traditional costumes.

Loong was replaced by 'Sun Loong' in 1970 and, now retired, he is displayed in Bendigo's Golden Dragon Museum, which since 1991 has served as a regional beacon for the Chinese-Australian community.

The museum faithfully preserves the history of Chinese Bendigo for both the local community and passing tourists. Its walls are lined with hundreds of images, black-and-white portraits and stills that capture the lives of Bendigo's old Chinese migrant community members and their descendants, some of whom played footy.

ı | | ı

In the museum, there's a painting of Chin Kit, a Toishanese gold rush migrant who came to Victoria in 1856 and was, at one stage, a very important Bendigo interpreter and head man of the Chinese Eureka village. In 1882, his son, Henry George Chin Kit, made his debut for the Ironbark Football Club aged 17, becoming the first known Chinese-heritage Australian Rules footballer.

Henry Chin Kit was the first known sportsperson of Asian heritage to play for a sporting club in Australia and his short football career ended when his family moved to Launceston, soon anglicising the family name to Kitt and assimilating into mainstream Tasmanian life.

Henry became an engineer, photographer and oil painter of note and his son Keith Kitt became a legend of northern Tasmanian football, winning the first ever McAuley Medal in 1926 as Launceston Football Club's best and fairest player that year.

Another image in the museum is of Yan Cheong Wong Ying, a Cantonese migrant who was the owner and publican of Ying's Terminus Hotel in Dunolly, a former goldfields hotspot and satellite town of Bendigo. Yan Cheong's son, William Ying, won two premierships as a wingman with Dunolly in 1903 and 1907.

William Ying's portrait is located next to his father's and shows a 26-year-old renaissance man, equally at home working as an assayer in the mines or pursing his hobby of photography – some of his images of landscapes and cars are kept in the State Library of Victoria's collection.

After he finished working in the mines, William Ying became a serious car collector and in 1931, at the age of 47, he officially became a mechanic to professionally indulge his passion for motor vehicles. He opened his garage in Alma Street, Maryborough, which still stands to this day adorned by the sign: 'W.H. Ying Garage'.

One stunning black-and-white photograph shows Louey O'Hoy, who came to Australia from Toishan and established a successful and famed general store in the old Bridge Street Chinatown that was inherited by his six children. He is seated with his wife and flanked by 18 family members all dressed in traditional Chinese formal wear to celebrate his 80th birthday.

Louey's great-grandson, Trevor O'Hoy, played reserve grade football for St Kilda in the VFL and would spend time in Bendigo as a young boy, visiting his extended family who lived in the old Bridge Street Chinatown.

He recalls receiving 'a glass of raspberry lemonade' as a reward every time he fetched his father for dinner from the Chinatown pub on his three-wheel bike.

There are portraits of Percy Wee Hee, a first-generation Chinese migrant – who once cared for the parade dragon Loong – and Percy's son Ron.

In the 1950s, Ron Wee Hee was a leading footballer in Bendigo, known locally as 'the Fireman Footballer'. In the portraits, his father, Percy, is dressed as the Easter Parade's 'General' in elaborate Ming Dynasty military uniform, while Ron wears his fireman's uniform.

Ron Wee Hee played with Sandhurst, won two senior premierships with White Hills and trialled with Collingwood before playing six games for Brighton in the VFA.

Ron's three sons, Grant, Rodney and Jeffrey, all continued the Wee Hee football tradition with Grant winning the Heathcote District Football League best and fairest award in 1991 and six best and fairest medals for his father's old club, White Hills.

As Grant says about his father's legacy: 'The Wee Hee name remains very strong in football circles.'

One large portrait on the museum wall features Samuel Ah Dore, a Toishanese market gardener who was labelled one of Bendigo's 'chief sporting men' by the *Barrier Miner* in July 1897 and was a popular figure on the greyhound racing circuit, causing a stir when he gave his dogs 'long heathenish names' like Changshafoo.

Samuel also took to the football field when he represented Bendigo against Eaglehawk in an all-Chinese charity match in 1896.

'Sadly, I never got to meet Samuel, but I heard a lot about him from my father who shared some of his wisdom,' Ah Dore's grandson, Russell Goldfield Jack, said.

'My father used to say, "if you live somewhere – it doesn't matter where it is – you got to give back. Don't take, give back."'

Russell Goldfield Jack served as president of the Bendigo Chinese Association for more than three decades. The Golden Dragon Museum, locally known as 'the house that Jack built', was his crowning achievement.

In 1993, he was made a Member of the Order of Australia for his contribution to preserving his hometown's Chinese heritage.

While Russell's short-lived football career is often forgotten among his many community awards and accolades, the game played an important role in his life as a 'Bendigonian'.

Russell Goldfield Jack was born in Bendigo in 1935, the son of a Hong Kong Chinese father and a Chinese-Australian mother. His parents named their children with grandiose middle names and for Russell, they landed on 'Goldfield'.

His first leadership position was as captain of the Long Gully Primary School football team.

A natural, all-round athlete, Russell honed his footy skills for hours on a vacant block of land across from his school.

Although he clearly looked Chinese, he received almost no racism in the schoolyard. 'Footy and the other sports cut across a lot of the barriers for me,' he says.

'It helped me a lot being a leader. I didn't have to fight to be captain at school; they just told me I was.'

Russell's daughter, Anita, says old timers called her father 'the Cazaly of Bendigo', referring to Roy Cazaly, the famous South Melbourne VFL footballer who took high marks despite his small stature and inspired the 1979 cult song, 'Up There Cazaly'.

'I don't want to sound big-headed, but high marking came easy to me,' Russell recalls.

As a young teenager, Russell watched Eaglehawk play in the Bendigo Football League and was amazed by the size of the crowds and how seriously fans and players took the game.

One of the Eaglehawk players was Ian 'Snowy' Chinn, a Chinese-Australian who had returned to Bendigo after playing two seasons in the VFL and then serving in World War II. Chinn kicked 28 goals over 17 games in 1940 and 1942 with the South Melbourne Swans.

In 1946, not long after he was discharged from the Army, Chinn was instrumental in delivering Eaglehawk a premiership. 'I remember Ian Chinn playing for Eaglehawk. He had all the skills and a big kick,' Russell says.

'We knew he had a Chinese background, which was exciting.'

In 1949, Russell was selected for the Bendigo regional schools' team that travelled to Melbourne to participate in the Victorian Schoolboys Carnival.

Russell played strongly and the tiny Chinese winger from Long Gully won the trophy for best and fairest player at the carnival, ahead of future VFL legends, such as Collingwood premiership winner and Hall of Famer Thorold Merrett, and future Brownlow Medal winner and Carlton Team of the Century half-back flanker John James.

After his return to Bendigo, Russell was promoted to Eaglehawk's senior side at age 17. He was already on the radar of VFL team Richmond, and the Tigers' president, Maurie Fleming, would travel to visit the Jack household to try and woo Russell to join Richmond.

Russell's priority, though, was earning money to help his family. 'What you have to remember is that everybody was poor,' he says.

'I was one of nine kids who ate like hungry horses. So I told Mr Fleming that I was grateful for the offer but I want to stay at home and help my mum who was sick. Cooking, washing laundry by hand, managing the fire – I did it all.'

Instead of finishing his final years of high school, Russell joined the Railways as a boilermaker and retired from football in 1953, after a single season of senior football.

'When I look back, I think I would have made it in footy,' Russell says. 'But as a boy in a Chinese family I had obligations that went beyond sport.'

In 1956, the Melbourne Olympic Games were held in the Southern Hemisphere for the first time and Australia's remoteness, once seen as a disadvantage, helped shield the Olympics from an uncertain post-war world.

The Suez Crisis had pitted Israel, Britain and France against Egypt, antagonising the Arab world and prompting Egypt's withdrawal from the Games. Soviet tanks crossed the River Danube to quell the Hungarian uprising, which led to the infamous 'blood in the water' water polo match between the USSR and Hungary at the Melbourne Olympics.

In China, the last of the Kuomintang forces were defeated in the north by Mao Zedong's communist forces and bloody riots took place between communists and Kuomintang in Hong Kong.

Due to the Republic of China's participation, the People's Republic of China would not partake in the 1956 Olympic Games, denying the Chinese-Australians, who had been living behind the White Australian curtain for 55 years, a chance to see them participating in the modern sporting world.

Their absence was offset by the participation of the ROC, who sent 20 athletes, and culturally familiar Hong Kong, who were represented by Kin Man Cheung and Shiu Ming Wan in swimming.

The Games were to be the first televised to the world and sport would again be required to project the possibilities of positive human co-operation.

Nothing embodied this global fraternity more than the cross-border Olympic Torch Run, a logistical miracle, which began in Greece, the original home of the Olympics, and then travelled an estimated 13,750 kilometres through Istanbul, Basra, Karachi, Calcutta, Bangkok, Singapore, Jakarta and Darwin before arriving in Cairns for a gruelling 4500-kilometre hand-to-hand overland relay to Melbourne, the longest single route in modern Olympic history.

The 1.8 kilogram aluminium 'Flame of Olympia' torch was carried for 13 days and nights, from Cairns to the Olympic Cauldron at the Melbourne Cricket Ground, a feat involving 3118 runners.

The torch bearers ran through floods, humidity and storms, cheered on by enthusiastic crowds.

When the torch finally reached Bendigo, it was handed to 21-year-old Russell Goldfield Jack, who completed his leg of the run and then travelled to Bendigo Town Hall to join the other torch bearers, letting the cheers of an estimated 12,000 people wash over him during the lavish celebrations.

Russell had been selected to represent the Bendigo Chinese community, one of 26 torch bearers from the City of Bendigo.

His selection was due to his sporting prowess, an acknowledgement of his excellence in football, baseball, and especially athletics where he held local records for many years, especially the long jump.

When the Olympic Games were held in Sydney in 2000, Russell had long retired from all sports but he was again given the honour of carrying the 'Flame of Olympia' torch for his work as President of the Bendigo Chinese Association and as a Life Governor at the Bendigo Hospital.

Over the 20th century, Bendigo's Chinese influence would gradually fade as the community's old people passed, its young ones assimilated and the town gradually forgot its Chinese history.

This erasure was captured in the book *Chinese Footsteps*, produced by the Golden Dragon Museum:

> Bendigo was a developing city with no desire to retain Chinese names associated with former Chinese pioneers.
>
> As Chinese moved on to their Celestial kingdoms, Australians were able to access the land, demolish the old huts, and forget the past by associating their own names with the land or businesses.
>
> There was no attraction to retaining Chinese names in a union dominated community of 'Australia for White Australians'. Chinaman's flat, Chinaman's swamp and even Ah Chew's bridge were all quietly excised from the official record and replaced with more contemporary 'Australian' names.

For Russell, the loss of the old Bridge Street Chinatown was a major blow. After all, he'd spent some of his youth there among lively restaurants and late-night games of mahjong.

The Jack family continued its connection to Chinese culture through Russell's uncle, Waysoon Louey, a larger-than-life character who was a comedian, cook and cultural man, and Russell's mother, Gladys, who passed down her recipes to Russell's Anglo-Australian wife, Joan.

Joan's cooking became so famous that the Jacks once owned a chain of four Chinese restaurants in the region.

Beyond the Easter Parade and Chinese restaurants, Russell wanted more done to preserve Bendigo's Chinese history. His father, Harry Louey Jack, had always encouraged Russell to be proud of his Chinese roots and wanted him to have a community leadership role.

'He would always call me by my Chinese name,' Russell explains. 'And he would say Louey Yeung Man, when you grow older, I want you to look after the Chinese population here in Bendigo.'

ı | | ı

In the mid-1980s, Bendigo City Council began a program to support organisations that could help attract tourists to the region. Sensing an opportunity, Russell developed a plan for a museum. He went on a study trip to China to learn about Chinese design principles in public buildings, temples and museums.

'I learnt so much on that trip about architecture and culture, which helped make the Golden Dragon Museum more authentic,' Russell explains.

Russell chose the site of the old Chinatown, which had been turned into a council carpark, and raised $3.25 million from a variety of sources, including grassroots fundraising, government grants and philanthropy. 'The words "no" and "can't" are not in my dictionary,' he says.

The Golden Dragon Museum was completed in 1991. What had originally been planned to be a permanent home for the parade dragons and processional regalia, blossomed into a full photographic history, home of community artifacts, library, archive and a conference centre.

The dedicated Chinese history Museum, the first of its kind for a regional Australian town, would help revitalise and celebrate Bendigo Chinese culture, and provide a place for the Chinese community, both new and old, to celebrate their heritage.

By the mid-1990s, a new generation of migrants and tourists would arrive in Bendigo to learn about the region's Chinese history – and meet 'Loong', the 100-year-old retired parade dragon.

Joining them would be schoolchildren, historians, local Bendigonians and domestic and international tourists, who would all come to learn about a hidden part of Australian history – pilgrimages of respect to 'the house that Jack built'.

CHAPTER 14

The Last of the Rice Eaters

For the football fanatics in country towns scattered across Victoria, the 1990s phenomenon of the merging of country football clubs impacted them deeply and emotionally.

Changing attitudes to contact sport, more diverse opportunities for recreation and an exodus of the towns' best and brightest to bigger cities, led to player shortages and weekly scrambles to fill teams.

Some clubs folded, unable to field teams or meet increased running costs, and they disappeared forever, their history consigned to the local historical society, fleeting player reunions and nostalgic social media posts.

Others took the more practical survival approach by merging, pooling resources and players and combining names and colours to create a new entity.

Rarely were these mergers welcomed. Fusing two groups of players who had been historical bitter rivals for, in some cases, over a century was at times a seemingly impossible feat.

Mergers ranged from 'common sense' to 'forced marriages' to 'hostile shotgun weddings', especially if a stronger club dominated the terms on colours, name, nickname, home ground and committee representation.

At the turn of the 21st century, Victorian footy clubs had been reluctantly merging with their rivals down the road, bound in many cases only by a primordial need to keep the game they loved alive.

Paul Daffey is the author of *Behind the Goals: The History of the Victorian Country Football League* and has written extensively on country club mergers that, according to him, range from 'harmonious to rancorous'.

For Daffey, the high rate of 1990s club mergers was all about survival in the face of rapid depopulation of the townships' young men, and even successfully merged clubs have a limited window to survive – a trend that Daffey has observed across the state:

'There's the initial euphoria, then a rush of enthusiasm and energy and efficiencies, and that lasts for three years,' he explains.

'Then it really relies on how the people at the top get along or one club gets subsumed or they just fold.'

The quintessential merger story for Daffey is a club called Ouyen United, near Mildura, which according to his research is the result of 32 mergers over 100 years, the latest strand being in 2000 when the Ouyen Rovers merged with Tempy-Goyra-Patchewollock.

In 2001, the club merger phenomenon finally reached the football stronghold of Eastern Ballarat and its two clubs, the Golden Point Rice Eaters and East Ballarat – bitter rivals who had shared the same ground for 57 years – began to negotiate terms.

From its humble early years, the Golden Point Rice Eaters became a force of Ballarat football with a sustained run of success spanning 15 senior premierships from 1910 to 1987.

Their merger partner, the East Ballarat Football Club, had won six premierships since 1944.

The people of Eastern Ballarat lived and breathed footy, but commercial reality and a declining pool of quality players willing to commit to a long career of football eventually took its toll.

In 2001, the committees of the Golden Point Rice Eaters and East Ballarat Football Club sat down to negotiate terms for a merger, with a compromise name and colours agreed after some robust debate.

One argument they avoided was where to base themselves, as their joint home was Eastern Oval, one of the most historic sporting venues in Australia – a mystical place that has hosted the intersection of many key moments in Australian history and a source of pride for Ballarat's 'easterners'.

English cricket titan WG Grace was so enamoured with the ground when he played there on the 1873–74 tour of Australia, that he reportedly planted a Dutch elm tree, which has grown to a mighty size on the northern side of the ground.

In 1854, the British Army's 12th and 40th Regiments stopped in front of where the main grandstand is today, to regroup before marching to quell the Eureka Rebellion taking place up the road.

The first Chinese-Australian Rules football teams, 'The Miners' and 'The Market Gardeners', first played their 'Celestial Match' on the ground in 1892.

By the late 1990s, Eastern Oval was in decline but in 2001–2002 it was redeveloped back to its former glory.

In 2002, a new chapter of history was written at the ground when the East Point Kangaroos played their first game as the newly merged entity. The Golden Point Rice Eaters and East Ballarat FC were no more.

The Kangaroos had a slow start, finishing last in 2002 and 2003, but they were financially stable and survived. Success was elusive for the club initially, but its first premierships were secured in 2018 and 2019.

Located between today's East Point Kangaroos clubhouse and the canteen is a set of old change rooms that hold the memories and ghosts of the Golden Point Rice Eaters, the Australian Rules football team that represented and was named after the old Chinese gold rush community of Ballarat.

When the merger was made official in late 2001, a much-loved symbol and authentic Chinese community institution from the old days of Ballarat's Chinese community went with it.

Steven Tung was a teenager when word came through that the club he had grown up wanting to play for had been renamed the East Point Kangaroos.

After an initial adjustment, he and his teammates continued to call themselves the Rice Eaters, as did their opponents.

As a young football fanatic, Steven had been inspired to play football by his first hero, his third-generation Chinese-Australian grandfather, Kevin 'Pop' Tung, who once played for local side Ballarat Imperials: 'Him playing footy made me want to play footy.'

Steven looked forward to visiting his grandfather's place when he was young because his parents wouldn't let him play footy before he was 10 years old.

When he turned 10, his reasons for joining the club were as much geographic as genetic: 'The Rice Eaters' home ground was White Oval, which was just around the corner from Nan's place where I played kick-to-kick with Pop in the backyard.'

The timeless repetition and large blocks of time playing kick-to-kick built their relationship and gave Steven a glimpse into a reserved man: 'My pop was a very staunch fellow, quiet, bold and gruff.'

The one time he recalls his grandfather showing emotion was at his 60th birthday, when Steven presented him with a photo that featured him winning the Golden Point under-12s best and fairest award.

The Tungs were an old Ballarat footy family and Steven has fond memories of watching matches together in 'Pop's kitchen', but the one thing they disagreed on was which club to support. 'He went for Collingwood and hated that I went for Richmond,' Steven explains.

For a young Steven, seeing a family member compete on the green fields of Ballarat was inspiring. Sadly, his grandfather never got to see him play senior football, passing away when Steven was 14.

Playing for the Golden Point Rice Eaters was a source of family pride and Steven still has his old training tops, including one special shirt that has a rice-eating dragon as the club logo.

He was taught the Chinese heritage of the Golden Point Rice Eaters by his under-12s coach, Wayne Barclay, who educated the team about the history of the gold rush and the Chinese community in Golden Point and what the club represented.

Tung says he and his teammates were proud of the Rice Eaters' heritage, but for opposition teams they were a target for derision and racist taunts. 'Some other clubs were definitely punching on us a little bit for being the Rice Eaters,' he remembers.

'Some kids would do Chinese accents and think they were funny.'

From the earliest days of the Golden Point Rice Eaters, there was a Chinese presence in their player lists.

The Rice Eaters was the only sporting club of its kind in Australia that carried a Chinese nickname, in this case spanning the duration and beyond the end of the White Australia policy.

According to club historian, Michael Walsh, the club was first given the nickname 'Rice Eaters' in 1901 by members of the

Chinese community leaving Ballarat after the White Australia policy was implemented.

The 1904 Golden Point team included Willie Wun Hym, who was also the captain of the Ballarat Chinese team that would engage in challenge matches in the region.

Willie was the first Chinese-Australian to cross over from the Ballarat all-Chinese teams into a mainstream football club, and he was the uncle of Jack Wunhym who would take Willie's pioneer lead further by playing for Footscray in the VFL in the 1920s.

Other early Chinese heritage players included the Sing Brothers, and Clarence Lepp who became the first Chinese-heritage captain of the Golden Point Rice Eaters in 1922.

Joining Clarence, as he proudly ran onto Eastern Oval for the first time as captain, were three teammates of Chinese heritage including a member of Ballarat's pioneering Chung family.

Clarence Lepp was the son of the first Chinese-Australian umpire, James Henry Lepp, and he had been working as a bacon curer before answering the World War I call to arms for country and empire.

Clarence was wounded twice in France serving in the Australian Imperial Force's 24th Battalion and earned the Military Medal for gallantry and endurance in carrying messages under heavy fire at Pozières.

Clarence's grandson Mark Lepp recalls one family story his auntie shared with him – of his grandfather Clarence being very angry when he heard a story about one of his children being teased in the playground for being Chinese.

Mark says his auntie recalled Clarence yelling out in anguish: 'Why is this happening, their father didn't serve in the First World War.'

There is a number of black-and-white images of Clarence in his military uniform and his face seems frozen cold in a middle-distance gaze of detachment.

This contrasts with a team shot of the Golden Point Rice Eaters in 1922 where he is the captain, in the centre of the photo and holding the ball.

There is a sense of animation in his gaze to the camera, as though the football field was one place where he found peace.

ı | | ı

While none of the Chinese-Australian players in the Golden Point Rice Eaters is widely known in Ballarat football circles, their most passionate and loyal fan is.

William Lung, aka Billy Butterfly, was an intellectually disabled Chinese-Australian who, for more than 70 years, attended Golden Point matches at Eastern Oval dressed in a suit, tie and hat and shouted his support in mixed English and Cantonese.

Billy got his nickname from his love of flying butterfly kites with his father Ah Lung, who was the captain of the town's Chinese Fire Brigade, dedicated to fighting fires in the Chinese camp.

He lived in his own hut in White Flat, eking out a living fossicking for gold alone.

He was loved and accepted by the Golden Point football community and was proud that he had played a few games for the club in the early 1900s.

Billy's old hut on Llanberris Reserve was removed, but the City of Ballarat officially commemorated the life of William Lung with the naming of Butterfly Lane, located next to the site of his old hut.

In tribute to his tireless support, his barracking area under the scoreboard at Eastern Oval is affectionately nicknamed 'Butterfly Hill'.

In addition to supplying players and fans, the Chinese-Australian community in East Ballarat also contributed off the field.

One of the trainers for the Golden Point Rice Eaters in the 1920s was Clarence Lepp's cousin Freddy Foon, the son of a Chinese herbalist.

Freddy and Clarence's time playing at the Rice Eaters in the 1920s represented the peak of Golden Point, which at the time was alive with the energy of human exchange, a thriving suburb of more than 1000 Chinese community members serviced by three Joss Houses and two fan banks (lotteries) running daily.

The Chinese community would slowly deteriorate from that point, as Chinese migration to Ballarat would dry up due to the restrictions of the White Australia policy and the descendants of the community assimilated or went underground after the final landmark, the Main Street Joss House, was levelled in the 1960s.

While he has never really thought of himself as the last of Ballarat's old Chinatown community, 87-year-old Bill Moy says he has noted a change in attitude over time: 'We used to hide being of Chinese heritage and now everyone wants to talk about it.'

Moy is a fourth-generation Chinese-Australian and still lives in Mount Pleasant, the suburb that alongside Golden Point was the main East Ballarat Chinese hub.

The community kept a low profile, but Bill explains that he knew where he could find his hidden tribe: 'Always look in the back row, you wouldn't hear a word from them.'

Bill remembers the spiritual heart of the community was the Red Lion Hotel and its publican, William Henry Mong, who ran the pub until 1955.

Mong inherited the Red Lion from his father, William 'Chow' Mong, who had provided the half-time entertainment in the original 1892 Ballarat Miners vs. Market Gardeners match.

William Henry Mong, who was widely known as 'Monger', would take care of the Joss House temple and assist elderly members of the Chinese community who were suffering hardship.

The Red Lion Hotel still exists today and when Bill Moy drives past, it triggers fond memories of going there with his father, Harold: '"Monger" would always put a raspberry lemonade on the counter for me and that was like Christmas.'

Bill Moy played 75 games in the back pocket for the Golden Point Rice Eaters in the late 1950s, keeping the old Chinese footy tradition alive at Eastern Oval.

One of his most prized possessions is a beautiful blue bomber jacket from his playing days featuring a Golden Point Rice Eaters logo on the back. His memories of his time as a 'Rice Eater' are only fond ones: 'The league was big in those days, and I played in front of crowds of more than 10,000 people especially against the big clubs Redan and North Ballarat.'

Special venom was reserved for the local derby with East Ballarat with whom they would later merge. East Ballarat and Golden Point shared a home ground so the bragging rights often led to a 'bloodbath' when they played each other.

'You couldn't move in the stands,' Bill says.

Bill's father, Harold John Moy, a teacher who became headmaster at the local Golden Point Primary school, was also a football player who later served as Secretary of the Rice Eaters.

He found fame as a sprinter and controversially came second in the 1925 Stawell Gift professional sprint race.

Bill says: 'I can't tell you how many old timers said, "your old man won the race" but they took it off him because of his Chinese blood.'

A week later, Harold put the decision beyond the reach of officials, storming home to win the 1925 Bendigo Easter Gift.

While Bill does not recall receiving any racism on the field, off the field he had moments. 'It was out on the playground and in the streets that you copped it,' he says.

'From kids singing "Ching Chong Chinaman" or saying you've got "Ching Chong eyes" to adults muttering things in shops that you could hear.'

Bill recalls returning home from school crying after being teased for being Chinese, and his father, Harold, telling him to 'just to walk away and ignore it'.

Harold Moy kept his community links quiet but, according to Bill, would head out for clandestine Sunday night card games with other members of the Chinese community.

Bill was proud to continue the Rice Eaters' tradition of Chinese community players and he was educated by his father on club pioneers such as Clarence Lepp and Freddy Foon: 'Those early players that played for the Rice Eaters before me always interest me because the Chinese community never pushed themselves into the limelight, particularly the earlier ones because they were walking straight into animosity.'

Playing for the Rice Eaters was a key part of Bill's social identity and, through the club, he developed lifelong friendships: 'I made a lot of mates for life through footy, some real good mates but sadly they all died.'

'I'm one of the last, if not the last, of my team.'

When Bill Moy retired, the Chinese connection to the Rice Eaters was most notably maintained in the 1970s and 1980s by the Young family, led by Norm, Max, Colin, Ron and John, who collectively played 409 games for the club. Off the field, Frank Young Jr, Bill Young and John 'Jocka' Young served as coaches and trainers.

One of Bill Moy's fondest memories of the old Ballarat Chinese world is of a Chinese market gardener called 'Paul' who had a beard and an old Manchu pigtail and would famously go around the district on his horse and cart delivering vegetables.

'I'd go down and give him a penny and he'd give me a couple of carrots,' says Bill. 'It's funny but I ended up doing the same job.'

Bill has kept his links alive with the Ballarat Chinese community and in 2008 became a board member of the Chinese Australian Cultural Society of Ballarat, taking an active role in community activities and cultural preservation: 'They ripped everything down but we're still here,' Bill says.

Michael Walsh does not have Chinese heritage but he is a proud Anglo-Australian 'Rice Eater', having played 209 games for the club in the 1970s.

When Golden Point amalgamated with East Ballarat to form the East Point Kangaroos in 2001, he was initially disappointed but rallied behind the new entity, becoming the club's president in 2003.

Now in his 70s, Walsh is the club's memorabilia manager and historian. And while he supports the new East Point Kangaroos, he is a Golden Point Rice Eater to the bone.

When the club secured a big sponsorship from the Rice Growers' Co-operative in the 1980s, it was Walsh who dressed up as the rice grain mascot at the Begonia Festival Parade and at matches.

He recalls doing a range of things to keep his sponsor happy including 'Throwing rice packages into the crowd, creating the banner the players ran through that read "Point Rice Power, It's Magic" and selling Sunfarm Rice Cakes at the canteen at games.

'It was a dream partnership ... there were pallets of rice everywhere.'

Although the sponsorship was successful, in the 1990s Walsh began to encounter questions about the 'Rice Eater' name and whether it was offensive to the Chinese community in the new era of political correctness.

When the merger came, the potential controversy made it an easier decision to lose the name, Rice Eaters being replaced by 'Kangaroos'.

Walsh had strong views on whether the Rice Eaters name was offensive but was reluctant to drag the club's name through a negative process, so the decision was taken to retire the name.

'All the people we spoke to loved the Rice Eaters name and what it stood for: the magnificent old Chinese community who are the co-founders of Ballarat,' Walsh says.

'Removing the Rice Eaters removed the last institutional link to that community.'

'The only hope for the Rice-Eaters nickname appears to be in the revival of the Golden Point senior football club,' *The Age* reporter Paul Daley wrote in 2004.

But Walsh was unconvinced: 'I think those days are gone.'

The Rice Eaters' Chinese history lives on through stories of old Chinese community players and also the fans who became minor celebrities in the town, screaming their support in loud Cantonese.

Along with 'Billy Butterfly', Michael Walsh's favourite fan was diehard Jimmy Louey, the owner of the best Chinese restaurant in Ballarat, located near the Eastern Oval club rooms.

According to Walsh, Louey would attend every Rice Eaters home game and stand on 'Butterfly Hill' and 'yell obscenities in half

English and Cantonese,' before leaving early to get his restaurant ready for the after-match dinner crowd.

After their post-match beers, Walsh and his Rice Eater teammates would go to Jimmy Louey's restaurant, 'starving!'.

'I'm sure we were the only club in Australia that used to pack a saucepan in their bag – to collect dimmys and fried rice after the game,' Walsh says.

He understands that time changes things, but he'll never forget a club that brought the Anglo and Chinese communities together for 90 years.

While the name can disappear publicly, what matters now for Walsh are the personal links between old members: 'It always makes me smile when the old players at reunions greet each other as "G'day Rice Eater".'

Meanwhile Steven Tung's football career took off in high school and he left the Golden Point Rice Eaters to play for the under-16 Ballarat representative team and the North Ballarat Rebels who played in the statewide under-18 TAC Cup.

He played in the Rebels for three years, notching up 39 games against the best young players in Victoria.

Some VFL clubs showed interest but for Steven it was a tough option: 'VFL is a great comp with great history.'

'But you have to have a full-time job on the side because you don't get paid to play.'

He chose to earn money in 'bush footy', playing for a range of country clubs including Maldon, Smythesdale, and Lexton where he won a best and fairest award.

His work as a police officer took precedence over his footy career but, at 30, the lure of coming home and playing with his brothers, Jamie and Daniel, brought him back to the Eastern Oval.

Daniel Tung had made a name for himself in the Ballarat Football League, winning the 2015 East Point best and fairest player award and, together with his brothers, Steven set off on a mission to win the East Point Kangaroos their first premiership – and this they achieved in 2018, and again in 2019.

Steven feels a sense of melancholy when he is reminded that he's one of the last playing members of the old Golden Point Rice Eaters: 'At the moment with East Point there's only me, Brad Whitaker and my brother Jamie that are original Golden Point boys.'

'That's going to be sad when the last one retires – the last of the Rice Eaters.'

Maturity and fatherhood have made him increasingly proud of his Chinese heritage.

'I'm very proud of having my surname,' he says.

'My ancestor's surname was Ah Mong, he was on the run from trouble in China and survived. The name changed to Ah Leong over time and then changed again to Tung. All the generations leading to me survived and it's an honour to carry on the Tung name.'

Steven hopes his son can continue the family's football tradition: 'I'll always have the spirit of the Golden Point Rice Eaters in my blood. Having that Tung background and history, hopefully my boy Theo will continue it on after that.'

CHAPTER 15

Saint Sarah Loh

Sarah Loh knows the precise moment when she first felt Australian. It was 1977, and seven-year-old Sarah was with her Malaysian-Chinese father, Poh Chean (PC) Loh, at Moorabbin Oval, the home of St Kilda Football Club.

PC Loh was not a football fan. Like many Asian parents, he was hesitant to venture into alcohol-fuelled environments in case his family became a target for abuse.

But after his daughter discovered a free club membership in her Kellogg's breakfast cereal box, she begged and badgered him to take her to a game until finally he relented.

At first, PC's fears were realised, with fans of both sides saying nasty things to him and his daughter as they stood on the hill at Moorabbin.

'We got all sorts of rude comments – "go back to where you come from", "what are you doing here",' Sarah recalled. Still, she focused on the footy, determined not to leave early despite the discomfort.

Unwittingly, she was complying with the timeless Australian football adage that 'real fans stay till the end' and her persistence soon wore the taunters down.

As the siren sounded for full time, and the St Kilda players celebrated their win over the South Melbourne Swans, a group of St Kilda fans picked Loh up, threw her in the air and caught her, completing a bittersweet and highly unusual rite of passage.

'They put us through some crap, but they saw how serious I was and I won them over,' Loh recalled. 'From that moment I became a fanatical St Kilda supporter – lived it and breathed it. That was my Australian moment!'

Three decades later, in 2016, Loh was appointed chief executive officer of the South Metro Junior Football League (SMJFL), one of the biggest grassroots leagues in the country, which boasts more than 10,000 players.

In doing so, Loh became the first woman and Asian-Australian to rise to such an esteemed executive position in running a community football league in the country.

On her first day as CEO, she was called in to the boardroom to meet the chairman, Peter Ryan, who told her the board had already fielded a 'stack of complaints' about her appointment.

'It's because you're female and because you're Asian,' Loh recalled Ryan telling her, before promising her that she was the best person for the job and that he would have her back.

'It's important,' he continued, 'that you are ready for anything that comes your way.'

Ryan could not have known the deep reservoir of strength possessed by his new CEO. Loh's 30-year journey from being racially abused by St Kilda fans to sitting in the CEO's chair at the SMJFL's headquarters in Moorabbin is a story of patience, resilience and an undying love of footy.

ı | | ı

Sarah Loh was born in Malaysia and arrived in Australia with her parents in 1977. She was the youngest of three children in a Malaysian-Chinese family that settled in Noble Park, 25 kilometres south-east of Melbourne's CBD.

Loh's mother, Doris, was a student nurse and an athlete who had studied in Melbourne's Austin Hospital in 1959, during which time she'd watched many footy games at the Melbourne Cricket Ground.

Doris had chosen to live in Melbourne because of the city's famed sporting culture, and she knew that sport would be her children's gateway to acceptance.

'Growing up, a typical Asian kid had to play the piano and become a doctor,' Loh recalled. 'But Mum said, "you've got to make friends in this country; you're Australians now – so just go play sport." I loved it.'

During summer, Loh imitated Australian fast bowler Dennis Lillee in frontyard cricket. In winter, she emulated St Kilda's high-marking hero Trevor Barker in games of kick-to-kick at Silverton Primary School.

But when she asked her teacher if she could join the school footy team, he just laughed.

'Sarah, you're a girl,' Loh recalled him saying. 'Over my dead body will a girl ever play football for me or in this country.'

That was the first challenge for Loh to overcome. In 1983, aged 13, Loh was a driving force behind the creation of the first Victorian high school girls' round-robin tournament – a competition that still exists today.

Although it wasn't a full season, the round robin allowed schoolgirls – at least for one day of the year – to cross the white line, contest the footy, make tackles, take 'speccy' high marks and kick goals.

'It was all driven by my Carwatha High School,' Loh recalled. 'We advocated the hardest and I was the persistent one, pushing our teachers – especially Ms Farrell, the best PE teacher in the world.'

Loh was a regular Australian teenager. Her mother packed her 'dreaded' white-bread sandwiches for lunch and she spent hours learning the subtle art of kicking the oval-shaped Sherrin football.

'I've always been obsessed with the Sherrin,' she says.

Like many women of her generation, Loh stopped playing when she left high school and in her case she directed her footy passion into supporting St Kilda.

During her twenties, the Victorian Football League expanded into a national competition, and the Saints moved away from their spiritual home at Moorabbin to the much larger VFL Park in the city's south-east.

'As a long-term Saints member, I support them financially and in return they deliver a sense of normality and belonging,' Sarah says.

Supporting St Kilda gave her a joint mission of pleasure and pain with hundreds of thousands of fellow Australians. 'I have developed a very simple formula to succeed in Victoria. It's the "Three F" philosophy: Fishing, Food and Footy,' she explained.

'If you want to get good jobs you need to be able to talk the local language, which is footy. It automatically makes you belong to some secret society. Footy opens conversations which opens doors. If you've set down roots in Victoria and you want to belong, footy is the way.'

During the 1990s, there were few avenues for women to play footy but Sarah joined the nascent St Kilda Sharks in the Victorian Women's Football League. Although they were an amateur outfit, the Sharks shared a suburb and the red, white and black colours of her beloved Saints.

When she ran onto St Kilda's Peanut Farm Reserve with her Sharks teammates, she was reintroduced to the rough and tumble of the game. 'I nearly killed myself, broke my ribs and nearly lost my eye, but I loved every second and even getting bumped felt good,' she said.

After one premiership-winning season, albeit sidelined by injury and unable to play in the grand final, she gave the game away for a second time, tired of being negatively stereotyped as being 'butch' and having to explain her black eyes to workmates.

'All sorts of girls played football, yet we were all embarrassed to tell people because there was a "tomboy" stigma,' she said.

'Now people have accepted that all types of women can be footy fanatics but back then you kept it quiet. If I wasn't being constantly embarrassed about it in other parts of my life, I most likely would have kept playing.'

Nearing 30, she turned her attention to her biggest challenge: finding a job in the footy industry.

Between 1988 and 2016, Sarah Loh applied for 10 significant manager-level jobs and other smaller roles in football. For 28 years, she received one rejection after another, and did not even get a single interview. She would get discouraged for a few years and then try again to no avail.

'No one thought my experience was worthwhile,' Loh recalled.

'That's a long time to be rejected after putting in my résumé to the AFL, VFL and even local clubs. I couldn't break into anything and the best I ever got was to become a trainer at a local club. At one stage I would have taken any job in football!'

But Loh knew her worth and never gave up, accumulating a wealth of experience outside Australian Rules football – including a number of jobs in other sports.

In 2016, she saw a job ad for CEO of the South Metro Junior Football League (SMJFL).

She called the recruiter immediately and, after 10 minutes on the phone, her knowledge, enthusiasm and authenticity landed her an interview. She was the standout candidate in a highly sought-after role, which received more than 1000 applications.

During her six-year term, Loh turned around the SMJFL, improving junior participation, boosting the umpire academy, doubling the number of staff and increasing revenue to the point where the SMJFL had the biggest corporate turnover of any community league in the country.

Her facilities strategy reaped rich dividends for the six local councils in her catchment, which shared over $30 million in investment into local grounds from a mix of AFL and state government funding sources.

'No one made me feel welcome. It was easy to tell that they thought I had no idea what I was doing and they needed someone from footy,' Loh said.

'At first all the other League CEOs didn't take me seriously, I had to do a lot to prove my worth.'

During the COVID-19 pandemic, the SMJFL was the only league in the nation to make a profit. Remarkably, the league did not lose a single sponsor as its corporate partners all continued their support through lockdown.

During the cancelled season of 2020, while other leagues suffered massive hits to registered participants, Loh drove SMJFL to start a COVID-19-adapted 'Football for Fun' program, the only league to return at the end of 2020.

Of the 500 teams within the SMJFL, 250 chose to return for the four-week season under strict COVID-19 protocols, which included no tackling and wiping down balls and equipment between games.

'We kept the business alive when others closed,' she said. 'And we only had a 3.5 per cent drop in participation for the following season.'

Perhaps Loh's greatest legacy, though, was to take a stand against harmful industries, refusing access to the SMJFL members from any entity involving alcohol, gambling, tobacco and junk food messaging.

Loh's vigilance against harmful industries soon attracted the attention of VicHealth, the largest government-funded health promotion agency in the country. In 2022 it made her an attractive offer to replicate her achievements in the SMJFL across the state, with a $45 million budget over three years.

'It was everything I'd ever desired on a platter, working with 78 councils and in the sport and health industry,' Loh said. 'It was as big as you're going to get.'

Loh was 'shattered' to leave the League and broke down in tears when she handed in her resignation to the board. As she walked out after a 'festival of goodbyes', she left the SMJFL in a much better place than she found it – the most important metric for leadership succession.

Although footy is no longer Loh's full-time job, she has returned to the game as a participant, turning out for Waverley Warriors in the over-35's AFL Masters competition.

Her form and enthusiasm elevated her to player–coach of the Warriors, coach for the Victorian Masters team at the 2017 national carnival, and she is now a board director for the AFL National Masters Board.

Forty-six years on from attending her first St Kilda game at Moorabbin Oval, Loh continues to support the Saints and is now a proud multicultural ambassador for the AFL.

'I can't hide from my culture, and I'm no longer embarrassed about who I am,' she said.

'I didn't fit the mould, but I changed a lot of minds. I look back on the struggles as a badge of honour.'

And she has one piece of advice for those wanting to follow in her footsteps: 'Always stay to the end of the game.'

CHAPTER 16

'The Time Has Come': Lin Jong and the New Generation

Lin Jong had only played football for three years when he was picked at No. 9 in the 2012 AFL Rookie Draft by the Western Bulldogs.

The 18-year-old midfielder, who spent most of his childhood playing basketball, had registered outstanding results and alerted clubs to his talents after completing the AFL-partnered Draftstar program, a talent identification pathway run by ex-players, Ben Dixon and Robbie Campbell.

As the news of his AFL recruitment was still sinking in, he was soon on the phone fielding questions from reporters about his East Timorese-Chinese and Taiwanese heritage.

'Hopefully it might inspire some kids to start playing footy,' Jong responded. 'But I'll just try to do my best and whatever happens, happens, really.'

Others in the AFL industry were more excited.

Jiaming 'Jamie' Pi, the host of a footy segment on 3CW Chinese Radio, wrote an opinion piece for afl.com.au about Lin's potential to shift perceptions of Asian-Australians and sport.

'The time has come,' Pi wrote. 'Asian migrants have now settled in this land. Their offspring are now growing up and making decisions for their next generation. Now is the time to engage the Asian community through pioneers like Jong.'

Seven months later, after Lin made a solid debut for the Bulldogs at the Melbourne Cricket Ground, *Sydney Morning Herald* sports reporter Andrew Wu wrote that the AFL had 'kicked a vital goal in its quest to spread the code beyond its traditional fan base'.

Wu interviewed AFL national multicultural manager Ali Fahour, who noted that for first-generation Chinese migrants to Australia, 'education was the most important thing, sport was not a priority'.

Lin Jong was one of those kids torn between sport and study. His mother, a college-educated accountant from Taiwan, wanted him to be a doctor. 'I suppose growing up in an Asian-Australian family, sport is not a big thing,' Lin later told *Liminal* magazine.

'My dad was really supportive of me playing sports, whereas Mum thought it was a bit of a waste of time and wanted me to focus on studying.'

Lin's father, Vitor, left East Timor in 1975, only a month before the Indonesian Army invaded the country and sparked a long war of independence. With his Portuguese passport, 18-year-old Vitor went to Macau first, then to Japan, before meeting his future wife, Faye, in Taiwan.

Although they had come from very different backgrounds, they were both of Chinese heritage and both spoke Mandarin courtesy of Vitor's language lessons as a boy in East Timor. They moved to Melbourne in 1985 and had six children. Lin, the youngest, was the only boy.

Their journey started in a small house in Footscray public housing, followed by another move to the Richmond public housing estate before settling into their final destination, Clayton South, 20 kilometres south-east of the Melbourne CBD.

Basketball was Lin's first passion, and he only took up football for the social aspect. 'Growing up, footy just wasn't on my mind but my mates kept hassling me to have a go, so at 15 I joined my local club, the Glen Waverley Rovers, for a bit of fun,' he says.

After being selected in his Brentwood Secondary College team, he began to enjoy the game.

But even when he caught the 'footy bug', he did not have the traditional family structures to support his skill acquisition through kick-to-kick or drills in the backyard with family members.

'I would go out with my sisters in the backyard,' Lin remembers. 'I would kick it to them, and they'd just drop the mark and throw it back to me. At least they tried!'

When Lin was drafted by the Oakleigh Chargers under-18 TAC team for the 2010 season, he gave up basketball to chase his footy dream. Although he was a star of that Oakleigh side, he was apprehensive about sharing his success with friends and family.

'I had a barrier in my head – and I imagine a lot of other kids had it – that Asian kids don't play footy and even if they do, they certainly don't play in the AFL,' Lin recalls thinking.

'There was some hesitation, because I just didn't have that role model and didn't want to be the only Asian player out there.'

When he told his parents that he wanted to pursue a career in the AFL, he received a mixed reaction. Vitor, who was a serious sports fan and had happily taken on driving duties for Lin's football and basketball games, was easy to convince, but his mother, Faye, was doubtful.

'I cried and said *why?*' recalls Faye. 'The game is so tough and it's so easy to get injured. I thought he should study and become a doctor, not a sportsman. In our culture, kids go to school and university into a good job – I was never thinking about sport.'

As Lin moved through the pathways towards the AFL, he left his junior teams and close friends behind and became increasingly lonely among 'a lot of private school people', often wondering if he was being judged on his background rather than his ability.

The feeling of being an outsider was amplified when he was on the receiving end of vicious racism from opponents.

He recalls a traumatic moment in one junior under-16s game against Lilydale: 'I was being continually insulted by one player, saying the most racist stuff and telling me to go back to China.'

'The umpires heard it, and everybody heard it, and the most disappointing thing was my teammates not doing anything and sort of laughing about it, too. Nothing was done about it afterwards. That was a sad moment in my junior career, and it still hurts to this day thinking about it.'

The self-doubt continued through Lin's first season with the Western Bulldogs in 2012.

During his early period of uncertainty, it was Bulldogs legend and club development coach Rohan Smith who stepped in to help.

'He was really good and positive and spent time with me,' Lin says. 'He told me to keep backing myself and looking back it was so important to have someone like him in my corner.'

Lin persisted and was rewarded for his consistency in the Bulldogs VFL team with selection in the senior team to make his debut against Richmond.

On Sunday 12 August, 2012 he took the field to the delight of 30 of his closest friends who had made the trek to the MCG to support their friend, who had miraculously graduated to playing top-flight AFL football only four years after first taking up the game.

His selection caught his parents by surprise. They were on holiday in New Zealand, having made the trip assuming he was playing in the lower-tier VFL.

'We were in the hotel room getting ready to watch the game on Foxtel,' recalls Vitor. 'And then we hear the commentators announce our son's debut.'

For Rohan Smith, coaching Lin in the early stages of his career was a pleasure. 'He would leave no stone unturned and do everything I asked him to do,' Smith recalls.

'He was appreciative of my time and had courage, speed, talent – he was as determined to be the best player he can be. That's all you can ask for as a coach.'

Smith took a particular interest in Lin's early games, and one in particular stands out. 'In his third game, against Geelong, here's this kid backing into a pack and taking contested marks where nobody else would go.'

Lin played in the final four games of the season, each a heavy loss with the Bulldogs floundering to fourth-last by the end of the season. The Bulldogs website mentioned his 'courage in the contest' in their season summary.

'They were some of my best AFL games,' Lin recalls. 'But it felt like a sink or swim moment.'

Before he could play a single game in the 2013 AFL season, Lin broke his leg – the first of many injuries that would plague his career and this one ruled out his entire season. Then, at the end of the season, he received the coldest of reality checks.

'Our coach told me: "You're lucky to be here. Half of us want you gone, half of us want you to stay",' Lin recalls.

'That shifted me in the right direction to realise how hard it is to play at the elite level. And some of the sacrifices you have to make.'

Once his leg recovered, Lin returned to training with renewed zeal.

The Western Bulldogs went international for their 2014 pre-season, organising the team's training camp at high altitude in the US state of Colorado. The rarefied mountain air and focus did Lin wonders, and he returned to Australia as fit as he'd ever been.

Despite only making six senior appearances for the Bulldogs in 2014, Lin helped the club's VFL side to a premiership victory and played with renewed freedom under head coach, Chris Maple.

'I used to have a tagging role, an important but negating role trying to stop other people from doing their best. I never really wanted to be a tagger but you play whatever role you can in a team,' Lin says.

'Towards the end of the season, Chris said, "alright, we're just gonna let you play your footy and do you own thing".'

The results, Lin says, were immediate: 'In the final five games of the season I really flourished and that form carried into winning the VFL premiership. That decision from Chris launched my belief and self-confidence. I wasn't just focused on this one person I was tagging, and I started to have fun as well.'

In 2015, Lin became a fully fledged AFL player after making 13 appearances for the Bulldogs. In early May, veteran footy writer Rohan Connolly described a defining moment in *The Age* that marked Lin's arrival as a senior player.

In an article headlined 'Lin Jong a Western Bulldog who belongs', Connolly wrote:

In round two, the Western Bulldogs were getting on top of Richmond late in the last quarter, one more goal certain to close the deal, when Jong, running with the flight of the ball, took a terrific strong mark over the Tigers' Dylan Grimes 25 metres out. Well, not officially. Umpire Shane McInerney, unsighted, called for a ball-up, much to the disgust of the Bulldog faithful. And to the displeasure of Jong, who in his 12th game, proceeded to tell the AFL's most experienced umpire, with more than 400 games to his name, exactly what he thought.

Beyond Lin's 'spray' at the umpire, Connolly praised the busy midfielder who 'ranked third for the Dogs in tackles and inside 50s, fourth for contested ball and fifth for clearances, and managed a couple of goals in last week's big win over Adelaide'.

However, after the Round 2 game, Lin learned that he'd been racially abused by an opposition fan. 'I didn't hear it but other people heard it and called it out,' he recalls.

'I still don't know what he said to this day, and I don't want to know. I accepted [the fan's] apology and moved on.'

In 2016, Lin was in the final year of his Bulldogs contract, and his good form attracted interest from Collingwood.

At the invitation of Collingwood coach, Nathan Buckley, Lin agreed to tour the club's facilities. When a photo emerged of Lin in rival territory, it sent Bulldogs fans into a fury.

'It was my biggest mistake and they let me know about it,' Lin says, adding that his coach, Luke Beveridge, 'tore me a new one'.

The captain of the Western Bulldogs, Robert 'Bob' Murphy, was more sympathetic. Lin says Murphy told him to get on the front foot and 'make light' of the saga.

Bob mocked up a photo of Lin in a Collingwood jumper, much to the delight of his Bulldogs teammates who felt Lin had showed sufficient contrition. As Murphy later explained to SEN Radio: 'it was done because we loved him.'

That year, Lin established himself as an elite footballer, playing 16 senior games, kicking 13 goals and racking up 268 disposals before breaking his collarbone in an elimination final against West Coast Eagles in Perth.

'I didn't know if it was my last game for the Bulldogs,' Lin recalls. 'I was coming off contract and thought I was out for the finals, which cut me deep. It was just so disappointing and overwhelming.'

It was a heartbreaking moment watched by fans across the nation as the cameras zoomed in on the Bulldogs bench and captured a powerful scene of Lin Jong with his arm in a sling being consoled by club doctor, Gary Zimmerman.

As Lin wept in the change rooms in the arms of close friend, flatmate and teammate, Fletcher Roberts, his team went on to defeat West Coast by 47 points and secure a spot in the semi-finals.

'He was shattered and very emotional so I tried to calm him, and then had to help him get out of his clothes,' Roberts would say later.

However, as his team celebrated their victory, Lin was on the midnight 'red-eye' flight out of Perth to Melbourne and after scans confirmed the break, he was straight into surgery at 4 pm less than 24 hours after the injury.

In an astonishing recovery, Lin made it back in time for the VFL grand final, held the week before the Bulldogs were to play the Sydney Swans in the AFL grand final.

As a current AFL player dropping down to play in the VFL, Lin knew his injured collarbone would be targeted by his Casey Scorpions opponents at grand final intensity, later telling AFL Media: 'I knew what was coming.'

To counter this potential onslaught, the Bulldogs coaching staff decided to strap the opposite collarbone to his broken one with layers of tape. The trick worked, Casey targeted the wrong shoulder and Lin played like a colossus, helping the Bulldogs to a 31-point victory.

Lin picked up 29 disposals – an equal team-high – and was awarded the Norm Goss Medal for best on ground, a hard-earned reward playing with a cracked collarbone.

Despite his VFL heroics, the Bulldogs chose not to pick Lin for the AFL grand final a week later, instead selecting Fletcher Roberts, his close friend and housemate.

'There were rumours floating around that Jongy had recovered so well that I might not hold my spot,' Roberts says. 'It was an awkward time in the house, but it fell my way.'

After the Bulldogs won the AFL grand final against the Sydney Swans to clinch the club's first premiership in 62 years, Fletcher made a point of spending some quiet time in the rooms with Lin and another close friend, Jack Macrae.

'We let Lin know that we were playing for him, and that he played a massive part in the season that led to the win,' Roberts recalls.

As the Bulldogs club song 'Sons of the West' echoed around the MCG changerooms, Lin sang along in suit and tie, wondering what might have been. He knew he was a spiritual part of the victory but, officially, he was an outsider to the grand final legacy.

'It was tougher to swallow because 2016 was my best year at the club,' Lin explains.

The setbacks continued in 2017 and 2018 as Lin injured his hamstring, his anterior cruciate ligament (ACL) and his collarbone.

The darkness closed in and, in 2019, he took a break from football.

'I now feel it's the right time to make my mental health a priority, and I also think it's important to be upfront and honest, as there's nothing to be ashamed or embarrassed about,' he posted on Instagram.

Lin, who was diagnosed with depression, continued to train with the team but was withdrawn from selection. It was the first time he had given himself time to reflect and process the setbacks and barriers he had faced in his journey to playing AFL. 'Looking back, it ate me up inside,' he said in an interview with Beyond Blue, one of Australia's leading mental health support organisations.

'There were times when I was in high school when I vividly remember coming home from footy and I'd sit in the car for an hour, just miserable. Then I'd front up to my family and make sure everything seemed okay to them.'

At least part of the reason for his withdrawal, Lin says, was due to abuse – some of it race related.

'I'm just trying to fight my own battle. And if others follow suit, then so be it. I'm not standing up against racism to impress anyone – it's because I think it's the right thing to do. If that's something that encourages others to do the same, it's a bonus.'

In the end, Lin returned to play four more games during the COVID-19-affected seasons of 2020 and 2021, before retiring at the age of 28 after a final hamstring injury. When news broke of his retirement, passionate fan tributes poured in – a mix of awe, sympathy, gratitude and regret.

After Lin's announcement, former Western Bulldogs captain Bob Murphy was asked on SEN Radio whether he thought Lin would have been a 150-plus game player if not for the injury setbacks.

'Yeah I think so,' Murphy responded. 'He was tough. Proper tough.'

Lin was awarded life membership of the Western Bulldogs for 10 years at the club and will always be remembered by Bulldogs fans for his fearless approach and his brave best-on-ground performance in the 2016 VFL grand final. But it was a headline on afl.com.au that best summed up his career: 'Injury-plagued Dog calls it quits after 65 games in 10 years'.

'I've had nine surgeries,' Lin says. 'I've also played with a broken hand, (had a) wrist reconstruction, knee reconstruction, groin reconstruction, two broken legs, two broken collarbones, ACL injuries, ankle surgery, three significant grade-three hamstring injuries, a fractured jaw and had my appendix removed mid-season.'

In retirement, Lin became an ambassador for Movember, the AFL Multicultural Program and began work with Beyond Blue.

Depression, he says, is 'now a part of my identity. I'm male, I'm a footballer, I'm Asian, I am right footed, I have depression. None are more unusual than the other for me now.'

After a decade of covering up, Lin has finally become comfortable in his role as a pioneer for Asian communities in the AFL. 'All I was doing was playing footy, but I have now embraced the fact that my background was unique and a big deal,' he says.

'When I first played as a junior, I didn't want to stand out, I wanted to be like everyone else. I really didn't know what being a trailblazer really meant, but now I embrace it and realise that it's good to be different.'

Two years into his retirement from life as a professional footballer, he can now see why he was positioned as a symbolic figure in engaging new audiences for the AFL.

'There is a big Asian population in Australia and if I can inspire some kid out there who is like me and hesitant to join the sport because he doesn't have a player they see themselves in – in name or look – well, I'm that player! I understand them. I always felt uncomfortable growing up playing footy and if I can help a kid feel comfortable and even proud, then that's good enough for me,' Lin explains.

Lin is proud that his mother, Faye, eventually became a footy fan. In 2016, during the Bulldogs premiership run, a video of her celebrating a victory went viral after being leaked from the family WhatsApp chat.

'To see how passionate she was watching a game of AFL footy – when she never knew anything about it and didn't want me to play – was nice,' Lin says.

'Everything I have achieved during my career and after my career is from my values, which come straight from my family. As clichéd as it sounds, my family means everything to me, and I have a much bigger appreciation of the sacrifices my parents made for me.'

CHAPTER 17

Bailey Banfield –
the Pearl of the Northwest

In Bailey Banfield's first season as a professional footballer, his parents, Rob and Debbie, travelled thousands of kilometres around the country to watch him play.

They were there to witness his AFL debut in Adelaide, and his first goal in Canberra. They were among the 49,021 fans at Perth's newly opened Optus Stadium for his first win as a Fremantle Dockers player, and joined him for post-match chats at footy grounds in Melbourne, Sydney and Brisbane.

'They come down into the rooms and I have a chat with them after every game which has become part of the routine,' Banfield told the Fremantle club website in 2018.

Bailey Banfield is a 190-centimetre, hard-running, versatile all-rounder, at home in the midfield or as a forward.

By the end of the 2022 season, he had kicked 31 goals for Fremantle across his 61 games. In defence, he won a reputation as a hard tagger, excelling at keeping key opposition players from dominating the game.

For as long as anyone in the family can remember, Bailey wanted to be a footy player. His father, Robert, a successful West Kimberley footballer for the Broome Bulls, was his first junior coach. As a child, he would spend hours kicking a soft footy with his Chinese grandmother, Shirley.

'When Bailey was five, someone gave him a life-sized red Sherrin football easter egg, which had all the teams on the back. After that he learnt every team and the ladder. In any round, I could ask him, "What's the ladder this week, baby?" and he could tell me,' his mother, Debbie, recalled.

'He told us he wanted to be an AFL football player. I was a stay-at-home mum for Bailey and he was always practising. We had a park close and a long driveway so I would be out there, trying to wear him out.'

‖‖‖

The Banfield family home is in Broome, a town on Western Australia's Kimberley coast, where the family had owned a sheep farm and a bus service before settling into the pearling trade.

To get to Broome, most visitors travel by plane from Perth, passing over dry salt lakes, red earth, spinifex and the brilliant white sands of Indian Ocean beaches.

One of the westernmost towns of Australia's 'Top End', Broome is also the country's original multicultural jewel. It was, for many years after the turn of the 20th century, a majority Asian city.

After Western Australian senator Staniforth Smith visited Broome's 'Asiatic Quarter' in 1902, his observations were published in the *Kalgoorlie Miner* in January 1903:

One might be excused for thinking that a small portion of Asia had been detached and grafted onto the side of Australia.

Here was gathered together from all quarters of the earth, the most heterogenous collection of nations, creeds, languages and races I never saw, a veritable ethnological museum.

Asian migration to Broome was catalysed by the pearl trade, which was the reason for the town's founding and existence; it once supplied 80 per cent of the world's mother-of-pearl shell.

The fan-shaped *Pinctada maxima* is the largest species of oyster in the world, growing up to 5 kilograms in weight and 30 centimetres in length.

The largest of them lie off the coast of Broome and an industry formed around their collection by mostly Asian diving communities whose very presence defied the White Australia policy.

When the pearl lugger ships returned to Broome filled with mother-of-pearl shell after months at sea, the town would celebrate wildly and it was a harvest time for the town's pubs, restaurants and hotels including those in the Chinatown precinct.

The incredible mix of races created a cultural melting pot that today would have been marketed as a 'foodies' paradise'.

When the pearl-shell industry was made largely redundant due to the global adoption of plastic buttons, a lot of the Asian community stayed in Broome and their descendants celebrate this history and diversity every year through the pan-Asian Shinju Matsuri festival, which translates to 'Festival of the Pearl' in Japanese.

Today, the Banfields are the inheritors of this pearling tradition, running the successful Willie Creek Pearl Farm and the Pearl Luggers museum in the heart of Broome's Chinatown. They are proud to 'tell the story' of pearling in Broome, even if their life

The Last of Ballarat's Golden Point Rice Eaters Football Club. From left to right: Jamie Tung, Ron Young, Bill Moy, Steven Tung. Michael Walsh is seated. (Courtesy Michael Walsh)

Lin Jong of the Western Bulldogs hand-passes the ball during the 2020 AFL Round 5 match between the Western Bulldogs and the North Melbourne Kangaroos at Melbourne's Marvel Stadium on 4 July 2020. (Photo by Michael Willson/AFL Photos)

Sarah Loh, captain of the Waverley Warriors AFL Masters team celebrating her team's first ever win on 11 September 2018. Sarah was the first Asian-Australian to manage a major grassroots Australian Rules football league.
(Photo by Robert Keeley)

Bailey Banfield of the Fremantle Dockers kicks the ball during the Round 23 AFL match between the Fremantle Dockers and St Kilda Saints at Blundstone Arena in Hobart on 22 August 2021.
(Photo by Steve Bell/AFL Photos)

Keifer Yu is chaired off the ground by his Claremont Football Club teammates after reaching the 100 game milestone at Claremont Oval vs. Peel Thunder on 18 August 2018.
(Claremont Football Club)

Sophie Li of the Adelaide Crows leaps for a spectacular mark attempt against Carlton's Tayla Harris during their Round 4 AFLW match at Richmond Oval in Adelaide on 1 March 2020. Carlton's Darcy Vescio is watching on.
(Photo by Mark Brake/ Getty Images via AFL Photos)

Rebecca Beeson of the GWS Giants handballs during the Round 7 AFLW match between the Greater Western Sydney Giants and the Western Bulldogs at UNSW Canberra Oval on 18 March 2017.
(Photo by Mark Nolan/ Getty Images)

Ryan Lim has been a standout player for the Claremont Football Club and was awarded life membership of the club for reaching the 150 game milestone in 2022.
(Claremont Football Club)

Jiaming 'Jamie' Pi with St Kilda player Shane Savage prior to the Port Adelaide vs. St Kilda game at Jiangwan Stadium on 6 June 2019.

(Supplied by Jamie Pi)

Joanna Lin of the Magpies celebrates a goal during the Round 6 AFLW match between the Collingwood Magpies and the St Kilda Saints at RSEA Park on 1 October 2022 in Melbourne.

(Photo by Morgan Hancock/Getty Images via AFL Photos)

The Ah Chee Brothers, Callum (left) and Brendon (right), captured before their first game against each other in 2020, have both played for two different clubs at AFL level and hail from an Aboriginal-Chinese family in Broome.
(Brisbane Lions Football Club)

Hawthorn's Connor Downie and the Western Bulldogs' Marcus Bontempelli contest the ball during an AFL practice match at Footscray's Whitten Oval on 24 February 2021.
(Photo by Daniel Pockett/ AFL Photos)

Carlton's Darcy Vescio kicks the ball during the 2022 AFLW Round 7 match between the Carlton Blues and the St Kilda Saints at Carlton's home ground, Princes Park, on 19 February 2022.
(Photo by Dylan Burns/ AFL Photos)

Sam Pang played in the Collingwood Under 19s team and for three years in the VFA for Prahran and Preston before becoming a broadcasting pioneer, co-hosting the award winning *The Front Bar* Channel 7 football program with Mick Molloy and Andy Maher.
(Photo courtesy The Front Bar)

Broadcast pioneer Nat Edwards performing MC duties during the 2022 AFL First Semi-Final match between the Collingwood Magpies and the Fremantle Dockers at the Melbourne Cricket Ground on 10 September 2022.
(Photo by Michael Willson/AFL Photos)

Roy Poy was a rover for the Albury Football Club in the 1950s, part of the Poy family football tradition in the Riverina district.
(Poy Family Collection)

is very different from the perilous conditions endured by the early divers.

'I remember taking trips out to the Pearl Farm when I was younger,' Bailey wrote on the company website:

Just getting out there was an adventure – it was always exciting taking the 'bumpy road' out and a couple of times when the tide was up, driving on the tidal flats was awesome!

Being one of three siblings, and pretty close in age, we used to fight a lot, particularly my brother and I.

At the farm though, Dad always had a ready-made threat to get us to behave … the resident croc, Nigel. We'd go out on the boat, definitely looking for the croc but not sure if we wanted to find it or not, and not sure if Dad would actually follow through on the threat and throw us in.

The other thing I loved about the farm was the tides. I couldn't believe how the whole jetty and a couple of flights of stairs could just disappear and reappear in a matter of hours.

Bailey's forebears may not have been pearl divers but his Chinese-Australian story also begins in the Top End. His matrilineal great-grandfather, Clem Fong, migrated from Canton to Broome in the early 1930s, where he married a local woman, Daisy, herself a child of Chinese parents.

Bailey's grandmother Shirley was born in Broome in 1937, but his mother, Debbie, grew up in Perth, where the family entered the restaurant trade.

The first business – Chan's Oriental Restaurant in Wembley – was a family affair.

'Dad worked seven days a week and when Mum finished school teaching, she worked there as well,' Debbie recalled.

'We would do our homework at the restaurant, and then just hang around until it was time for Mum to take us home to bed.'

Later, Debbie would also work at the restaurant for $10 a night and a free feed. Yet despite her Chinese parents and their 'Oriental' restaurant, Debbie was mostly disconnected from her Chinese heritage.

'When I was about eight or nine, Dad decided he wanted my brother and I to learn Chinese and go to the Chung Wah Chinese Association,' Debbie recalled. 'We didn't want to go and that was that: I never learnt Chinese.'

That break in the Chinese family cultural line meant that Debbie's children grew up looking – but not necessarily feeling – Chinese. Bailey still listened respectfully to stories told by his Chinese grandparents but his upbringing was not so different from that of his non-Chinese mates.

His childhood in Broome was free and easy, which influenced his approach to football. 'The grounds are big and hard,' he said, 'so Broome footy is less focused on defence and more on playing at a high pace with great skills.'

At age 13, after completing Year 7 in Broome, Bailey moved to Perth to attend Scotch College, one of the state's most prestigious boarding schools.

'I loved boarding school – 30-odd blokes on a massive new adventure and, of course, lots of sport,' Bailey remembered.

After a brief spell playing rugby union, he switched back to footy to chase his AFL dream. On weekends he played for the Claremont Colts, and in his senior school years he was selected for the Western Australian schoolboys side.

After the disappointment of being overlooked in the 2016 AFL Draft, Banfield was selected to play for Claremont's senior WAFL side, joining fellow Chinese-heritage players Keifer Yu and Ryan Lim at the Tigers. It was a pivotal year.

When Bailey arrived to play League football at Claremont in that 2017 season, he felt 'very much the young fella coming into the team and the first time playing with grown men'.

A familiar face was there to greet him – fellow Broome player Keifer Yu.

'When you've got that Broome connection, there's always something to talk about and we had a few chats,' Bailey explains.

'He's the nicest bloke but on the footy field he's as tough as nails – I used to admire his big, big boot when he would launch them 60-odd metres!'

Another Chinese heritage player, Ryan Lim, also took Bailey under his wing: 'He looked out for me as well and acted as a bridge between the young boys and the senior players.'

Was their shared Chinese heritage ever mentioned between Ryan Lim, Keifer Yu and Bailey?

'It's all unsaid, but Keifer and Limmy definitely looked out for me,' Bailey says.

Bailey had a strong year in 2017, averaging 24.8 disposals per game, and the teenager ended up winning the E.B Cook Medal for Claremont's best and fairest player.

Claremont coach Darren Harris spoke glowingly of Bailey at the annual presentation night and noted the reaction to his medal win. '(It was) one of the most popular outcomes I have witnessed, to be honest.

'His season performances were consistently high. He was team first in all he did and set an example to our whole club well beyond his years in how to prepare effectively. The way he presented himself and spoke also set a great example and showed his level of maturity. He is a ripper!'

But it was one particular game, against South Fremantle in Round 16, which proved to Bailey that he could make it against much more experienced men.

'We were on their home ground and I was tagging Tim Kelly, a gun player who got drafted that year, and their boys got stuck into me pretty heavily,' he recalled.

'I was feeling a bit isolated – all these men were coming at me, getting in my grill physically and verbally trying to get into my head.'

By standing up to them and holding his nerve, Bailey unknowingly impressed the Fremantle Dockers scouts who were watching on.

'The key people at Fremantle have said to me since: "that was the game where we saw you go up against AFL level opposition and you went pretty well",' Bailey said.

'It's funny: the game I came out of feeling pretty crap ended up being the one that got me drafted. In hindsight, it was a really great lesson of the good that can come out of bad.'

After being called up to Fremantle Dockers via the rookie draft, Bailey 'trained the house down' in the 2018 pre-season and was selected to make his AFL debut for Round 1.

At his jersey presentation, Dockers captain, Nat Fyfe, spoke of Bailey's non-traditional journey and persistence in getting to the big time.

'Bailey has come in, in a slightly different way,' Fyfe said. 'But he had no respect, really, for natural progression and waiting his turn to be picked. He's just come in and made a big impact.'

The different way that Fyfe referred to was Bailey's setbacks until that point – not being picked up in the 2016 AFL Draft and almost missing out in the 2017 AFL Draft.

'I missed out on the first AFL Draft then the Rookie Draft, missed out on the second AFL Draft and then got picked up in the Rookie Draft,' Bailey explains.

'There were 209 players picked ahead of me in those four drafts.

'I just squeaked in, so I had all the fuel I needed.'

He enjoyed a breakout season for Fremantle in 2022, playing 23 games (his current career tally is 61) and kicking 18 goals.

He has not forgotten the pain of being overlooked in two AFL Drafts, nor those years of doubt playing for Claremont. He remains hungry to live out his childhood dreams.

'I don't automatically get picked and I always feel on the edge of selection,' Bailey said.

'I'm happy with life but don't think I'm happy with footy yet. I've got more to prove and more of my story to write.'

CHAPTER 18

Keifer Yu, Ryan Lim and the WAFL's Nicky Winmar Moment

The opening game of the Western Australian Football League's 2018 ANZAC tribute round was held at grand old Leederville Oval, once the home of West Perth but in the fluid world of professional football, now jointly tenanted by East Perth and Subiaco.

Subiaco was hosting Claremont on a crisp Thursday night and 2378 fans came out to sit in the grandstands and on the terraced hill in the hope that Claremont could somehow compete with the might of Subiaco.

Subiaco's fans were burning, still recovering from their team having won the previous two minor premierships in 2016 and 2017 and then stumbling to lose both grand finals.

In the 2017 home-and-away season, Subiaco had compiled an imperious 19–1 win-loss record and Claremont, a team in transition, finished seventh with eight wins and 12 losses.

A decade before, Subiaco and Claremont had enjoyed a strong rivalry but their recent games had been one-sided affairs, and in their two matches in 2017 Subiaco had beaten Claremont comfortably by 55 and 40 points, respectively.

Subiaco had opened the 2018 season with an extraordinary 118-point thrashing of East Perth. In the following two rounds, the Subiaco Lions won by margins of 58 and 96 points and emerged as the clear premiership favourites.

By contrast, Claremont's 2018 season in the lead-up to the game against Subiaco featured a win, a loss and a bye.

Having fallen short of premiership glory in the past two seasons, Subiaco were men on a mission and only the Claremont true believers thought they were in with a chance.

True to form, Subiaco demolished Claremont by 86 points in that Round 4 encounter and would go on to complete the season undefeated – and finally win the grand final they felt was their right.

But what should have been a routine win on Subiaco's march to glory was tarnished by allegations of racism from their player Josh Deluca.

Keifer Yu, a Claremont player of mixed Aboriginal, Chinese and European heritage, had filed an official complaint against Deluca for allegedly using a racial slur against him during the game, an accusation that rocked the WAFL's administration, which was both inexperienced and underprepared for what was to follow.

The history of racism against Aboriginals and Asians in Australian Rules football runs deep; the footy field becoming a frontline in the battle for social acceptance.

Of the early Chinese VFL/VFA, pioneers, Wally Koochew and Les Kew Ming notably suffered racial abuse.

In 1872, a Gunditjmara man named Albert 'Pompey' Austin, from Framlingham Mission near Warrnambool in south-west Victoria, played one game for Geelong and reportedly suffered racial abuse and humiliation.

Other Indigenous pioneers, such as Polly Farmer and Sir Doug Nicholls, also suffered racial taunts from fans, with Nicholls – who would later become the Governor of South Australia – receiving second-class citizen treatment from Carlton players. After over-hearing derogatory remarks about him from his teammates, Nicholls chose to leave Carlton, joining Northcote.

In the 1990s, racism was still used as a tool to put players off their game according to former Collingwood premiership captain Tony Shaw, who shared his thoughts in a groundbreaking interview with Caroline Wilson in *The Age* in 1991.

'It's a business out there,' said Shaw, who played 313 games for Collingwood over a 16-year career that spanned three decades.

'I'd make a racist comment every week if I thought it would help win a game.'

In 1993, two years after Tony Shaw's frank admission, St Kilda's Aboriginal star Nicky Winmar took a famous stand in response to virulent racial abuse from Collingwood fans at the club's home ground, Victoria Park.

He lifted his shirt and pointed to his stomach, showing pride in his skin colour and the moment was famously captured in an iconic photograph seen by millions of Australians, and immortalised in a bronze statue outside Optus Stadium in Perth, WA.

Nicky is a proud Noongar man, from a Western Australian Aboriginal nation that has produced approximately one-third of all Aboriginal players in the AFL/VFL, from old-school VFL legends, such as Polly Farmer, Barry Cable and the Krakouer brothers, to modern superheroes like Lance 'Buddy' Franklin.

Nicky's on-field stance, combined with Michael Long's racism callout two years later, came to redefine race relations in sport in Australia and led to two important initiatives: the AFL's first campaign, 'Racism: The Game is Up' and a new AFL rule, Rule 30, which was aimed at combating racial and religious vilification.

Rule 30 declared racist abuse to be against league rules and sent a strong message that there would be zero tolerance and strong punishments meted out to offenders.

Winmar's message was slow to reach parts of the Western Australian Football League, where he represented South Fremantle for four years before moving to St Kilda in the VFL where he played 230 games.

For some players out in football's western outpost, casual racism was still a tool to unsettle players, a continuation of Tony Shaw's 'whatever it takes' mentality.

'It should be the WAFL's Nicky Winmar moment,' wrote veteran football journalist John Townsend from the *West Australian* after Keifer Yu proceeded with his official racism complaint against Josh Deluca.

'Just as Winmar made a stand 25 years ago in response to being the target of constant racist abuse in the AFL, Yu's decision to say, "enough is enough" should be a watershed moment for the State league,' Townsend wrote.

Keifer had previous racism experience earlier in his WAFL career when he was abused in a match during NAIDOC round, the annual celebration of Aboriginal and Torres Strait Islander participation in the game. He was told by one player to 'Go back to where you came from'.

Keifer still scratches his head at that previous incident.

'This was the second time it happened and I was like "nah, not again",' explained Keifer. 'I had to do something otherwise I'd probably go insane.'

For Townsend, there was only one good thing that could come of the affair – clarity.

'The WAFL should apply a black and white approach to vilification,' he wrote.

For Keifer and Ryan Lim, it was more than a black-and-white issue.

Ryan was also racially abused for his Chinese heritage during an ANZAC-themed WAFL round. In the aftermath he had a similar experience to Keifer when he was asked to adjudicate on the level of punishment his offender was to receive for the incident.

By the end of the 2018 Claremont season, the careers of Keifer Yu and Ryan Lim diverged.

Keifer would play 19 games and retire at the end of the season, having reached the 100-game milestone for the club.

He would be chaired off the field and promptly returned to his hometown, Broome, to start a family and finish his career, winning three premierships with his beloved Cable Beach Greenbacks.

Back home on the big open fields of West Kimberley, he had asked to play full forward where there was more skill and fewer high-impact collisions.

It was a precautionary move because Keifer was renowned at Claremont for a hard, tough playing style, which on some days came at a price.

'I got a couple of head knocks at Claremont and was advised by a couple of doctors that I shouldn't play,' he says.

'I used to thrive off hard clean footy and was not afraid to put my head where it wasn't supposed to go.'

In that same WAFL season, Ryan Lim was entering his fourth year at Claremont with 58 games under his belt. He was an established player and the decision to promote him to vice-captain was an indication he was being groomed for future leadership opportunities.

Both were one-club stalwarts who had attended Hale school in Perth. However, their ancestral journeys to arrive at Hale and Claremont Football Club represented different strands of the Chinese diaspora migration story in Australia.

Keifer Yu was brought up as a Yawuru Aboriginal man, with Chinese heritage via his grandfather Johnny Yu, who migrated to Broome in the 1940s to work on a pearling lugger.

Johnny worked as a tender on the luggers and had the crucial and trusted role of communicating with the pearl diver below on the sea floor, who was risking his life in the low-tech suits connected by an air hose.

Keifer's mother Sarah is an anthropologist and historian and his father, Professor Peter Yu AM, is a man who walks at the apex of two worlds with an Aboriginal mother and a Chinese father.

He's a Traditional Owner and land rights leader of the Yawuru people of West Kimberley and, in 2010, was elected as a Western Australian ambassador for the Chinese community for the centenary celebrations of the Chung Wah Association.

As part of his role as a Yawuru Traditional Owner, Peter was a key negotiator on behalf of the Yawuru Native Title Holders with the Western Australian state government to secure the 2010 Yawuru Native Title Agreement.

Peter works in Canberra in his role as Vice President First Nations at the Australian National University and loves his footy, serving as the Deputy Chair of the AFL Aboriginal Advisory Committee, a role he treasures.

He remembers his father, Johnny Yu, as a gentle, wise and highly intelligent man who could be firm and resolute when required, and who would stay in touch with world affairs and read the Chinese newspapers sitting on benches outside Broome's Chinatown shops.

Johnny grew up in an impoverished fishing village called Tai O on an island located in Hong Kong's New Territories. Tai O was originally a Tanka or 'sea gypsy' colony before Hakka families, such as the Yus, joined them living on boats and traditional stilt houses over the water.

Peter has taken his family a number of times to visit their relatives in Tai O and they have always been welcomed: 'They accepted us back as family and were accepting of our Aboriginal side, which made us all happy.'

Keifer was amazed at the reception he and his family received in his ancestral village: 'They were very traditional and, because my grandfather was first born, we were warmly welcomed.'

The trips to Hong Kong were a revelation for young Keifer, who said he: 'found it amazing that Johnny Yu came all the way from there, living on the sea, to settle in Broome.'

Every year Keifer and his family pay tribute to Johnny Yu at Broome's annual Ching Ming festival, where the Chinese families of Broome sweep their ancestors' graves and bring offerings to respect their memory.

'He gave my family a lot of good things,' says Keifer in gratitude.

'And he taught my dad to cook, which has been passed down to me.'

Once he established himself in Broome, Johnny Wu married Margaret, an Aboriginal woman who had been brought up on a Catholic mission and was a member of the Stolen Generation.

Their frontier relationship was typical of many in Broome where traditional race barriers were dismantled in favour of values such as reliability, hard work, loyalty and a sense of humour.

Peter remembers a strong parental partnership that somehow thrived under an ever-present threat of personal disruption and pressure through different discrimination laws including the 'Aborigines' Act, which made it technically illegal for his father, an Asian, to cohabit with his Aboriginal wife.

'My mother was Aboriginal but not a citizen of the country. So, she was constantly under threat of deportation back to the mission and my father was under threat of deportation out of the country,' Peter says.

Keeping the family intact involved some close shaves and Peter remembers his father telling him that he had to pay off the police a few times to keep the family out of trouble.

Out on the streets of Broome, Johnny Yu was a popular figure and a man of integrity who kept his word, according to Peter.

It was his father's work ethic that also stood out. 'In addition to his work, he built a house, would fish, grow vegies, look after goats and chooks. The ocean was our supermarket,' Peter explains.

One important life lesson that Johnny Yu shared with his son was about respect for Aboriginal people: 'He sat me down when I was about four years old, and he said to me, "this is your mother's country. I am a guest here, so you best learn the Aboriginal ways".'

That philosophy gave Peter the grounding and permission to walk in both worlds: 'So, we participated in Chinese rituals and events in town, but we grew up under Aboriginal lore.'

Peter recalls laughing long and often with his father who, despite being discriminated against, would find a way forward through humour: 'That's what made me angry, such a funny, generous guy who gave so much, was treated differently to everyone else.

'Yet he still managed to have a laugh.'

While Keifer Yu's Chinese grandfather came to Australia as an indentured labourer during the White Australia policy era, Ryan Lim's ancestral story represented the next phase of Chinese heritage migration into Australia – post-White Australia migration.

Ryan was born in Perth in 1996 to a Malaysian-Chinese father, Paul, and a Scottish mother, Mary, from Perth.

They met while working in a restaurant together in Spain and, according to Ryan, his mother 'coerced Dad to come and live in Perth.'

The parents of Ryan's father, Paul, migrated from Fujian province in China and he was born in Kuantan on the eastern peninsula of Malaysia.

Ryan begrudgingly acknowledges his father for passing down some athletic ability based on his basketball career: 'I have to give that one to Dad.'

He was raised by his parents to work hard and 'always put your best foot forward'.

'I've never been the most naturally gifted so it's always just about hard work.'

His father never pushed the Malaysian-Chinese cultural side onto Ryan but led by example, particularly in the kitchen.

'We stopped going to Chinese restaurants for a while because Dad's cooking was better,' Ryan recalls.

Peter and Keifer Yu inherited their love of football from both the Chinese and Aboriginal sides of the family – and Johnny and Margaret offered a study in cultural and personal contrasts when they were watching Peter play football in Broome.

'My father, Johnny, loved football but he used to stand on the other side of the oval because my mother was one of those vocal barrackers,' Peter recalls.

'She had a fiery reputation, and sometimes if me or a teammate were hit hard, she wanted to jump the fence and thump someone.'

There was no structured Auskick juniors program when Keifer Yu was growing up in Broome, which meant his skill acquisition came from playing with the older kids, especially his cousins who cut him no slack.

He attributes his later on-field toughness directly to his upbringing in Broome with his older cousins: 'I got that from trying to compete with them, if I cried, they teased me so I was toughened up here before I went down (to Perth).'

In Year 7, his mother and father moved with him to Perth so he could attend Hale School, a quality independent school that had a reputation as 'a good footy school'.

Keifer was following in the footsteps of his father, Peter, who had attended Clontarf High School in Perth, a Christian Brothers school that specialised in teaching Aboriginal children and in 1970 he captained the under-16 team to an undefeated record.

Peter played football for three years and remembers a turbulent and occasionally dangerous time where he had to defend himself on and off the field against racism.

'But footy saved us for sure,' Peter explains.

Keifer's sisters moved with him to Hale School and, with his family close to him, he was able to ward off homesickness – although nothing could replace Broome and his beloved hunting, fishing and camping activities.

He tried to fill the void with football and there was plenty of it in the footy capital of Western Australia. Keifer was no different from all of the aspiring footy kids in Perth: 'I wanted to play in the AFL, which was a lot of kids' dream.'

Keifer was a late bloomer. He was not selected in rep teams and only started playing in the Hale School first team in Year 12.

After his high school finished, he stayed down in Perth to play for Claremont Colts.

It was the logical club for Keifer as the West Kimberley Football League was a feeder league for Claremont and the club had invested time in Broome developing the game in the off season.

In 2010, Keifer made his debut for Claremont and, for the next nine seasons until his retirement, he played a physical brand of football, always putting his body on the line.

His peak years were his final ones at the club, according to Claremont coach, Darren Harris: 'I had him for his last three years and he was important to me from a leadership point of view.'

'He didn't need to say a lot because he has such a strong set of values. He listens to everything and is honest and when he speaks it hits right between the eyes.'

Beyond his leadership, Keifer possessed an 'elite skill set', according to Harris.

'Keifer is one of the five best kicks of the football I've seen in 25 years of coaching – he was just pure, his timing, his power, his distance.'

But it was his toughness that endeared him to his teammates and Harris puts it down to one word: 'courage'.

One of Keifer's closest teammates was Claremont captain, Jake Murphy, who led the team for the final half of Keifer's nine-year career.

It was Keifer's ability to lead by example, with a mix of 'hardness and courage', which left a mark on Murphy.

'There was one season when he kept getting injuries, concussions, broken bones – all from putting his body on the line in intense combat and collisions,' says Murphy.

'And we'd all look at him in the rooms and we would see just how committed he was and it drove us on.'

||||

While Keifer Yu was starved of traditional AFL programs in Broome, Ryan Lim grew up in a sports-mad household in Floreat, a well-resourced football heartland just north of the Perth CBD.

Ryan's elder brother, Brendon, forged a pathway into representative football and Ryan was able to progress in his wake: 'I followed his footsteps in every way.'

Brendon would later go on to play a senior game in the WAFL for Claremont, a proud moment for the family.

Although their Malaysian-Chinese father, Paul, didn't understand Aussie Rules, he was still happy to participate in his son's passion, throwing the ball up in the air for hours in the front yard developing their marking skills.

In his early days, Ryan was a big kid for his age and excelled in key positions for the West Coast Junior Football Club before going to Hale where he took it up a notch, winning best and fairest awards in under-13s and under-14s and making the WA state team in under-15s.

The following year, Western Australia won the national under-16 championships under coach Rob Wiley, and Ryan's outstanding form was rewarded with selection in the Australian Institute of Sport (AIS) Academy camp in Canberra, his squad mates including AFL stars Angus Brayshaw and Christian Petracca.

The AIS squad toured the country and made a trip to New Zealand to play the national team. It also toured Europe where Ryan played against a combined European Union side.

Ryan was picked again to represent Western Australia against South Australia in 2013, and got to experience a victory at Adelaide

Oval: 'I remember kicking a goal from outside 50 metres and thinking that I now have a launchpad to go to the next level.'

With two years of representative footy under his belt, he was supremely confident going into the under-18s national championships in his final year of school. He knew the stakes were high with AFL scouts watching their every move.

At this crucial point of their football careers, the Western Australian team were delivered a brutal reality check: 'We didn't perform well and only won one game,' Ryan recalls.

When AFL Draft day came and he didn't get named, Ryan was devastated and fronted up to pre-season training with Claremont feeling disenchanted: 'It was difficult but after an initial period of being down, I tried to use the disappointment as fuel.'

In 2015, he made his debut in the Claremont seniors team but was dropped for the next two matches.

He fought his way back into the team and grew in confidence as a defensive midfielder, securing a spot in the team for the finals – and has been playing in the team ever since.

Teammate Lachie Martinis is in awe of Ryan's durability and work ethic: 'He's only missed one game of footy in nine years and that was for an exam.

'And that is a testament to him being a super hard worker … Which is why he's been so good for so long and is a big finals player.'

Ryan Lim has one on-field moment that soars above the rest. In the second match of the 2022 season, 14 Claremont players were struck down with COVID-19 and he was appointed captain of a team of inexperienced, mostly reserves players.

It was Ryan's first game as captain and his appointment appeared to be a poisoned chalice – an impossible task against the full-strength reigning premiers, Subiaco.

Shocking the 1585 fans in attendance, the rookie Claremont team clawed their way to a famous victory and Lim's herculean effort echoed throughout the league, winning the WAFL's player-of-the-round award for his performance.

For Claremont coach, Ash Prescott, it was an extraordinary moment: 'The highlight of my coaching career,' he says.

'The club was on its knees with so many players out and Ryan couldn't have done a better leadership job in the way he galvanised the young group, but also the way he performed, which is ultimately the measure of a leader.'

Lachie Martinis was one of the players sidelined by the pandemic and forced to watch a live stream of the game from home.

'It was a crazy and bizarre game and I can't really explain the feeling but Ryan played unbelievably well,' Martinis recalls.

Ryan will never forget the 'most special moment' of his career and the unique post-match atmosphere. 'The change rooms were just electric and all of our families came together,' he recalls

'And it was the only time I captained, so my record is 100%.'

Late in the 2022 season, Ryan Lim celebrated a notable playing milestone when he turned out for his 150th WAFL game, earning him life membership of the Claremont Football Club.

For Prescott, the Claremont coach, Ryan is one of a kind: 'First and foremost he's just exceptionally focused and team orientated.

'He's also very nurturing to the younger generation coming through, which is the sign of a good club man and a really good human being.

'And importantly he has humility and is always open to improving himself, which sets a great example, and he drags a lot of players with him – what a great person to have around.'

ı | | ı

When Ryan Lim was on the receiving end of racial abuse playing for Claremont, the WAFL contacted him and asked him what he wanted to do about the incident – and the resolutions ranged from an apology to proceeding to an official tribunal hearing.

Ryan chose not to go to the tribunal: 'I kept it pretty quiet but it was pretty bizarre that the decision was left completely up for me to make.'

He was more concerned for the offender's welfare than punishment: 'I thought for a guy to say that, he must be in a pretty dark place so I was more interested in him learning as opposed to punishment.'

Ryan recalls his response was to opt for the player to apologise and undergo counselling and education.

He also happened to be on the field when his teammate Keifer Yu was abused: 'That was pretty definitive and in his case the offender was multicultural and in my case he was Aboriginal.

'It's hard to believe that people still think one culture is better than another.'

ı | | ı

For Keifer Yu, an apology for his second incident with racial abuse was not enough.

The responsibility for deciding on a punishment for Josh Deluca's racial taunt was left to the victim, Keifer himself. The incident went to mediation and Deluca received the maximum three-week suspension with Keifer Yu cast as a villain by some fans on social media and some opposition players.

Keifer's stand came at a cost to his mental health and he shared his side of the story with the *West Australian*: 'I was a bit rattled the week after the South Fremantle game when a few boys gave me a bit of flak and I was made to feel like I had done the wrong thing.'

As a mentor to younger Aboriginal players, Keifer explains that he had no choice but to decide on the maximum punishment for Deluca to provide a deterrent.

A big part of his stand was to make a statement on behalf of other Aboriginal players he had spoken to who did not trust the system after their previous cases were lost or weakened in the maze of semantics and mediation.

In a number of columns in the *West Australian*, Townsend railed against the WAFL process that Keifer was subjected to: 'It is an obvious flaw in the system that the victim is the sole arbiter of the crime and in Yu's words, he was required to be the judge and jury of the matter.'

Keifer is adamant that the matter was handled badly by the tribunal: 'I shouldn't have been the one making the decision on a suitable penalty.'

ı | | ı

For all that initial unpleasantness, Keifer Yu's decision has left the game in a better place.

According to Townsend, since that incident six seasons ago, things have improved for minority players in Western Australian football.

'But there have also been re-education sessions run by the WAFL and its clubs, the widespread presence of Aboriginal players at every club, the growing number of African players in the league, as well as society's trend towards self-censorship of inflammatory language, have all contributed to a "cleaner" football environment.'

'It may be that the Yu matter had a positive impact on cleaning up the game,' Townsend says, a testament to the bravery of Keifer Yu's stand.

CHAPTER 19

Fourteen-hour Shifts and Footy: Sophie Li on the AFLW Movement

In 2017, the AFL launched a new professional women's league, called the AFLW. The inaugural AFLW competition, featuring eight teams from across the country, was won by the Adelaide Crows.

Sophie Li, a proud South Australian and longtime Crows fan, was one of many women inspired by the new competition. She had dreamed of playing in the AFLW since it was formally announced in 2016 but missed the first season due to travel commitments.

While travelling across Europe, she kept up her football fitness by playing kick-to-kick with her partner and dreamed of one day being drafted.

When she returned to Australia, she was selected by the Norwood Redlegs for the first season of the South Australian National Football League (SANFL) Women's competition, which also launched in 2017.

Four SANFL affiliated men's clubs – Norwood, North Adelaide, Glenelg and West Adelaide – joined the SANFLW, which was described by SANFL CEO Jake Parkinson as a 'stepping stone' for players to make it in the AFLW.

Sophie knew that a good season would put her directly into consideration for AFLW recruiters, who were locked into an increasingly competitive market for talent. After two rounds, Sophie had kicked three goals to help Norwood to back-to-back wins.

The highlight of the season were the rivalry matches between Norwood and North Adelaide, two SANFL clubs with a combined 268 years of history. In 2017, the women's teams representing the old SANFL blueblood rivals qualified for the first ever SANFLW grand final.

At three-quarter time, Norwood held a six-point lead over North Adelaide before storming home to clinch a 65–38 victory. The AFLW scouts were watching closely and it was impossible to miss Sophie Li, who won the best-on-ground award with two crucial goals and 23 disposals. 'I was really humbled to win as it was the first ever SANFLW final,' Sophie recalls.

Sophie's exceptional season was acknowledged by the SANFL when she finished runner-up in the competition's best and fairest award. Statistically, Sophie was the highest-ranked all-round player in the game, with the most kicks, second-highest number of disposals and second-highest number of tackles. In other words, Sophie had met every key metric to convince the recruiters that she was ready to play AFLW.

When the regular Adelaide season commenced, she went back to her local club, the Adelaide University Blacks, and helped them win the premiership alongside several teammates who would soon graduate to the AFLW, including Courtney Gum, Jess Edwards, Ruth Wallace and Ebony O'Dea.

For Sophie, it was her second premiership in 2017. 'We had a really talented team,' she recalls. 'I loved having a good time and playing with some of my best friends above all else.'

Fittingly, she was with her friends at the Adelaide Uni football club's rooms when the 2017 AFLW Draft was conducted. A few of her Adelaide University teammates were draft hopefuls and they decided they would ride the highs and lows of the journey together.

Although Sophie had been given a strong indication that she would be picked, she knew that player drafts were complex and unpredictable. When her name was called at No. 28 for Carlton, the room erupted in joy.

'There was a lot of screaming and jumping,' she recalls. 'I think I may have appeared the calmest in the room, but internally I was just overwhelmed with excitement and nerves.'

To chase her dream of playing in the AFLW, Sophie took leave without pay from her job as a paramedic in the South Australia Ambulance Service. She had become a paramedic at her sister's suggestion, and healthcare ran deep in her family. Sophie's mother Liz, a teacher, had met her father, Peter, while working casually for him as a dentist.

Peter Li's ancestral village is Sunhui (Xinhui) in Jiangmen in Guangzhou, but he was born in Hong Kong after his grandfather moved there to work in a tea and grocery shop.

Peter arrived in Australia as a 17-year-old student, withered from seasickness from the seven-day boat trip. Although his English was poor, he adapted quickly to Australian high school life and eventually went into practice as a dentist.

Sophie's mother was born in New Zealand from parents of English descent and moved to Melbourne when she was 14.

Liz and Peter raised four daughters in Adelaide without the Cantonese language, although the Li siblings were immersed in Chinese culture whenever they visited their grandparents, five minutes' drive away.

'They didn't speak English,' Sophie recalls. 'Every time we visited, we took our shoes off at the front door, went upstairs to where they spent the majority of time watching Chinese soaps on their La-Z-Boy chairs, gave them a kiss on the cheek and they would grab our cheeks and smile and say things in Chinese to us.'

Sophie's grandparents provided her biggest connection to Chinese culture through family outings for hot pot, yum cha and Chinese sweet buns; Chinese New Year was a time for celebration and homemade dumplings. It was only as she got older and started visiting other people's houses that she began to realise the difference between cultures. No other father she visited kept a fridge filled with durian, the pungent Asian spiky fruit.

Sophie also reconnected with her Chinese heritage on a trip back to Hong Kong with her father and sister where they 'food-crawled' around the city. They stayed with her auntie and uncle, who kept them well fed and Sophie and her sister learned about their father's early life. 'It was amazing to be able to put a place to all the stories Dad told me about,' she says.

Importantly, she gained an understanding of the living conditions that drove him to migrate to Australia: 'They all lived in one room, sleeping on a bamboo mat on the floor when it was hot.'

When Sophie flew to Melbourne to begin her AFLW football career with Carlton, she was able to set up her new life in a familiar environment, living with her sister. 'I was awestruck, excited and terrified,' she remembers.

'It made the transition to a new city a lot easier, having someone I know so well and feel comfortable with.'

The one element she could not control, though, was Melbourne's famously fickle weather: 'I hated it and still do – I'm not built for the cold.'

Her 2018 AFLW season started well when the Blues beat Collingwood in the first game. 'I remember standing out in the middle of the field moments before the siren was about to go off and it was just unbelievable to be playing in front of such a huge crowd, wearing the navy blue and knowing the game was being televised live!' she recalls.

Although Carlton ended up finishing last on the ladder, Sophie had a strong season with 34 kicks and 20 handballs across seven games. Most of all, she was excited to be at the frontline of change for women's sport.

'The beauty of AFLW is that it's a movement – it's breaking gender stereotypes and breaking glass ceilings for women in so many ways – to be part of that is incredible,' she told afl.com.au.

Although Sophie was contracted to Carlton for another season, she received word that the South Australia Ambulance Service was not able to extend her unpaid leave.

And due to differences in clinical guidelines, Sophie would have had to undergo significant retraining and reaccreditation to work as a paramedic in Victoria. 'If I wanted to keep playing in Victoria,' she recalls, 'I would have had to quit my job.'

Due to her difficult circumstances, Carlton gave her permission to break her contract on compassionate grounds and return to Adelaide to begin working as a paramedic again.

She signed with the Adelaide Crows, the team she had grown up supporting along with Geelong.

ı | | ı

As a child, Sophie had collected footy cards, watched AFL games on television and played kick-to-kick at school. But like many girls of her generation, she had also been told to focus on other sports because there were no footy teams for girls.

'I wanted to be a boy just so I would be allowed to play football and take marks like Tony Modra!' recalls Li, referring to the former Crows player who made 118 appearances for the club, kicking 440 goals.

Receiving her first Adelaide Crows uniform was a personal moment to savour. 'It was so nice but also surreal,' she says. 'I never thought I would be wearing a Crows guernsey and training in The Shed.'

Sophie spent the 2019 season juggling the demands of elite women's football with 14-hour shifts as a paramedic at Murray Bridge, an hour's drive east of Adelaide.

On the job, she would deal with car accidents, motorcycle crashes and a variety of medical emergencies such as heart attacks, seizures and strokes. On the field, she had a busy season for the Crows, playing in all nine games and laying 30 tackles to go along with her 54 disposals.

In the preliminary final, Adelaide thrashed Geelong by 66 points in front of 13,000 fans at Adelaide Oval, which set up a grand final match the following week against Sophie's former club, Carlton.

Playing at Adelaide Oval for the Crows was the fulfilment of a 'childhood dream', Li told *The Advertiser*. 'And (next week) to run out again with this group of girls, and play against Carlton on my birthday, it's just this strange kind of whirlwind of coincidences and it's going to be incredible.'

The 2019 AFLW grand final was one of the most significant moments in the history of Australian women's sport. More than 53,000 fans swarmed into Adelaide Oval, a record for a women's domestic league sporting match in Australia.

Big crowds at 'AFL level' had been the one missing ingredient from the spectacle of AFLW and, for the next generation, this crowd was a glimpse of a commercially viable and sustainable future.

When the Crows scored their first goal, Sophie was shocked.

'The crowd erupted and it was the loudest, most deafening sound I had ever heard,' she recalls. 'I felt very emotional, humbled and proud and it was an incredible moment.'

The Crows defeated Carlton 10.3 (63) to 2.6 (18) and, after the game, Sophie's teammates serenaded her live on national television to celebrate her 31st birthday. 'I feel quite privileged to be in the position I am in, as part of the movement of AFLW,' she told reporters.

'Seeing the impact that AFLW is having ... little girls come up to you and they want to play and tackle each other, they see they can do what the boys can do. And the boys can see people with the strength like Erin [Phillips] get injured and cry, and that it's okay, and that's strength in itself – the boys can learn from the AFLW.'

The grand final celebrations went on into the night in a private room and, despite the scarcity of tickets, somehow her father, Peter, made it in. He had never been known to drink alcohol, but in the delirium of victory he took a swig from the premiership cup.

It was the highlight of her short-lived AFLW career.

After five games in 2020, Sophie decided to retire, unable to continue juggling full-time work with a footy career and her plans to start a family. 'I had to use all of my annual leave to play football, so it meant that I never really had a break,' she says.

'I was also conscious that at some point soon I wanted to start a family, so it was the logical step to retire on a high after winning a premiership.'

CHAPTER 20

Beeso the Giant

In the first round of the AFLW 2022 season, Greater Western Sydney (GWS) Giants midfielder Rebecca Beeson scored her first goal of the season. It was a goal that showcased her attributes – quick hands to pick up the ball, speed to evade her opponents and a smooth kick off the outside of her right boot.

In the entire 2021 season, 'Beeso' as she been nicknamed by her teammates, had only scored one goal and an early-season 'major' was a positive omen for the year ahead.

Her goal helped lay the foundation for a 15-point win against the Gold Coast Suns and she looked forward to helping GWS improve on their 2021 season where they placed ninth out of 14 teams.

Rebecca's 2021 season was a personal best where she had averaged in double figures per game for key areas – 11 kicks and 10 handballs. Her average of 21 disposals per game ranked equal 11th in the league.

For the GWS Giants coming into their sixth season, Rebecca Beeson was their taliswoman and she was building a solid AFLW career on the back of a five-year 'streak' of uninterrupted matches, playing every game since the inaugural AFLW Round 1 in February 2017 without injury.

Journalists described her as a 'stalwart'.

Rebecca had played 38 games straight when she ran onto Whitten Oval in Footscray to play against Fremantle in Round 2 of the 2022 season.

For Rebecca, it felt like any other game but, after a shot at goal, she got her leg caught under a Fremantle player and clutched at her right ankle in pain.

Lying on the turf, she knew her life had changed. The streak was over, and she had returned to the pack of injured mortals.

'I was pretty lucky up until that point to be injury free,' Rebecca explains. 'But that happens when you play contact sports; you're eventually going to get those types of injuries.'

Although Rebecca had assembled an impressive streak, she knew it would end at some stage. 'That's the brutal part of the game; it can be taken away from you pretty quickly.'

In her first year in 2017, she had watched her good friend and teammate, Mai Nguyen, suffer a dreaded ACL injury, restricting her career to just three AFLW matches.

Mai's pioneering role as the first Vietnamese player in either the AFL or AFLW was brutally cut short by knee injuries, but she wasn't alone.

After the opening round of the 2022 AFLW season, the talk was not of the players on the field but the players who were taken off the field, supplied with crutches and facing the prospect of lengthy rehabilitation for their damaged ACLs.

Images of three of the game's drawcards – Brianna Davey, Kate Lutkins and Isabel Huntington – clutching their knees devastated the AFLW community.

A range of biological theories were put forward for the high injury rates for AFLW players but for Adelaide Crows legend Erin Phillips, it was simply down to the player's semi-professional status.

Phillips had a unique vantage point, having previously played nine seasons in the professional Women's National Basketball Association (WNBA) and winning an Olympic silver medal with the Opals.

'I do feel very confident that if girls were given the opportunity to play year-round and put the time and effort and money and practice into their body – just being purely paid as an athlete – you've got to believe that there's going to be less injuries,' Phillips told the ABC's W Podcast. In the 2019 AFLW grand final, Phillips tore her ACL in the third quarter – despite this, she still won the medal for best afield.

Rebecca's recovery from her ankle injury meant five games on the sideline and upon her return she suffered two concussions from heavy tackles that finished her season. She was moved to the dreaded 'inactive playing list'.

The streak was now a distant memory and after playing five full seasons uninjured, the Women's AFL website now described her as 'injury-prone'.

To play every game consecutively for five years is an achievement she will cherish in future years, but the concussions triggered a broader personal reflection for Rebecca.

'I think the concussions have been more challenging than the ankle,' she explains.

'It's really changed my perspective and I'm just so grateful to be able to play this great game because no one can play forever.'

It was an important lesson to learn: 'I think a lot of elite athletes think they're invincible and I was no different. But you're invincible till you're not.'

Rebecca Beeson was born in Sydney in 2002 to Alan, her Anglo-Australian father from Gunnedah, and Jin, her Taiwanese-born mother.

She was an unlikely candidate to become a professional footballer.

She was a female and there was no AFLW when she was growing up to aspire to. She had Asian heritage, a rarity in the Anglo-Celtic and southern European–dominated world of AFL clubs.

And she was from the New South Wales Central Coast, an hour north of Sydney, a hardcore rugby league area where Australian rules football was both exotic and rarely sighted.

'I loved watching footy on TV but there was nowhere to play it,' says Rebecca.

Growing up, she was a classic all-round athlete playing everything that was available to her including cricket, Oztag, touch football and soccer.

ı | | ı

The story of Jin's journey from a small village in Taiwan to the Central Coast of New South Wales is a constant source of inspiration for Rebecca.

Jin's father worked in construction and her mother managed a mixed fruit farm, which involved a relentless daily grind of growing and picking the fruit, transporting it to the market and then selling it at the family's market store.

While Jin and her four siblings helped out their mother on the fruit farm, or walked the many kilometres to the local school, she dreamed of travelling overseas and seeing the world.

Her first stop was to the municipality of Kaohsiung City on the southern tip of Taiwan where she worked in a steelworks by day and studied by night, before getting a visa and moving to Australia.

Rebecca has visited Taiwan twice, the second time when she was 17 and travelling with her mother to stay in their ancestral home. She found the language barrier a challenge to connecting with her relatives.

'And of course, my main memory is of the amazing food, the noodles, the dumplings, the stir fries,' she says.

For Rebecca, the trips to Taiwan engendered waves of respect and appreciation for her mother's journey to Australia, Jin being the only one of her extended family to leave the village.

'She decided she wanted to experience life outside Taiwan and she was brave to leave, worked hard to pay her own way to Australia and start a new life. Just amazing,' Rebecca says.

Living on the New South Wales Central Coast, an hour away from the closest Taiwanese community in Sydney, Jin could have felt culturally isolated, but Rebecca admires how she adapted and coped.

'She speaks regularly with her family in Taiwan and has a couple of friends in Sydney she catches up with,' Rebecca says.

'She found a way to make it work.'

Although her trips to Taiwan were a 'whirlwind', Rebecca always made time to spend in the company of her maternal grandmother, Ah Mah, who raised five children and was a 'tremendously strong woman'.

When reflecting on the source of her work ethic and drive, Rebecca feels her female line is the most likely source: 'I come from a line of tough, strong women who fought bloody hard to make a life for themselves, and I reckon this mentality has definitely helped me in my sporting life.'

While Rebecca is thankful for her hard-working DNA sourced from a small farming village in Taiwan, she is also grateful to her father,

Alan, for infusing her with a love of sports and developing the week-to-week resilience required for elite athletic success.

When Rebecca was 12, her family moved to Western Australia for work opportunities, and being transplanted from the NRL heartland of New South Wales to the AFL heartland of Perth opened exciting new possibilities for her.

She immediately signed up to play in the closest Aussie Rules competition and remembers not being able to contain her excitement when her father took her down to the Swan Districts Wednesday night competition for girls: 'I loved everything about it and was hooked,' Rebecca explains.

By the time the Beeson family returned to the Central Coast three years later, Rebecca committed to playing footy which involved travelling down three times a week to train and play for Macquarie University in north-western Sydney and later for the UNSW-East Sydney Stingrays.

She also took up rugby sevens, part of the 'gold medal fever' national athletic talent search prior to the introduction of rugby sevens as an Olympic sport for the Rio 2016 Olympics.

Rebecca was part of the first generation of young women who were sought out and pursued for their raw athletic talent in contact sports.

When Rebecca missed out on making the NSW representative rugby sevens team, she made the decision to focus on the game she loved – Australian Rules football.

After Rio, the more financially powerful AFLW and NRLW semi-professional competitions were launched and they joined the search for outstanding women athletes, cannibalising each other's talent pools.

When Rebecca and her father drove around the suburbs of Sydney to train, play and grind through seasons in the AFL Sydney women's competition, the concept of playing for money and in a professional environment was never discussed.

'It was just purely for enjoyment, I never thought that it could be a career,' says Rebecca.

When the AFLW competition was announced, it was a momentous day for many women who had been denied the chance to play the sport they loved at an elite level. For Rebecca, it was just another day in high school.

'It wasn't a big thing to me, I was just a schoolgirl and the dream wasn't on my radar,' she explains.

'But later I learnt that some of the older girls had waited their whole adult lives for this moment.'

When Rebecca Beeson's name was read out as pick No. 32 in the 2016 AFLW inaugural draft, it was something of an anticlimax for the teenager. She knew in advance that she was being drafted to the Greater Western Sydney Giants, who had an obligation to take any players developed in New South Wales.

After a strong pre-season, she made her debut against the Adelaide Crows on 4 February 2017, and played every match of a disappointing season in which the Giants came last with only one win.

Her form and consistency improved and, in the first match of the 2018 season, she won a prestigious NAB Rising Star nomination.

Rebecca was on a mission to improve her football skills, demonstrated by her committing to two off seasons with Hawthorn in the VFLW competition to 'hone my craft' in the footy capital.

It was her great leap into the unknown – a strange city with new friends – but the move paid dividends in 2018 when she tasted premiership success with the Hawks at Etihad Stadium.

For the girl from the football backblocks of New South Wales to fit into the culture and succeed with a heavyweight club like

Hawthorn was a big moment: 'Everything just clicked and I have nothing but good memories from that year.'

The Hawthorn VFLW premiership experience boosted Rebecca's confidence and accelerated her growth as a player.

On her return to GWS for the 2019 season she took her game to new heights, winning the Gabrielle Trainor Medal for the club's best and fairest player.

In a year of consistently elite performances, Rebecca cemented her role as a midfielder and ranked 12th in the AFLW for clearances, seventh for handballs and averaged a hefty 16.3 disposals per game.

Rebecca's breakout year released her from any self-doubt about her ability at the top level.

'I learnt that year that it's about establishing yourself, gaining confidence and learning,' she says.

In recognition of her form, she was named in the 2019 Virgin Australia AFL Women's All-Australian 40-player squad, an honour she takes great pride in.

Starting in 2020, the COVID-19 pandemic restricted personal movement and wreaked havoc with sports in Australia, leading to season cancellations, stringent daily testing, crippling lockdowns and access-restricted player 'bubbles', which hit the AFLW players particularly hard.

The average annual salary for AFLW players in 2020 was $18,088, an amount that could not cover their living costs. Unable to work in their full-time or part-time jobs that required physical attendance, some players were traumatised and sought help.

Rebecca was one of the players who suffered a financial crisis during lockdown and her dilemma was so frustrating it drove her to write an article for the *Guardian Australia* that was a cry for help.

Her story documented a slice of life in the COVID-19 bubble, with her and her teammates' lives in limbo, facing the grinding pressure of training four nights a week yet having to apply for and work in part-time jobs.

Rebecca and her teammates constantly felt aggrieved at having to 'carry the weight of the competition's infancy' on their shoulders.

While Rebecca and her 419 fellow AFLW players in 2020 were still experiencing the glow of being able to play a sport denied to the generations before them, the cold financial reality had taken off the shine, their optimism replaced by a pessimistic view of the future.

Rebecca wrote in the *Guardian Australia*: 'What scares me the most is the possibility that I'll be done with football in my 30s, with only a couple of dollars to my name and no proper career path to step into. Hopefully in the not too distant future, the game will move from a semi-professional space to a fully professional game. With any luck, I'll still be young enough to be playing AFLW when that time comes.'

In October 2020, the AFLW world was rocked when Rebecca's GWS Giants teammate, Jacinda Barclay, took her own life after a brief but intense period of mental illness. Barclay had been a baseball champion before playing AFLW, having represented Australia at five World Cups.

It was a desperately sad time for Rebecca and her GWS teammates and she penned another moving story for *Guardian Australia* to honour the memory of her teammate.

Rebecca was glad to see the end of a wretched 2020 in which she suffered a form slump. She embraced 2021 with optimism and energy, returning to her 2019 form levels and polling second in the GWS Giants best and fairest award, the Gabrielle Trainor Medal, behind Alyce Parker.

The lesson she took out of her 2020 experience was the importance of a 'Plan B' to transition into life after professional sport.

She completed her double degree in Commerce Media and has done a lot of work separating her identity from her sporting achievements which, she has learnt, 'can leave you vulnerable if your self worth as a human is based on how well you played on the weekend'.

'After my injuries it's become apparent to me that it's really important to have an identity and balance away from footy.'

Rebecca has increasingly enjoyed her role as a pioneer, using her cultural background to inspire young girls of Asian heritage to take up the game.

'I'm pretty much an Aussie but I understand that seeing someone make it is important,' she says. 'The game has welcomed people from a variety of cultures and welcomed me with open arms so I will do the best I can to help people feel included.'

Alan McConnell was the GWS Giants AFLW coach from 2017–2022. He oversaw Rebecca's development from raw rookie to polished high-performance player, and he valued her contribution on a number of levels.

He described her key attributes as: 'drive, diligence, connection to the team and elite hands and composure.'

The pair shared tough times in the COVID-19 player bubble and McConnell found a silver lining from the ordeal when he saw Rebecca's personal growth and resilience 'flourish', evolving from a player trying to get selected every week to one who really cared about her teammates.

He also sees significant potential left to realise: 'Prior to the injuries, Rebecca was destined to become one of the very best players in the competition,' McConnell says. 'And hopefully that still occurs.'

CHAPTER 21

Jiaming Pi – the Player Agent

Jiaming 'Jamie' Pi is a 400-game grassroots player, the AFL's first Mandarin-speaking commentator and the first Chinese-Australian AFL player agent. Having moved to Australia from China at age 12, he is a shining example of footy's power to change lives.

Growing up in the city of Urumqi, almost 3000 kilometres west of Beijing, Jamie knew nothing of Australia or its native code of football. He was an only child, a legacy of China's one-child policy, which was in place from 1980–2016 to contain Chinese population growth.

In 1993, Jamie's life was upended when his father secured an Australian skilled migration visa to work as a chef at a friend's restaurant in Dandenong in south-east Melbourne. The Pi family left their hometown for a step into the unknown.

'It was a pretty ballsy move to be honest to take a punt like they did, because not many people migrated where we were from,' Jamie says. 'They didn't speak any English.'

The Pi family landed in Melbourne in January 1993, in the middle of summer, and when he went to visit the restaurant for the first time he was amazed at the lack of people on the streets.

'It was the middle of the day and hot and there was nobody on the road,' Jamie says. 'It was shock to the system coming from China where there are people everywhere.'

Before Jamie could study at high school, he had to attend Noble Park Language School where he did three terms and he had a great time despite the language barrier. 'We had people from Sudan, Somalia, Afghanistan, Palestine, Vietnam,' he says. 'I don't know how we spoke to each other in broken English, but it was always funny and fascinating.'

When Jamie finally arrived at Dandenong High School with barely intermediate English, he discovered Australian Rules football. 'A bunch of kids were kicking around a yellow footy at lunchtime,' Jamie recalls. 'I can clearly remember the first time I went to have a crack at it and that was my introduction to football.'

The kid that owned the 'yellow footy' was Travis Hyland, who lived around the corner from Jamie, and they became best mates. Jamie, often left alone by his parents who worked late at the restaurant, was adopted by the Hylands and says: 'they became my Aussie family.'

The Hyland family matriarch, Kathleen, changed his name from Jiaming to Jamie, 'to make it sound more Aussie', and Jamie Pi was born.

While his parents worked in their restaurant in the evening and on weekends, Jamie began training with the St Gerard's Football Club (now the Dandenong Saints).

He turned up to his first pre-season training session on his own, having ridden his bicycle 2 kilometres to the Dandenong Showground. He trained hard and learnt the fundamentals of the game. 'I had no idea what I was doing, but I loved it,' he recalls.

Overjoyed at making the St Gerard's under-14s team in 1994, he rode his bike to home games and was ferried to away games by the coach, who was a schoolteacher.

St Gerard's won a premiership in his first season, and Jamie was hooked, looking to help out wherever he could: 'I trained with both the under-14s and 15s and loved being the water boy for other teams. I was in and around the club three or four nights a week. My English improved and you learn a lot of sayings, improve your social skills.'

It was also the first time he came across racism. 'Early on in my career in one game my teammates told me that they heard me get called a "gook",' he recalls. 'I didn't hear it and even if I did, I didn't know what it meant.'

It was his teammates' reaction that impressed him: 'It was a pretty big moment, they stuck up for me and it was an all-in brawl. I remember it well.'

He was less impressed with the tribunal when the player who racially vilified him didn't even show up to the hearing and escaped reprimand.

Jamie was suspended for striking, with a member of the panel telling him if he was going to play football, 'you're going to have to cop stuff like that'. And cop it he did.

One day, in a game against Seaford, he remembers being punched and spat on. 'I had blokes laughing at me and someone in the crowd yelling "hit the chink" – I won't ever forget it,' he says.

He started lifting weights and learnt to handle himself on the field, hitting hard and getting his revenge the legal way. Over time, he learned to 'brush it off' and use the experience to make him stronger.

He also feels very strongly that racism is a problem that is wider than one group: 'It happens in all cultures, man. You go to China, and they'll call you names.'

That year, 1994, was also a pivotal one for Jamie off the field. It was the year he found one of the great loves of his life – the Collingwood Magpies Football Club.

The Collingwood–Melbourne game at Waverley Park in Round 6, 1994 is seared into his memory; particularly one incident when Collingwood's Gavin Brown was collected by a head high tackle but not given a free kick.

Pi, who had arrived at the ground unsure of which team to support, felt the unfairness of the umpire's call to his new favourite player and started following the Pies: 'A young boy obsessed with everything black and white.'

'I loved the us and them mentality and following the Pies gave me an instant conversation starter,' Jamie explains.

The sense of belonging that came with supporting Collingwood changed Jamie's life; so much so that he recalls becoming emotional watching Collingwood legend Tony Shaw's final game: 'I was crying on my own at home watching it – crazy how much I loved that team.'

Jamie's football career has involved a number of clubs but his heart is with Keysborough, his first senior club who he still plays with for now, at the age of 42, where he answers to his old nickname of 'China'.

His journeyman career includes a premiership with St John's Collegiate, stints on the road with Hawthorn Amateurs and Box Hill North, playing for and being the first president of the all-Asian Southern Dragons team, playing for and sponsoring Ainslie Football Club in Canberra and playing for two years in Germany as a co-founder of the Düsseldorf Lions Club in the Australian Football League of Germany (AFLG).

Sadly, Jamie's parents only watched a handful of his junior games because they worked on Saturdays and Sundays. Now they have retired, Jamie says, they have no excuse.

'They've watched a lot more of my footy now that I'm 42 years old – playing thirds footy at nine o'clock in the morning – than they ever have,' he says.

In addition to playing, Jamie also tried his hand at coaching, getting his Level 2 certificate and serving as Assistant Coach for the St Kilda VFLW team: 'Coaching was a great experience and I learnt so much about the game but I felt my skills could be better served elsewhere.'

His coaching career peaked when he was appointed player–coach for Team China at the 2014 International Cup, held every three years in Australia. For the first time China managed two wins in the tournament, against India and East Timor, which were a cause for celebration. Jamie says: 'Each one I can still remember clearly.'

In 2010, Jamie moved in a new direction when he became the first official AFL commentator speaking in Mandarin when the AFL partnered with Melbourne Chinese radio station 3CW to build awareness for the 2010 Shanghai exhibition match between Melbourne and Brisbane.

Jamie was the logical choice, having previously been the 3CW footy pundit since 2006.

His first gig was in Shanghai, calling the game in China, which was beamed live on Chinese television.

Later, he would commentate at a number of AFL events including some Port Adelaide home matches, but he will never forget his first night of commentary in Shanghai.

He remembers arriving at the ground and, after failing to find the commentary box, was told he was in the wrong place, and to go to a broadcast studio across the other side of the city in busy Shanghai traffic.

Jamie arrived at the studio in a panic. When confronted by security, he realised he'd left his passport in the hotel and had no ID to show. After some negotiating, he showed the security guard his ANZ business card and was let in with 10 minutes to spare. Then, he was told that his co-commentator – normally the basketball commentator – had arrived at the ground late and would not make it to the studio in time.

'So, I had no partner and was about to go live on Chinese TV,' Jamie recalls. 'We were about to start and there were already two guys in the studio commentating the Phillip Island Moto GP, which had just finished. When they were leaving, the producer asked one of them to do commentary with this bloke who has come over from Australia.'

When the commentary began, his conscripted co-commentator told Jamie in Mandarin that he had no idea what was going on.

Jamie recalls him saying, '"Mate, you just do the commentary and I'll ask you things I don't know, and we'll put on the show." That's what we did, and it was a lot of fun. And to this day, I don't even know his name.'

Jamie Pi was the first Chinese-heritage person to enter the cut-throat world of AFL player management when he got his accreditation to operate as a player agent in 2019. He's been successful as an agent, finding a niche with a stable of 32 players in the growing AFLW market, including Collingwood's Taiwanese-Australian player Joanna Lin.

As the only player agent of Asian background, he felt like an outsider at the annual player agents' conference. 'I work in a white man's world, you have to understand that,' he says.

'You're unknown, you're isolated, you sit on your own at conferences but I have forged a pretty good stable for myself, so I'll stick in there.'

Part of being a player agent is watching games and sometimes Jamie will watch all nine AFLW games a week, especially when one of his clients is playing. 'I just love it,' he says. 'It's my passion.'

Although he experienced a time when he felt he didn't fit in to either world, Jamie now feels comfortable in both – a proud Aussie of Chinese heritage.

Asked if the Chinese had a name for Australian Rules football, Jamie recalls a debate over a couple of different names. Eventually, he says, they chose 'Boshiganinqou' or 'Australian Style Olive Ball'.

The overwhelming emotion Jamie feels towards the game is gratitude: 'I was very, very fortunate to have football. I cannot tell you how fortunate … because that really shaped what I am and who I am, and it's really spread into a lot of other things including helping with my banking career.'

And now he is a married father, of course his family has become Collingwood fanatics.

Pi is clearly delighted to carry on the tradition of the early Chinese-Australian football pioneers.

'We've always played the game and we'll always play it,' he says. 'It's our game too, no matter what anybody says.'

CHAPTER 22

'I Found My Tribe': Joanna Lin on Football, Family and Fitting In

Every footy player dreams of their first goal sailing through the big sticks and being greeted by the roar of the crowd.

Unfortunately for Joanna Lin, her first goal for Collingwood – a textbook right-foot snap against Geelong – occurred on Valentine's Day, 14 February 2021, during the middle of the COVID-19 pandemic in Melbourne.

With the city in lockdown, Joanna's personal milestone occurred in front of an empty Punt Road Oval stadium, the old home ground of the Richmond Tigers.

Melbourne's residents were living under a 'circuit breaker' hard-lockdown in which leaving the home was deemed illegal except for grocery shopping, essential services work, exercise and caregiving. Face masks were to be worn at all times outside the home and fans were banned from stadiums for Melbourne teams playing that weekend.

Despite the silent atmosphere, Joanna jumped up and down and was mobbed by her teammates, who did their best to make up for the lack of noise. 'A lot of things raced through my mind including the memory of practising snaps so many times in junior footy,' she says.

'I can so clearly remember the ball just going through the posts and it wasn't just me jumping around, it was my 10-year-old self who would not have thought this moment possible.'

Joanna Lin was born in Melbourne in 2002, the middle daughter of Taiwanese immigrant parents.

Her mother, Wen Ju, had already been on a unique journey, migrating to Australia from Taiwan at 16 to complete high school and work in her grandfather Jang Cherng Hour's Chinese takeaway food shop, Rai-Rai, in Chadstone, in south-east Melbourne.

For Joanna, her grandfather's life in Australia is a source of inspiration for its resilience: 'I have no idea how he survived, because his English wasn't great at all,' Joanna says.

'But he had Mum at the front of the shop to manage things and they got by.'

Joanna's mother embraced her new life in Australia, studying at Richmond High School and then Monash University where she graduated to become a teacher.

After graduating, Wen Ju moved back and forth between Taiwan and Australia until she fell for Yu Sung, a bus driver she met while working in a Taiwanese kindergarten. They decided to get married and moved to Melbourne together to start a new life.

'I don't think about it too much,' Joanna reflects. 'But it's an amazing story how I came to be in Australia.'

For as long as she can remember, Joanna Lin loved footy and followed Collingwood.

'My brother William told me to be a Collingwood fan and that was that,' she recalls.

Her first heroes were Alan Didak and Dane Swan, and one of her saddest childhood moments was watching Collingwood lose the 2011 AFL grand final to Geelong.

There were few opportunities for her to play junior football, though, so she played basketball and futsal instead. Her first experience of footy came through school and, although she had no idea what she was doing, she loved the camaraderie and freedom of running.

In Year 10, she was invited by a friend to join her local football club, the Bulleen Templestowe Bullants. At her first training session, she learned how to kick and pass the Sherrin, and soon she was drop-punting it with the best of them.

Football, she recalls, felt 'weirdly natural and second nature', but her parents were less than impressed.

'Mum and Dad didn't want me to play [footy] because of how rough it was,' Joanna says. 'And it wasn't a sport that they thought you could sustain a career in.'

But she was a fast learner and, between 2017 and 2019, Joanna helped an all-conquering Bullants side win three consecutive premierships in the Yarra Junior League.

'I found that footy was a family, a connection that was deeper for me than the other sports,' she says. 'All the friends I made then, I still call them close friends and they all came from so many different backgrounds.'

Things got serious in 2019 when Joanna was nominated by her coach to trial for the Oakleigh Chargers, a strong side in the under-18 NAB League.

Still new to the sport, she had low expectations for the trial but was invited along to pre-season training. 'From there, I thought to myself, "This is actually pretty cool",' Joanna remembers.

'We started doing gym and I hadn't even come close to a gym. So, I had to learn the basics including how to move your body in the right position – it was an eye opener!'

While Joanna was adjusting to the demands of semi-professional football, in 2019 the AFLW was in its third season.

Two clubs, North Melbourne and Geelong had joined the party, increasing the number of teams to 10 and resulting in the competition being split into two five-team conferences for the first time, a source of season-long angst for fans who felt one group was much stronger than the other.

This new generation of players was enjoying the benefits of what journalist Kate O'Halloran described in an ABC story as: 'uninterrupted pathways to elite football for the first time.'

Beneath the AFLW, the VFLW was thriving in its role as a developer of talent, with 13 teams participating, a mix of old VFL Clubs and AFLW feeder teams, which were fed in turn from talent produced by the NAB under-18s clubs.

Girls' grassroots participation was on the rise and the next generation of female footballers would experience less obstacles in their journey from Auskick to elite football.

Those that made it to an AFLW team played in front of impressive crowds and to a growing and increasingly diverse and curious television audience.

While the demands of the march to professionalism took an increasing toll on their time, work and bodies, the AFLW player salaries were a constant source of debate and sometimes anger, with the majority of AFLW players earning $13,400 for the first seven-game regular season.

After the three years of operation, the AFLW started to flourish and mirror the core elements of the men's AFL competition that made it the major elite sporting code in Australia.

Media coverage began to increase and fans began to buy into the passion, red-hot rivalries, drama and controversies.

Role models, such as Adelaide's Erin Phillips, Carlton's Darcy Vescio and Melbourne's Daisy Pearce, displayed elite skills that provided inspiration to young girls watching in the stadiums and homes around the nation.

Vescio also led the fight for increased player payments and improved conditions as part of the Collective Bargaining Agreement, calling in legal firm Maurice Blackburn to help improve their deal.

So 2019 was a busy year for the AFLW, a year of change, turbulence and transition but on all metrics it was trending upwards.

Joanna Lin had been an avid fan of the AFLW since the first season in 2017. She followed the Collingwood's women's side and idolised club captain, Stephanie Chiocci.

'I was in awe of her,' Joanna says.

When she was drafted by Collingwood in 2021, the enormity of the occasion only sank in when she realised she would be playing alongside Chiocci and received a welcome phone call from her new captain.

'That was the point when I thought, this is real,' she says.

Among the many people wishing her well were members of the Asian community, from young girls and boys to grandmothers.

'It was so humbling when I had a number of Asian community members contact me saying how excited they were to see me get picked,' she recalls. 'Especially when it's been their dream as well – seeing someone else do it really built them up as well.'

The joy of being drafted was soon tempered when Joanna was made aware of racially insensitive comments aimed at her online. Until then, she had been 'under the radar' for journalists, without much media focus on her Taiwanese background.

'There were some not-so-nice comments online, including one that said that the club shouldn't have picked me because I'll give them COVID,' Lin says.

Collingwood acted swiftly, suspending the offender's membership and organising education programs. 'As it turns out it was a middle-aged woman who clearly didn't know any better,' she says.

The racial discrimination against Chinese-Australians relating to COVID-19 was not restricted to Collingwood fans. According to survey results published in 'Being Chinese in Australia', a Lowy Institute report released in March 2021, nearly one in five Chinese-Australians had been physically threatened or attacked in the previous year because of their Chinese heritage.

According to the report, the cause of the attacks was a mix of blaming China for being the source of the virus, worsening trade relations with Australia, cyber security threats and allegations of political interference.

This cocktail translated to an uncomfortable and at times unsafe environment for Chinese-Australians on the streets of Australia and more broadly for Chinese diaspora communities across the world who were called offensive names, treated differently and at times physically assaulted.

In response to this global phenomenon, on 8 May 2020, United Nations Secretary-General António Guterres spoke on the issue. 'The pandemic continues to unleash a tsunami of hate and xenophobia, scapegoating and scare-mongering,' he warned, and urged governments to 'act now to strengthen the immunity of our societies against the virus of hate.'

Dr Jennifer Hsu, a research fellow at the Lowy Institute and co-author of the report, said the increase in reported racist attacks and discrimination was a threat to multiculturalism's core values of cohesion and tolerance.

The report sadly acknowledged a decreased sense of Australian belonging for Chinese-Australians, with their attackers either ignorant or deliberately refusing to differentiate between ethnicity and nationality.

An Australia that had once proudly trumpeted its intentions to play a central role in the new 'Asian Century' was seemingly in a philosophical retreat to darker times.

For Joanna, it was a matter of moving on and playing footy.

'It didn't faze me too much, because the club took charge of it, dealt with it and supported me through it all while trying to make sure it doesn't happen again,' she says.

Joanna Lin's debut for Collingwood, on Saturday 6 February 2021, came as a shock. She was preparing in the change rooms for a practice match with the reserves when she got a tap on the shoulder from coach Steve Symonds.

At first, she thought she'd done something wrong, before Steve told her to get ready for the main game: 'I knew that a lot of draftees don't get to play in the first year, but I trained hard and pushed myself up for selection. But it was still a big surprise!'

Joanna grabbed her bag and moved to the senior team change rooms, where she was presented with her coveted first senior black-and-white Collingwood jersey and 'a lot of hugs' by her teammates.

Named on the interchange bench, she soon ran onto Victoria Park, the fabled home of Collingwood from 1892 to 1999, and she quickly overcame her nerves to collect four touches.

'My 10-year-old self would be jumping around the place,' she told media after her debut, barely able to contain her excitement. 'Actually, I'm jumping all over the place right now!'

Lin so impressed the Collingwood selectors in the midfield with her work rate, stamina, strength and decision-making skills that she went on to play nine out of 11 games that season, scoring her first goal less than a fortnight after her debut.

She attributes her elevation and consistency to her teammates, who she grew close to during a COVID-19-affected season that forced the players to spend time together in isolated 'bubbles' to restrict the spread of the virus.

Through the joint struggle of separation from friends and family – and the need to maintain part-time jobs – the team became a support unit.

'There were no fights in the bubble,' she recalls. 'I don't know how, but all our personalities mixed together regardless of if you were an introvert or extrovert. It was weirdly unsaid, but we knew when each other needed alone time or when we wanted to get up and about. We could all relate to each other in some sort of way.'

With momentum on her side for her second season, Joanna suffered a shoulder dislocation in pre-season training. She agonised on whether to 'patch it up' and play on or undergo shoulder surgery, which would put her out for a year but provide her with greater career longevity. In the end, she opted to go under the knife.

The season on the sidelines gave her new perspective on her football career and she learned to enjoy the moment. 'Because you never know how long it's going to last,' she says. 'It's tough when it gets taken away from you.'

ı | | ı

As one of nine known AFLW players with Asian heritage to have played since 2017, Joanna has done her best to honour her Taiwanese roots. Every Lunar New Year, she brings Chinese snacks for her teammates, who appreciate the cultural exchange.

'It's been a good thing for me to learn about her background and she has really embraced it within the club,' says Collingwood teammate Lauren Butler, who in turn took Lin to her family farm in regional Victoria.

Before COVID-19 stopped international travel, Lin would visit Taiwan every second year to reconnect with her relatives. They would spend time at her mother's village in Jiayi county with her paternal grandmother, Suh Thyy Hour.

'I can understand Mandarin completely,' Lin says. 'It's just a lot harder to speak it back at the level of my Taiwanese relatives. You get the stares because somehow they can tell, no matter what I'm wearing, that I'm not from there.'

In Australia, though, as a born-and-bred Aussie, football has been a key pillar of her life. 'I found my tribe with footy,' she explains.

'I've always been accepted, and no one ever thinks of me differently.'

CHAPTER 23

Auskick and the Next Generation Academy: Connor Downie's Journey to the AFL

When Connor Downie received an email invitation to join Hawthorn's Next Generation Academy, his parents realised for the first time that their 15-year-old son's football career was beyond a 'hobby'.

Connor had always loved the game and had been one of the better players at his junior Forest Hill Football Club. His parents also trusted his junior coach, Brian Rafton, who had been responsible for the Hawthorn invitation.

The Hawthorn Next Generation Academy was part of a joint program between the AFL and the Hawthorn Football Club that was piloted in 2016. It was designed to provide culturally specialised pathways to nurture multicultural players (Asian and African communities) who may not have had the same opportunity or grounding in the fundamentals of the game.

If the AFL was to increase the diversity of its player base through growth in under-represented communities, the Next Generation Academy program was their flagship initiative to achieve that aim.

The academy was a bridge for players from non-traditional football families to be exposed to an elite program with top-level coaches who would assist in their skill development, mental health, nutrition, healthy lifestyle and retention in the sport.

Each AFL club was given designated regions to run their academy programs at first-class AFL facilities and Hawthorn's areas were Gippsland in eastern Victoria, Katherine in the Northern Territory and Melbourne's Eastern Ranges zone, which included Connor's club, the Forest Hill Zebras.

In return for their efforts and investment, clubs such as Hawthorn would receive draft priority for any player that emerged from their program.

Connor Downie qualified for the academy by virtue of his Chinese heritage from his mother, Tracy.

Waiting for Connor at Waverley Park on the first day of the academy was program manager, Nathan Foley. Foley was the missing link – the supportive football mentor that some previous Asian-background young players had lacked in their football career development.

Foley had played 154 games for Richmond over an 11-year career and retired in 2015; he was appointed by the Hawks Next Generation Academy the following year.

When a young Connor Downie first appeared, Foley recalls a young player who was on another level: 'He's always been a star from day one,' says Foley. 'He was dedicated, respectful and polite, and he loves football.'

Foley's role as mentor covered any issues on and off the field, one-on-one training sessions and organising opportunities for Connor to train with the Hawthorn senior team.

In addition to building confidence in players from under-represented communities, Foley says that he wants to give them the best chance possible to be drafted.

'But it's very hard to get drafted and it's only through dedicated programs that we will see an increase in Asian and African heritage players on the television and on the MCG,' he says.

The success of the program depends on building trust with parents, and Nathan went to meet Graham and Tracy Downie to explain the program. Once they understood it, they fully supported Connor's commitment.

In addition to rising through the junior ranks, Connor stayed under Foley's tutelage until he was selected by Hawthorn in the 2020 AFL Draft, the Hawks Next Generation Academy program's second AFL success following South Sudanese heritage player, Changkuoth 'CJ' Jiath, who made his debut for the Hawks in 2018.

The experience culminated in Connor training with the Hawthorn senior team a number of times, which had a deep impact on a young player.

'It gave me a taste of AFL football,' Connor recalls. 'And Nathan prepared me for what it would take to play at the highest level.'

Connor Downie was born in East Melbourne in 2002 and he was followed by a younger sister, Mira.

His mother Li Xia (Tracy) Lin came to Australia from Xiamen in China at the age of 24, enrolling in a short English course in a language school.

She had been working as an English teacher for six years in China prior to her arrival but with her qualifications not recognised in Australia, she worked in a clothing factory and went to English language classes at night.

Studying part time, it took five-and-a-half years for Tracy to finish a Bachelor of Arts degree. Then, after completing a one-year Diploma of Education, she finally became a high school teacher in 1999, 10 years after her arrival in Australia.

Tracy met her Anglo-Australian husband, Graham, also a teacher, through a friend.

Tracy had no idea that Australian Rules football existed before her arrival and Graham wasn't really a fan of the game, preferring the company of his wife and reading books, the combination making the Downies a 'non-traditional' football family.

'My parents didn't put too much pressure or expectation on me,' Connor recalls of his upbringing. 'They're just proud and enjoy watching me play, which is good.'

Connor was given consistent exposure to his Chinese heritage and has visited his mother's hometown in China twice, first at age four and then when he was 13.

On his first trip, Connor met his Chinese grandfather, Minzeng Lin, and remembers a cheeky and fit character who used every opportunity to exercise, even when waiting for the bus.

In Melbourne, Tracy ensured that Connor maintained his Chinese connection by speaking to him in Mandarin when he was young and later enrolling him at a local Chinese language school.

Connor would rise at 7 am on Sunday to catch the bus to language school, a tedious experience for a young man who dreamed only of footy.

'I really didn't enjoy it,' Connor recalls.

'But now I'm really grateful because I can speak decent Chinese and hold a conversation and that's a skill I'm proud of.'

Regarding his academic studies, Connor says his mother was 'very traditionally Chinese'.

'She was big on discipline and would say to me that perseverance and patience are essential to achieve good things.'

'A lot of the habits I have now were instilled by my mum.'

While Connor's father, Graham, describes his sporting career as 'inglorious', his passion for reading books and history also rubbed off on Connor, triggering a lifelong love of reading, which helped him embrace the workloads for his high school studies.

For Tracy, the academic side always came before football but, over time, she became aware of the larger importance of Connor's role in the game.

Tracy now understands the significance of her son's position as a cultural pioneer, telling afl.com.au: 'I think definitely there is an opportunity for him to share his experience with Chinese people, so that a lot more Chinese will be able to play football as well.'

Connor's family represented the market the AFL needed to engage to grow beyond its cultural and geographic borders. His parents had no background or real interest in the game yet were willing to support their child on his grand adventure.

'A lot of Chinese people perceive football as a very physical and dangerous game and we originally thought it was just a hobby, but it was so much more,' says Graham.

For a father with little interest in the sport, Graham had a pivotal role in Connor's football development, including being the catalyst for the 'first moment'.

'We were in Federation Square close to grand final time and there was an AFL stall selling small footballs,' Graham remembers.

'So we bought him one and went to the Botanical Gardens where we played kick-to-kick.'

The mini-football sessions with his father continued in Alexandra Gardens in Kew where they would play kick-to-kick for hours.

'For a non-football father, I give him a lot of credit,' Connor says.

Connor's mini footy went with him to kindergarten and friendships were forged in the playground kicking the footy.

His new friends 'all loved their footy and Collingwood', so he started following the Magpies and then followed them to their local Auskick program at the Forest Hill Zebras.

Auskick is the premier entry-level program in Australian sport, a juggernaut with over 4000 centres scattered across the nation, run by AFL staff and an army of parent volunteers, teaching and promoting the game with religious zeal.

An extension of the original Vickick program, Auskick is aimed at providing a friendly and non-competitive environment to teach kids the unique skills required to play the game.

The skill development for kids wishing to play Australian Rules football was once the domain of schools but, as the game evolved, they could not reliably provide this service and the state bodies of the game intervened.

The program's pioneer, former Richmond player Ray Allsopp, added the element of fun and enjoyment to the skills development and launched Vickick in 1985, the initiative going national a decade later with the launch of 'Auskick', a program of clinics aimed at engaging with kids of all abilities and skill levels.

Auskick went to the next level in 2007 with National Australia Bank coming on as a major sponsor, high-profile celebrity ambassadors such as ex-Hawthorn legend Robert DiPierdomenico being appointed and a new campaign slogan launched: 'Where Champions Begin'.

Auskick became crucial in developing the game in 'non-footy' multicultural communities and the rugby league states of New South Wales and Queensland, where it was used to convert kids with intergenerational links to other codes.

With Auskick centres in place across the nation, junior football clubs had the perfect partner to feed kids into their junior teams with fundamentals of the game already in place.

When Connor graduated from Auskick, one fundamental that he brought across to the Forest Hill Zebras Football Club under-9s was a big left boot.

The kick-to-kick sessions with his father and schoolmates, combined with formal training under Auskick, had produced a coveted junior football asset.

Connor's size and good kicking skills were recognised early and, after a few games, he was moved up to playing against much bigger boys in the under-11s where coach Brian Rafton played him at fullback and gave him the responsibility of 'kick outs'.

He responded to the challenge by mastering the art of 'torps' – long, spiralling torpedo kicks that he would deploy to get the ball out of the Forest Hill danger zone and thrill the watching parents and coaches.

For Connor, kicking long was fun and all about timing. 'I'm not the strongest or most powerful player,' Connor says, 'but my timing allows me to find the sweet spot and get good penetration.'

He struggled for a while playing above his age but, by 14, his body grew and he developed new self-confidence – a key ingredient he previously lacked.

'I started to find my feet and thought "I'm a pretty handy player",' he remembers.

Although he was a relatively shy and reserved kid, Connor had plenty of people who believed in him.

His Year 8 physical education teacher, Jo Lane, thought Connor had something special and called an Eastern District Football League representative who attended one of his matches.

Connor recalls not being nervous and playing well: 'I didn't know what was at stake because I hadn't really known about rep teams or even know they existed really.'

His impressive performances led to selection in the Eastern Football League under-15s representative team to play in an inter-league carnival and, such was his form, he was awarded the best player trophy.

Connor was now in the mix with serious players and his performance in that tournament propelled his career forward with real momentum.

Looking back, he sees Jo Lane's 'guardian angel' intervention in reaching out to the league as crucial and sometimes wonders what would have happened if she hadn't.

'I'm very grateful for what she has done for me and she still checks up on how I am going,' he says.

After six seasons with Forest Hill, Connor switched to Vermont Football Club in 2017. He played there for his final three years of youth football and his good form earned him selection in the Eastern Ranges' under-16 team, the representative team of the Eastern District Football League.

His form continued for Eastern Ranges and Connor was rewarded with selection in the under-16 Victoria Metro team and remembers pulling on the famous Victorian navy blue 'big V' guernsey for the first time as a 'really eye-opening experience'.

But despite his representative achievements he still suffered from 'imposter syndrome'. 'You hear about these good players and I didn't really see myself as one of those,' Connor says.

Buoyed by his representative success, Connor committed to a brutal pre-season with his Vic Metro under-16s midfield coach, Anthony 'Ant' Phillips, who drilled him in skill work repetitions.

The following season he again played strongly for Eastern Ranges, resulting in selection for the Australian under-17 team to play against the New Zealand men's national team.

Connor's elevation to wearing the green and gold of his country had been stunning and he knew the source of his success: 'Things were happening because I was more sharp and more well-rounded and, importantly, I didn't make as many mistakes,' he says.

'All of that credit goes to Ant.'

In his late teens, Connor had developed into an impressive physical specimen with strong thighs enabling him to roost the ball 60 metres, wowing his teammates with the sweet timing of his kicking.

His under-18s Eastern Ranges coach, Darren Bewick, built on his skill foundation and showed considerable belief in him, giving him the freedom to roam: 'He just let me play my footy and use my strength – he really got the best out of me,' Connor said.

In an interview with the Eastern Districts Football League website, Bewick spoke glowingly of Connor's dedication, diligence and love of the game.

'More importantly he's a ripping kid – he's very humble and down to earth,' Bewick said.

Connor's form was rewarded with selection in the Victorian Metro under-18s team – a representative honour, which, combined with his great year in the NAB Cup, helped solidify his reputation ahead of the AFL Draft.

Connor's impressive 2019 season for Eastern Ranges saw him average 16.4 disposals and 3.8 inside-50s per game across his 14 appearances.

Bewick was so impressed with his development and temperament that, for the 2020 season, he gave Connor the honour and extra responsibility of captaining the Eastern Ranges' under-18s team playing in the NAB League – the statewide competition watched by every recruiter in the AFL.

Sadly, his hard-earned captaincy role did not eventuate, as the 2020 season was cancelled due to COVID-19.

Although he was disappointed at his 'lost season' and forced to train alone in the COVID-19 bubble, Connor felt he had done every-thing he could to entice the Hawthorn recruiters to believe in him.

The build-up to the AFL Draft can be the most harrowing period of a young player's life. The draft itself is a televised national event scrutinised by an army of journalists, pundits, player agents and expectant fans.

Most AFL players come through the draft system, from young rookies still in school to mature-age late bloomers. Their form is forensically examined and the chosen ones make a trip to the Australian Institute of Sport in Canberra to participate in the 'Combine', a suite of physical, mental and psychological tests.

Those with more than five expressions of interest from AFL clubs are invited to the Draft Camp for further intensive development and scrutiny.

After the Draft Camp, AFL club recruiters then monitor the players' local club and representative seasons.

But, for the first time, AFL clubs were denied the opportunity of watching their prospects when COVID-19 forced the cancellation of the 2020 grassroots season.

ı | | ı

In the 2020 AFL Draft, Connor Downie, a line-breaking midfielder with a long mullet and a big left foot kick, was selected by Hawthorn as draft pick No. 35 out of a total of 83 total selections.

'It was just a relief, and all the emotions hit me then. I just had a massive smile on my face,' Downie recalls. 'Most kids would say that getting drafted is their childhood dream, and I can definitely speak as one of those kids.'

In the weeks before and after the draft, 20-year-old Downie received an unusual amount of scrutiny including one headline on an AFL website story that read: 'Could a Next Gen Hawk become the AFL's answer to Yao Ming?'

'My Chinese heritage became a main story,' Connor says.

A key component of the Chinese story was that Connor was the first player to be drafted with direct mainland Chinese heritage (although his role model, the Western Bulldogs Lin Jong, had a combined East Timorese-Chinese and Taiwanese background).

Connor remembers seeing Lin Jong play and thinking it was unusual to see an Asian playing football, let alone playing in the AFL.

'Lin was a trailblazer and he certainly gave me inspiration to get to the highest level!' he says.

Beyond his pioneer role, Connor had great admiration for Lin's dogged football journey: 'I have a lot of respect for him coming back to play, especially after the injury run he had.'

Surprisingly they have only met once, during Connor's first year at Hawthorn when he played on Lin for a full practice match against the Western Bulldogs.

'I didn't formally meet him,' Connor recalls. 'I just said hello and shook his hand after the game.'

ı | | ı

For the opening round of the 2021 season, Connor Downie had one of the more unique AFL debuts in the game's 145-year history.

He was named as a medical substitute for Hawthorn's match against Essendon at Marvel Stadium, which means it was his official debut, but he never actually ran onto the field.

Connor's strange situation put him at the centre of controversy with many commentators expressing sympathy that his debut was marked in the record books, yet he didn't take the field.

'I didn't listen to any of that,' says Connor who viewed the experience through a positive lens.

'It was a great experience being part of an amazing group of guys that I had trained with for a long time.'

In Round 22 of the 2021 season he finally made his on-field debut, helping Hawthorn defeat the Western Bulldogs in Launceston.

Connor Downie had achieved his dream of playing an AFL game and finished with 12 disposals and two marks – a solid debut.

He says of his first game: 'I felt pretty comfortable and confident at a level that nothing really took me by surprise.'

'I guess I just embraced the occasion and really enjoyed it.'

His 2022 season was marred by injuries and he was delisted by the Hawks at the end of the season, a reminder of the sometimes cold and ruthless side of professional sport.

On the Hawks website, Connor's fledgling career was summarised as follows: 'Making his debut in 2021, Downie showed his ability as a smooth-moving outside midfielder with a raking left foot.

'Downie has been unable to break into the senior side after battling several injury setbacks, and unfortunately mid-way through 2022 he was ruled out with a further hamstring injury.'

Connor has no regrets and, in 2023, embarked on a fresh journey after signing with the North Melbourne Kangaroos VFL club.

He remains optimistic: 'I'll work my way back (to the AFL) through that avenue.'

Despite the setback, Connor's journey proved that AFL players could be produced from non-traditional football families through a combination of luck, open-minded parents, hard work and a series of mentors and specialised pathway programs like the Hawks Next Generation Academy.

For Connor's mother, Tracy, her son's journey has been one of mutual learning: 'My knowledge of football is a work in progress.'

'So, I have a lot to learn from Connor. In the meantime, Connor still has to continue with learning Chinese as well.'

Connor's Chinese heritage hasn't caused him any issues and besides a few 'throwaway lines' when he was playing in the juniors, racism hasn't been a factor.

And he has unfinished business as a role model for the Asian community: 'I'm really proud of my Chinese heritage and would love to use it to grow the game … and hopefully encourage more Chinese people to play footy.'

CHAPTER 24

Darcy Vescio: Carlton's Cantonese-Calabrian All Star

In late December 2021, less than a fortnight out from the new AFLW season, Carlton forward Darcy Vescio posted a note on social media. 'Just popping in to let you know that I am non-binary,' Vescio wrote of their newly announced gender identity, now classified as neither exclusively female or male.

'Sharing this feels a bit daunting but brings me a lot of warmth and happiness. I am most comfortable with they/them pronouns and will always respond to Darcy unless in trouble.'

At the time, the 28-year-old was the league's all-time leading goal-kicker and a two-time All-Australian player. Having spent all six AFLW seasons at Carlton, one of Australia's most popular football clubs, Darcy was a genuine marquee player – one of the few AFLW stars who might be considered a household name.

While Darcy wasn't the first AFLW player to reveal a non-binary identity, they were perhaps the most well-known to publicly state that they did not identify as either male or female.

'AFLW star Vescio changes the game on gender diversity,' ran *The Age* headline in the days that followed.

Two years later, Vescio was the only footy player to feature in the *Weekend Australian*'s 'Pride List', alongside television celebrities, actors, comedians and politicians.

One of Darcy's key supporters was Carlton coach Daniel Harford who earlier that year had elevated his star forward to co-vice-captain. Harford, an ex-AFL footballer in his mid-40s, admitted to the *Herald-Sun* that 'he didn't know too much about' non-binary people before Vescio.

'One of the things I've learnt during my time in women's footy over the past five years is that there are a lot of different parts of life that I wasn't aware of,' he said, adding that Vescio 'explained what the situation was and how they had come to rest (settle) on their identity.'

In many ways, Darcy – a child of an Italian-Australian father and a Chinese-Australian mother – was already accustomed to navigating multiple identities. Darcy had, for most of their life, been smashing stereotypes and acting as an emissary between footy's past and its future.

Not that Darcy had planned on it being that way, of course. To them, they were just like any other footy-mad country Victorian. In the 2018 documentary, *Bloodlines*, Vescio spoke about playing junior footy in boys' teams.

'Looking back, I remember maybe pre-game or post-game, that's when the biggest difference was, when I had to get changed elsewhere,' Darcy said.

'Whereas on the field, we're all just playing footy, so there's no differences or divides there.'

In 1982, a school teacher named Christine Louey walked into a pub in Wangaratta and met a barman by the name of Paul Vescio.

According to Darcy, they hit it off immediately and became a couple. Both were born to migrant parents who came to Australia after World War II, with Christine's Cantonese family hailing from Toishan, in Guangzhou in China, and Paul's from Calabria in southern Italy.

Together, they had three children: Zeb, Darcy and Louis. 'Myself and my two brothers often ask each other, how did Mum and Dad connect?' recalls Darcy.

The Vescios lived on a farm in Markwood, a small town located close to Wangaratta, 200 kilometres north-east of Melbourne. Christine and Paul ran cattle, while Paul's Italian parents up the road grew tobacco.

'I remember the smell of drying tobacco plants, collecting eggs and, once a year, salami making,' Darcy recalls. 'Nonna and Nonno didn't have great English, so it wasn't lots of conversation, but there was lots of love.'

Like most regional towns, the common language was football. The Vescio kids would play kick-to-kick for hours in the backyard and junior footy in the country leagues – first for the Whorouly Lions and then the Myrtleford Alpine Saints Football Netball Club in the Wangaratta and District Football League (WDFL).

'Footy was the heartbeat of the town. It was our way in for credibility,' Darcy explains.

'Dad is a big footy-head: he loves it and he taught me so much about the game. He knew that it was key to building friendships. There's a level of respect that comes from being able to play their game so, by playing it, we create a shared game.'

Although Darcy would eventually become a loyal Myrtleford player, their original allegiances lay with the neighbouring Whorouly

Lions where they played their Auskick and juniors, and were comfortable playing with the boys.

'They felt like my people although we always got belted and hardly won a game the two seasons I was there,' Darcy recalls.

Due to a shortage of players in Whorouly in 2007, Whorouly and Myrtleford decided to merge clubs to form two teams and Darcy was selected for the Myrtleford 'A' team, in a new club 15 minutes' drive down the road.

With a fresh set of teammates, Darcy had to prove they weren't a novelty and earn their respect – which they achieved immediately by kicking seven goals in their first game.

Darcy Vescio's footy dream came to an abrupt halt in 2007 after helping the Myrtleford Saints win the under-14 grand final.

In the documentary *Bloodlines*, Vescio's junior coach, Cesare Rizzi, recalled the bittersweet moment. 'I still remember when we won the under-14s grand final and I looked over and you were crying ... and I said "Darc, what's the matter?".'

At the time, Darcy was the only girl on the field and, under AFL Victoria rules, girls were to be excluded from playing in mixed gender teams past the age of 14, as part of the organisation's duty of care.

As there were no girls teams for Darcy to join, that grand final ended up being both their first premiership and their final game of junior competitive football.

'When I was forced to stop playing footy, I honestly didn't think I would play again,' Darcy recalls. 'It was over.'

Although Darcy knew that their promising footy career was coming to a halt, they needed help adjusting to a future without footy: 'Mum and Dad spoke to me regularly and did their best to prepare me for the gaping hole that footy would leave.'

When the following season began and Darcy wasn't part of Myrtleford's under-16 team, they felt indifferent rather than sad.

'That was the career of a gal living in "Wang",' Darcy says. 'You played with the boys till you were 14 and they went on happily and you hung your boots up and played netball, which I did.'

It wasn't something Darcy thought they could question as they genuinely believed they would never play competitively again and recalls a cold lack of options: 'I didn't know that an alternative world could exist.'

During school holidays, Darcy would travel to Melbourne to visit their Chinese grandfather, Cheong Lip Louey, who they called 'Goong Goong' or just 'Goong'.

At the end of high school, Darcy enrolled in a Bachelor of Communication Design at RMIT in 2012 and moved in to Goong's home in Melbourne's eastern suburbs.

'It was like a window to another world and helped me understand my mother better,' Darcy recalls.

Cheong Lip Louey grew up poor in Toishan, Guangzhou, living with his family in a one-room house with no running water. After World War II, he migrated to Hong Kong to work as an apprentice tailor and then to Melbourne, where he met and married a Chinese-Australian woman, Annette.

Together they started a fruit and vegetable store at the Queen Victoria Market where they served the community for decades.

Annette died before Darcy was born, so by the time Darcy moved in with Goong as a young adult, it was just the two of them in his Lower Templestowe home.

During their time together, Darcy developed a taste for Chinese cuisine – particularly bitter melon, pork baos, salty plums and fish balls.

'I always felt so lucky to live with my Goong and to have that day-to-day connection with him,' Darcy says. 'I was a bit of a messy student and he was so patient with me.'

As Darcy settled in to their new Melbourne life, they received a message from a friend from Wangaratta about the Darebin Falcons – Melbourne's sole 'women's only' senior football club, which had its own ground.

Curious, their dad made some calls and, two weeks before the 2018 season, Darcy decided to buy a mouthguard, dig up some old boots and check the Falcons out.

Darcy's new field of dreams was the AH Capp Reserve tucked away in West Preston, in the northern suburbs of Melbourne, an unlikely ground zero for a revolution.

It was a rough old ground and a local council blind spot but it was metaphorically appropriate for the struggle of women's Australian Rules football.

'It's tiny and mainly used for dog walking,' says Darcy who trained there with the Darebin Falcons for five years.

'But it was ours and it was sacred ground.'

Darcy's life changed forever when their car first pulled up at the nondescript ground and walked down the hill to find a tribe of like-minded women training to play footy.

'When I first walked onto that field, it was like another planet, a world I hadn't known existed,' Darcy recalls.

'Women all around me marking and drop kicking, so skilful – it wasn't just me that loved the game and I knew right then that someday this was going to be special.'

Darcy remembers a stoic, club-wide attitude of gratitude and not complaining about their grim facilities: 'I can't tell you how many times I rolled my ankle on dog holes,' Darcy says with a smile.

'If the Creek flooded there would be rubbish on the oval and you'd spend the morning before games picking up dog poo from the ground, but we loved it.'

After a practice match and the first couple of training sessions, Darcy was hooked again: 'I was raw and could not follow any structures, but I was playing footy again.'

It was a family affair, with Goong supporting Darcy at home and Mum and Dad helping where they could.

Darcy has a memory of looking up at training and seeing mother, Chris, waving a cheque in the air to confirm registration fees had been covered: 'Mum was just making sure I had the finances in order and I still have one friend who remembers Mum rocking up holding a cheque.'

While the memory still brings a smile, the symbolism of that moment was deep.

'Looking back I feel like she always played that role of removing barriers. She was always there, as long as we're happy, she's happy – as long as you're not injured!'

Back at home with Goong, Darcy struggled to explain their reignited passion for playing football: 'He was a soccer man but nevertheless he'd wish me well when I'd dart out the door when my teammates came to pick me up for training.'

Later when Darcy signed with Carlton, Goong was delighted and took their footballing endeavours more seriously – he was already a Carlton fan and understood the importance and history of 'The Blues'.

Darcy's debut for the Darebin Falcons was in a borrowed jersey and came with a shock: 'There were no sponsors, of course, but it was the first time I had seen the VWFL logo and realised I was playing in the top league.'

Darcy went on to win four consecutive premierships with the Darebin Falcons and showcased enough potential and talent to convince Carlton to make their move in the AFLW Draft in 2016.

On reflection, Darcy feels a debt to the Darebin Falcons for their personal development on and off the field: 'We weren't affiliated with a men's club so we had control over everything we wanted to stand for as a club, from no pokies to all decision-making.

'It gave me an idea of the possibilities and I am really proud to be a Falcon.'

In the off season between the Darebin Falcons' 2014 and 2015 seasons, Darcy's passion for football began to wane. The elation of winning a couple of premierships and the sense of community was life-changing but the commercial reality of making a living began to intrude.

It was time to get serious, having worked through a succession of jobs while playing for Darebin, including working in a data entry job at Glencore Grain, a bakery, and a furniture store before securing a part-time job at Carlton FC as a graphic designer.

Darcy's chosen career of graphic design was time-intensive and they began to feel the time invested in the Darebin Falcons was impacting both their income and career progression.

Seeking inspiration, Darcy caught up with Falcons teammate, friend and future AFLW legend Daisy Pearce, a country girl who had faced the same junior football gender barrier as Darcy while growing up in Bright, 320 kilometres north-east of Melbourne.

Daisy was working with the AFL and raised the prospect of Darcy becoming a Multicultural Ambassador and role model for the AFL's Multicultural Program.

Darcy recalls initially being 'perplexed' in response to Daisy's offer: 'But Daise! I'm not multicultural.'

Despite an Italian and Chinese–infused upbringing, Darcy had never felt at home with the label 'multicultural' and considered their family to be the norm. But they also understood that the game didn't reflect wider society in its player base.

'This moment kept me in footy,' Darcy explains.

'All of a sudden I had the opportunity to be more than a footballer and could connect with communities that didn't see themselves in the game.'

Darcy's new role as an AFL Multicultural Ambassador piqued their interest in their cultural identity and, in 2017, Darcy travelled to Conflenti in southern Italy and Hong Kong to reconnect for the Carlton-produced documentary *Bloodlines*.

For the Hong Kong leg, Darcy accompanied their mother, Christine, to retrace the final part of Goong's journey before he landed in Australia. They had wanted to go deeper into mainland China to his ancestral village in Toishan but securing visas and permission to film were too difficult.

Christine and Darcy walked around the streets of Hong Kong, visiting key areas including the site of the tailor shop where Goong served as an apprentice tailor, and meeting historians who provided insights into life under Japanese occupation in World War II.

The trip gave Darcy a new appreciation of Christine. 'She grew up in Melbourne her whole life in the Chinese community there, and ended up in Wangaratta,' Darcy says. 'Travelling with her in Hong Kong gave me a glimpse of her different worlds, and why she is so optimistic.'

They also gained a better understanding of Goong's escape from Hong Kong.

But their abiding memory of Goong, who passed away in 2018, is of him sitting in his 'special spot' on the first floor balcony of his house in Lower Templestowe, basking in the sun and people-watching.

'The fact he chose the path of sacrifice, getting on a tiny, packed boat that took a month to come to Australia with all that seasickness and then he set up our life – that makes me feel both humble and proud,' Darcy explains.

'No wonder he didn't get emotional about things; he'd already seen it all.'

On Friday 3 February 2017, 24,568 fans packed into a sold-out Princes Park to witness the newest edition of footy's most bitter rivalry – Carlton versus Collingwood in the historic first match of the Australian Football League Women's (AFLW) competition.

The eight-team league had been assembled at breakneck speed having been announced only 233 days previously, in June 2016.

The AFLW's inaugural game had originally been scheduled for the 5000-capacity Olympic Park, but such was the interest that the AFL was forced to shift the match to the much larger Princes Park.

'None of us had played a proper night game before,' recalls Darcy, who wore No. 3 on their back and their hair tied in a warrior-style topknot.

As the players of both teams lined up in the players tunnel before kick-off, Darcy recalls looking down at team mascot Olivia Brown – the seven-year-old daughter of AFL legend Jonathan Brown – and realised the magnitude of the moment.

'I'm looking down at a young girl that could have been me,' Darcy explains.

'And she is looking back at me, equally proud, because we've never been able to have this tradition with someone she can identify with so strongly.'

That game announced the beginning of the AFLW, with Darcy Vescio the instant star with a four-goal haul.

Darcy's best-on-ground performance helped Carlton to a 35-point victory. 'I was in a really good euphoric state and the crowd was reacting.'

'After I kicked a couple of goals, I was just floating in the electric atmosphere – the crowd was going nuts.'

That season, despite Carlton finishing mid-table, Darcy Vescio was the league's leading goal-kicker with 14 goals. In the league's first six seasons, Darcy was Carlton's leading goal-kicker three times, best and fairest once, and twice selected in the All-Australian side.

Darcy had become one of the league's most marketable athletes.

'Before AFLW when I went out to schools, I'd have to convince the kids I was a footballer,' Darcy says. 'Not any more!'

From their early junior days as a Whorouly Lion, Darcy was a prolific goal-kicker. After completion of the first five AFLW seasons, Darcy had kicked 44 goals to be the leading all-time goal-kicker in the competition.

In the lead-up to season six in 2022, there was speculation on how long it would take Darcy to become the first player in AFLW history to reach the 50-goal milestone.

Darcy was not keen to talk about the milestone and says: 'I'd shrug and say "maybe" when they asked. Goals are elusive, if you chase them, they run away.'

Jonathan Healy wrote glowingly on womens.afl of Darcy's growth and achievements in 2021: 'the veteran Carlton forward seems to be getting better with age based on [their] efforts this year.'

For the first six matches of the AFLW 2022 season, Darcy managed only two goals but kicked another two in Round 7 against Fremantle to bring their season goal tally to four.

Darcy needed a further two goals to reach the half-century when Carlton travelled up to Canberra to play the GWS Giants at Manuka Oval in Round 8.

Waiting for Darcy was GWS nemesis Pepa Randall, a very physical opponent who had given Darcy trouble in previous matches.

And, sure enough, Randall made Darcy earn every kick, at one stage knocking them to the ground in a late tackle – which Darcy felt was somehow fitting and emblematic of their sometimes rocky journey.

But the Blues' vice-captain was awarded a free kick, got up off the ground, dusted off the dirt and grass and strolled 50 metres up the ground to kick their second goal of the match.

Darcy Vescio, a Chinese-Italian Aussie from Wangaratta, who was once told they would never play Australian Rules football again, was etched into the records as the first AFLW player to reach 50 goals.

AFTERWORD

In my quest to document Chinese-Australian footy stories, I crisscrossed Australia and made visits to Darwin, Broome, Brisbane, Perth, Derby, Braidwood, Ballarat, Bendigo, St Arnaud, Minyip, Wedderburn, Dunolly, Maryborough, Hillside, Melton, Albury, Sydney, Melbourne, Beechworth, Geelong, Woodend, Macedon, Echuca, Mooroopna, Dunolly, Inglewood and Chiltern.

Along the way, I met some fascinating characters, learnt about others and heard a plethora of extraordinary stories.

There was Owen Ah Chee, who set up the bakery in Derby, Western Australia, in 1885, and whose descendants Brendon and Callum made it to the big-time, playing 163 games (and counting) between them in the AFL.

Then came Les Kew Ming, the 'fighting footballer' from Minyip, who was once considered the longest kick in the land. In the early 1900s, at the height of the White Australia policy, he overcame hardship on the World War I battlefield in France and Belgium, and discrimination on the football field in country Victoria, to become a warrior of both worlds.

More recently, the Fong brothers, Les and Neale, had incredible success at all levels of the game in Western Australia, as players and administrators. On the other side of the country, Lin Jong, who was a basketballer until his mid-teens, showed extraordinary courage to come back from multiple injuries to play for 10 years with the Western Bulldogs, and become a life member of the AFL club.

On the last stop on my journey, I was told about the inimitable Roy Poy who, in addition to playing 50 senior games with Albury, was a clerk with Murray River Electricity, a publican, taxi owner, cricketer, golfer, bookmaker and veteran who proudly served his country in the Vietnam War.

Roy's cousin, Lindsay Poy, is alive and well, and has fond memories of playing football for North Albury and Macquarie University in Sydney. He is proud of his Chinese heritage, sports a 'Chinese tattoo' and – like many of his Chinese-Australian brethren – remembers racial taunts when he was playing.

He stresses that most of the exchanges since he retired from football have been good natured. 'My mates call me Chinese Chicken Legs,' says Lindsay. 'Or ABC (Australian Born Chinese) or "8 per cent" because my Ancestry.com DNA test says I am 8% Chinese.'

I was fascinated to learn the stories of the all-Chinese 'Celestial' Victorian Goldfields matches in the 1890s to raise money for local charities; Melbourne's Young Chinese League team; Aboriginal-Chinese co-operation in the Darwin Buffaloes club; and the Golden Point Rice Eaters – yes, the club's official name – who kept the memory of Ballarat's old Chinatown alive for almost 100 years.

There were significant Chinese-Australian football families that spanned multiple generations – the Koochews, Wongs and Wunhyms, all proud of their legacy and continuing it with pride.

I was thrilled to witness the tradition expand and continue into the modern era through elite women's Chinese-heritage footballers such as Darcy Vescio, Sophie Li, Rebecca Beeson and Joanna Lin.

Football, in so many cases, has proved the catalyst for assimilation and acceptance into the community – notwithstanding the sadly inevitable racist flare-ups. The Macedon townsfolk rallied behind Wally Koochew when he was racially abused on the field; Billy Wong found his tribe of mates with the Mooroopna Cats; for Les Kew Ming, football was his passport to acceptance in Minyip; and Sarah Loh's childhood love for footy, and St Kilda, helped her land a dream job in the sport.

It was an honour to stitch together the lives of this group of individuals to illuminate a hidden chapter in the annals of Australian sport.

The list of players is by no means exhaustive – and to the many Chinese-Australian footballers who were not included in the book, there will be another time and place for your stories.

I should acknowledge and give a special salute here to the coaches, teammates and fans who helped give the Chinese-Australian footballers a sense of belonging and inclusion through the connective tissue of the great Australian game.

These stories provide a rich historical context for modern multicultural Australia and proof that if a love of Aussie Rules is a key marker of Australian identity, then the footy-loving Chinese-Australians have earned their stripes over 140 years as true blue members of the community.

ACKNOWLEDGEMENTS

The journey to write this book started in 2015 and there have been many people along the way who have helped – I truly stand on the shoulders of giants. The first thanks goes to all of the players, friends, families, teammates, librarians and historians who gave up their time and whose cumulative stories helped bring a hidden tradition to light.

Going back to ground zero, thanks to Mike Hytner from the *Guardian Australia* for believing in the original story, as bizarre as it seemed when I pitched it.

Kudos to Tom Parker, who was working at the AFL when the idea for this book germinated and for helping with the original submission. You were the project's true believer!

Thanks also to AFL International's Simon Highfield for your unwavering determination to steer things through.

A writer is only as good as their research and thanks to Nick Marshall for digging deep into Trove to dig out some nuggets.

On my journey across Australia, guardian angels emerged to guide me in collecting these stories.

In Ballarat, thanks to Michael Walsh, Stanley 'Digger' Roberts, Gary Snowden, and Charles Zhang who watched over me during a brutal bout with COVID-19 in freezing Ballarat.

I learnt a lot about the Chinese-Australian experience in Bendigo with special thanks to Leigh McKinnon, Terry Ilsey, Anita Jack and Di Dempsey.

My stop in beautiful Broome was a highlight and the mind-blowing history of the town was shared with me by Doug Fong, Sarah Yu, Chris Maher and Michael Torres.

In Perth, I was grateful to hear the stories of the Chinese community from Kayleen Poon of the Chung Wah Association. On the football side – thanks to Greg-Wardell Johnson – when I landed in Perth I knew of five Chinese heritage players in the WAFL and I left after learning about twenty!

In Mooroopna, Mark Lepp opened up his family history as did the historians at the Mooroopna Historical society, for which I am grateful.

In Darwin, a big shout out to the team at the Northern Territory Chinese Museum – Neville Jones, Roland Chin and Austin Chin. Also a special mention to Matthew Stephen and Charlie King who educated me on early Darwin Football history, and Bennie Lew Fatt who looked after me and gave me an eye-opening tour of historical Darwin.

In Melbourne, many have assisted with my journey, including Harold Chin Quan, Sally Keam from the CAFHOV, Mark Wang from the Museum of Chinese Australian History, AFL historian Col Hutchison, and AFL Club historians, especially Carlton's Tony de Bolfo, North Melbourne's Barb Cullen and Western Bulldogs' Darren Arthur.

To Reg Raghavan, Jake, Dee and my Cultural Pulse workmates and also to my friends and family – thanks for all of your unwavering support and spiritual guidance with a special mention to John Harms,

Nick Hatzoglou, Dom Bossi, Ashley Gray, my father-in-law Narayanan, my brother Adrian and Dion Woo from the Museum of Chinese in Australia.

A special thank you to all the team members involved in the project at The National Foundation for Australia-China Relations – especially Kevin Magee, Gavin Ku, Amber Miller-Greenman and Luke Coates.

To Dr Robert Hess – thanks for your time, energy, wisdom and guidance.

To the AFL's Digital team Monica Forlano, Beth Wallis and Bianca Smith – you've been amazing. Thank you to the team at the AFL who read early drafts: Patrick Keane, Dr Sean Gorman and AFL Historian, Swamp.

And finally to my family, Divya, Narayan and Priyana – your patience and support has been magnificent.

BIBLIOGRAPHY AND RELATED SOURCES

Adelaide Now 2019, *Adelaide Crows winger Sophie Li will face her old club Carlton in Sunday's AFLW grand final* https://www.adelaidenow. com.au/sport/afl/aflw/adelaide-crows-winger-sophie-li-will-face-her-old-club-carlton-in-sundays-aflw-grand-final/news-story/ d35ddaa6cedb57be3ad818f99b1721c9 (Accessed: Date Unknown)

AFL.com.au 2021, *Journey to the Draft: Connor Downie* https://www. afl.com.au/video/568978/journey-to-the-draft-connor-downie (Accessed: Date Unknown)

Ah Chee, K 2021, *Nomad Girl*, Aboriginal Studies Press, Canberra

Archer, G 2017, *Shinboners*, Slattery Media Group, Melbourne

Atkinson, B 2008, *It's A Grand Old Flag - West Perth Football Club 1885– 2007*, Fremantle Press, Fremantle

Atkinson, B 1985, *West Perth Football Club 1885–1985*, Action Press, Morley

Bagnall, K 2011, 'Rewriting the History of Chinese Families in Nineteenth Century Australia', *Australian Historical Studies*, vol. 42, no. 1, pp. 62–77, doi/full/10.1080/1031461X.2010.538419

Bailey, J 2002, *The White Divers of Broome*, Pan Australia, Sydney

Barker, A 2004, *Behind the Play: A History of Football in Western Australia from 1868*, WA Football Commission, Subiaco

Barned, B 1985, *Woodend on the Five Mile Creek*, Self published, Woodend

Baum, G 2011 *Rules of the game: no place for racism in today's AFL* https://www.theage.com.au/sport/afl/rules-of-the-game-no-place-for-racism-in-todays-afl-20110627-1gnmi.html (Accessed: Date Unknown)

Beaumont, J 2022, *Australia's Great Depression*, Allen & Unwin, East Melbourne

Beeson, R 2020, *AFLW players already stuck in limbo plunged into further uncertainty by Covid-19* https://www.theguardian.com/sport/2020/aug/11/aflw-players-already-stuck-in-limbo-plunged-into-further-uncertainty-by-covid-19 (Accessed: Date Unknown)

Beyond Blue 2021, *The break from AFL football Lin Jong knew he needed* https://www.beyondblue.org.au/personal-best/pillar/the-break-from-afl-football-lin-jong-knew-he-needed (Accessed: Date Unknown)

Bird, M 2015, *Athenians and Red Invicibles: The Origins of Queensland Football*, Sports Publishing Pty Limited, Brisbane

Bird, M 2018, *More of the Kangaroo: 150 Years of Australian Football in Queensland, 1866 to 2016*, Sports Publishing Pty Limited, Brisbane

Birrell, R 2008, *A New Bendigo: The Story of the Gold and Silver Mines of St. Arnaud*, Self published, Strathfieldsaye

Bongiorno, F 2015, *The Eighties: The Decade that Transformed Australia*, Black Inc., Collingwood

Bozyck, R 1971, *West Australian Football History 1885–1971*, Pilpel Print, Perth

Bradby, D 2022, *Ten Delightful Tales: Ovals of Ballarat*, Self published, Ballarat

Cai, M 1999, 'Astride two worlds: The Chinese response to changing citizenship in Western Australia, 1901–1973', PhD thesis, Edith Cowan University

Carlton FC 2018, *Bloodlines* https://www.carltonfc.com.au/video/256124/bloodlines-darcy-vescio (Accessed: Date Unknown)

Carter, R 2006, *Mixed Relations: Asian-Aboriginal Contact in North Australia*, UWA Publishing, Crawley

Cha, J 2020, *Chung Wah Association Perth, 110th Anniversary Commemoration Publication*, Self published, Perth

Chiu, E 2021, *For Honour and Country: Victorian Chinese Australians in WWII*, Museum of Chinese Australian History, Melbourne

Christian, G, Lee, J & Messenger, B 1985, *The Footballers: A History of Football in Western Australia*, St George Books, Stonyfell

Church, P 2003, *A Short History of South East Asia*, Wylie, Milton

Clark, M 1995, *A Short History of Australia*, Penguin, Docklands

Clark, M 1996, *Manning Clark's History of Australia: Abridged from the six-volume classic by Michael Cathcart*, 3rd edn, Penguin, Docklands

Collins, G 1993, *Memories of Mooroopna*, Historical Society of Mooroopna, Mooroopna

Connolly, R 2015 *Lin Jong a Western Bulldog who belongs* https://www.theage.com.au/sport/afl/lin-jong-a-western-bulldog-who-belongs-20150430-1mx6zv.html (Accessed: Date Unknown)

Daffey, P 2017, *Behind the Goals*: *The History of the Victorian Country Football League*, Self Published, West Melbourne

Dale, D 2010, *The Little Book of Australia*, Allen & Unwin, East Melbourne

De La Rue, K 2017, *A stubborn city: Darwin 1911*, Historical Society of the Northern Territory, Casuarina

De La Rue, K 2004, *The Evolution of Darwin 1869–1911*, Charles Darwin University Press, Darwin

De Lacy, H 1948, *The Sporting Globe Football Book*, The Herald and Weekly Times Limited, Melbourne

Dowling, G 1997, *The North Story: The North Melbourne Football Club*, Playright Publishing, Caringbah

Dragon Museum, G 2000, *Chinese Footsteps*, The Golden Dragon Museum, Bendigo

Dragon Museum, G 2001, *Chinese Memorial and Memories: the White Hills Cemetery, Bendigo*, The Golden Dragon Museum, Bendigo

Earl, C 2018, *In Their Footsteps*, Muso's Media, Kangaroo Flat

Edwards, H 1983, *Port of Pearls: a history of Broome*, Rigby, Adelaide

Edwards, P & Yuangang, S 2003, *Lost in the whitewash: Aboriginal-Asian encounters in Australia*, 1901–2001, Australian National University, Canberra

Egan, T 2019, *Outback Songman*, Allen & Unwin, East Melbourne

Egan, T 1997, *Sitdown up North*, Kerr Australia, Marrickville

Errington, S 2013, *Southerners Forever More: the triumphs and tribulations of South Fremantle's first six decades*, South Fremantle Football Club (Inc.), Fremantle

Evans, G 1995, *Australia's Foreign Relations In the World of the 1990's*, Melbourne University Press, Carlton

Fei, S 2011, 'Environmental Experiences of Chinese People in the mid 19th Century Gold Rushes', *Global Environment*, vol. 4, no. 7–8, pp. 98–117, doi.org/10.3197/ge.2011.040705

Fitzgerald, J 2007, *Big White Lie: Chinese Australians in White Australia*, UNSW Press, Randwick

Flett, J 1974, *Dunolly: Story of an Old Gold Diggings*, Hawthorn Press, Hawthorn

Flett, J 1970, *The History Of Gold Discovery in Victoria*, Hawthorn Press, Hawthorn

Flinders, C E 2016, *Kimberley Days and Yesterdays: 45 years in the Great Nor-West of Western Australia*, Hesperian Press, Carlisle

Friends of Mount Alexander Diggings 2010, *Chinese Snapshots*, brochure, Castlemaine

Fox, M 1915, *The History of the North West of Australia*, Hesperian Press, Carlisle

Ganter, R 2006, *Mixed Relations: Asian-Aboriginal Contact in North Australia*, UWA Press, Perth

Gervasoni, C 1998, *Castlemaine Petitions: Petitions for a Castlemaine Municipality and Petitions against the Chinese Residence Licence*, Ballarat Heritage Services, Ballarat

Giese, D 1995, *Beyond Chinatown: changing perspectives on the Top End Chinese experience*, National Library of Australia, Canberra

Glover, R 2018, *The Land Before Avocado: Journeys in a lost Australia*, HarperCollins Publishers, Sydney

Gock Yen, M 2022, *South Flows the Pearl: Chinese Australian Voices*, Sydney University Press, 2022, Sydney

Hankin, W 1978, *A History of the Golden Point Football Club*, Self published, Ballarat

Hankin, W 1993, *Ballarat Football League Centenary*, Ballarat Football League, Ballarat

Harrison, F & Lee, J 1976, *The South Fremantle Story 1900–1975 Volume 1*, South Fremantle Football Club, Fremantle

Herald Sun 2021, *Darcy Vescio's decision to reveal they are non-binary the toughest call* https://www.heraldsun.com.au/sport/afl/aflw/aflw-2022-carlton-coach-daniel-harford-backs-darcy-vescios-decision-to-reveal-they-are-nonbinary/news-story/4b92f84b026f9e144b0528a8c3342e22 (Accessed: Date Unknown)

Holmesby, R & Main, J 2018, *Encyclopedia of AFL Footballers*, 11th edn, BAS Publishing, Bayswater

Huang, R 1997, *China - A Macro History*, 2nd edn, Routledge, Melbourne

Hughes, R 2003, *The Fatal Shore*, Vintage, New York

Hunt, D 2021, *Girt: The Unauthorised History of Australia*, Black Inc., Collingwood

Hunter, A 2020, *Port Adelaide to Shanghai: Taking Australia's game to the world*, Wakefield Press, Mile End

Hsu, J & Kassam N 2021, *Being Chinese in Australia: Public Opinions in Chinese communities*, Lowy Institute, Sydney

Jaivin, L 2021, *The Shortest History of China*, Black Inc., Canberra

Jones, T 1997, *The Chinese in the Northern Territory*, NTU Press, Darwin

Keating, J 1996, *The History of the Woodend Fire Brigade 1896–1996*, Woodend Fire Brigade, Woodend

Keneally, T 2018, *Australians: A Short History*, Allen & Unwin, East Melbourne

Kennedy, A 2012, *Chinese Anzacs : Australians of Chinese descent in the defence forces 1885–1919*, A. Kennedy, Canberra

Krause, J 2021, *A Short History of Humanity - How Migration Made Us Who We are*, WH Allen, Docklands

Kuo, M F 2018, *Jinxin, the Remittance Trade and Enterprising Chinese Australians, 1850–1916*, Routledge, Melbourne

Kuo, M F 2013, *Making Chinese: Urban Elites, Newspapers and the Formation of Chinese-Australian Identity 1892–1912*, Monash University Publishing, Clayton

Lack, J 1996, *A history of the Footscray Football Club: unleashed*, Aus-Sport Enterprises, Melborurne

Lea, T 2020, *Darwin*, NewSouth Books, Randwick

Lovell, J 2011, *The Opium War*, Picador, Sydney

Loy-Wilson, S 2017, 'Coolie Alibis: Seizing Gold from Chinese Miners in New South Wales', *International Labor and Working Class History*, vol. 91, no. 3, pp. 28–45

Luck, P 1991, *A Time to Remember*, Mandarin, Port Melbourne

McGowan, B 2015, *The History of the Chinese People in the Hay, Deniliquin and Hillston Districts*, Museum of the Riverina, Wagga Wagga

McGregor, P 1995, *Histories of the Chinese in Australasia and the South Pacific: proceedings of an international public conference held at the Museum of Chinese Australian History, Melbourne, 8–10 October 1993*, Melbourne Museum, Melbourne

McKinnon, L 2015, *A biographical dictionary of historic figures in Bendigo's Chinese Community*, The Golden Dragon Museum, Bendigo

McKinnon, L 2018, *Chinese ANZACS of the Loddon Mallee Region*, The Golden Dragon Museum, Bendigo

McKinnon, L 2012, *Loong, Bendigo's Golden Dragon*, The Golden Dragon Museum, Bendigo

McKinnon, L 2015, *Places associated with Bendigo's historic Chinese community*, The Golden Dragon Museum, Bendigo

McLennan, D 1984, *History of Mooroopna, Ardmona and District*, Mooroopna Historical Society, Mooroopna

McWaters, V 2013, *The Peculiar Strangers*, Self published, Beechworth

Macknight, C 1969, *The Farthest Coast: A Selection of Writings Relating to the History of the Northern Coast of Australia*, Melbourne University Press, Carlton

Megalogenis, G 2017, *Australia's Second Chance: what our history tells us about our future*, Penguin Books, Docklands

Megalogenis, G 2019, *The Football Solution: How Richmond's Premiership Can Save Australia*, Penguin Books, Docklands

Milbourne, J 1982, *Mount Macedon - Its History and Its Grandeur, 1836–1978*, Cambridge University Press, Port Melbourne

Mueller, A 2019, *Carn: Game, and the Country that Plays it*, HarperCollins, Sydney

Navaratnam, D 2016, *Sly Dogs trick Scorpions with Jong's shoulder strapping* https://www.afl.com.au/news/127902/sly-dogs-trick-scorpions-with-jongs-shoulder-strapping (Accessed: Date Unknown)

Negrepontis, N 2021 *"Proper Tough" Jong could have played 150 plus games* https://www.sen.com.au/news/2021/08/04/proper-tough-jong-could-have-played-150-plus-games/ (Accessed: Date Unknown)

Nicholson, M, Stewart, B, de Moore, G & Hess, R 2021, *Australia's Game: The History of Australian Football*, Hardie Grant, Richmond

Nixon, A 1982, *Inglewood gold: gold town of early Victoria*, Sundowner Press, Greensborough

O'Halloran, K 2019, *Conferences, crowds and AFL cannibalism — the four AFLW controversies you need to get across* https://www.abc.net.au/news/2019-02-18/the-four-aflw-controversies-you-need-to-get-across/10821034 (Accessed: Date Unknown)

O'Halloran, K 2022, *Erin Phillips weighs in on the part-time demands of AFLW and round one's injury crisis* https://www.abc.net.au/news/2022-01-11/erin-phillips-injury-crisis-part-time-demands-w-podcast/100749348 (Accessed: Date Unknown)

Palmer, Y 1999, *Track of The Years - The story of St. Arnaud*, Melbourne University Press, Carlton

Pi, J 2012 *Jong on song* https://www.afl.com.au/news/531558/jong-on-song (Accessed: Date Unknown)

Poat, P 1988, *The Les Fong Story*, West Perth Football Club, West Perth

Postlethwaite, Y 2021, *St Arnaud and District World War I Diary*, ANZAC Centenary, Melbourne

Pountney, T 2018, *AFLW: Croweater becomes a true Blue* https://www.afl.com.au/news/41659/aflw-croweater-becomes-a-true-blue (Accessed: Date Unknown)

Poy, V 2015, *Heroes & Gamblers: Tales of Survival and Good Fortune of the Poy Family*, Calyan Publishing Limited, Toronto

Priestley, S 1965, *Echuca - A Centenary History*, Jacaranda Press, Brisbane

Pugh, D 2021, *Darwin: Growth of a City*, Self published, Darwin

Pugh, D 2019, *Darwin: Origin of a City*, Self published, Darwin

Pugh, D 2023, *Darwin: Survival of a City*, Self published, Darwin

Pung, A 2008, *Growing up Asian in Australia*, Black Inc., Collingwood

Ritchie, F 2004, *Guichen Bay to Canton Lead: The Chinese trek to gold*, District Council of Robe, Robe

Schultz, J 2018, *Griffith Review 61: Who We Are*, Griffith Review, South Brisbane

See-Kee, C 1987, *Chinese Contribution to Early Darwin*, Northern Territory Library Service, Darwin

Shee Ping, W 2019, *The Poison of Polygamy*, Sydney University Press, Sydney

Sickert, S 2017, *Beyond The Lattice - Broome's early years*, 2nd edn, Backroom Press Inc, Broome

Simpson, H 1990, *Horrie Simpson's Oodnadatta*, Oodnadatta Progress Association, Oodnadatta

Soutphommasane, T 2015, *I'm Not Racist But... 40 years of the Racial Discrimination Act*, NewSouth Publishing, Sydney

Stephen, M 2015, *Colour Bar: Remembering and Forgetting Northern Territory Football 1916–1955*, UniPrint NT, Charles Darwin University, Darwin

Tart, M 2003, *The Life Of Quong Tart: or, how a foreigner succeeded in a British community*, Wild and Woolley, Sydney

Townsend, J 2018, *Keifer Yu's decision to call out Josh Deluca should be the WAFL's Nicky Winmar moment* https://thewest.com.au/sport/wafl/the-tuesday-wafl-keifer-yus-decision-to-call-out-josh-deluca-should-be-the-wafls-nicky-winmar-moment-ng-b88822060z (Accessed: Date Unknown)

Travers, R 2004, *Australian mandarin: the life and times of Quong Tart*, Rosenberg Publishing, Dural

Tuohy, W 2021 *'Absolutely huge': AFLW star Vescio changes the game on gender diversity* https://www.theage.com.au/sport/afl/absolutely-huge-aflw-star-vescio-changes-the-game-on-gender-diversity-20211230-p59ky7.html (Accessed: Date Unknown)

Wang, S 1969, 'The organization of Chinese emigration, 1848–1888, with special reference to Chinese immigration to Australia', PhD thesis, Australian National University

Watson, D 1984, *The Story of Australia*, Thomas Nelson Publishing, Sydney

Watt, J 2020, *The Ghosts Have Never Left: Victorian Gold Rush Towns and the Stories They Could Tell*, Creatours Press, Hermosa Beach

Whimpress, B 1983, *The South Australian Football Story*, South Australian National Football League, Adelaide

Williams, M 2018, *Returning Home with Glory; Chinese Villagers around the Pacific, 1849–1949*, Hong Kong University Press, Hong Kong

Wood R, 2021 *Interview #183 – Lin Jong* https://www.liminalmag.com/interviews/lin-jong (Accessed: Date Unknown)

Wu, A 2012 *Spreading the word: Asian influences break down walls, one game at a time* https://www.theage.com.au/sport/afl/spreading-the-word-asian-influences-break-down-walls-one-game-at-a-time-20120817-24dww.html (Accessed: Date Unknown)

Yee, G 2006, *Through Chinese eyes: the Chinese experience in the Northern Territory 1874–2004*, Self published, Parap

Yong, C 1977, *The new gold mountain: the Chinese in Australia, 1901–1921*, Raphael Arts, Richmond

Yu, O 2017, *Billy Sing – A Novel*, Transit Lounge Publishing, Melbourne

Yu, S 1999, *The story of the Chinese in Broome*, Pindan Printing, Broome